A Short History of Early Modern England

A Short History of Early Modern England

British Literature in Context

Peter C. Herman

A John Wiley & Sons, Ltd., Publication

This edition first published 2011
© 2011 Peter C. Herman

Blackwell Publishing was acquired by John Wiley & Sons in February 2007. Blackwell's publishing program has been merged with Wiley's global Scientific, Technical, and Medical business to form Wiley-Blackwell.

Registered Office
John Wiley & Sons Ltd, The Atrium, Southern Gate, Chichester, West Sussex, PO19 8SQ, United Kingdom

Editorial Offices
350 Main Street, Malden, MA 02148-5020, USA
9600 Garsington Road, Oxford, OX4 2DQ, UK
The Atrium, Southern Gate, Chichester, West Sussex, PO19 8SQ, UK

For details of our global editorial offices, for customer services, and for information about how to apply for permission to reuse the copyright material in this book please see our website at www.wiley.com/wiley-blackwell.

The right of Peter C. Herman to be identified as the author of this work has been asserted in accordance with the UK Copyright, Designs and Patents Act 1988.

Library of Congress Cataloging-in-Publication Data

Herman, Peter C., 1958–
    A short history of early modern England : subjects, rulers and rebels / Peter C. Herman.
        p.   cm.
    ISBN 978-1-4051-9560-7 (hardback)
    1. Great Britain–History–Tudors, 1485–1603.   2. Great Britain–History–Stuarts, 1603–1714.
3. English literature–Early modern, 1500–1700.   I. Title.
    DA315.H44 2011
    942.05–dc22
                                                                    2010051057

A catalogue record for this book is available from the British Library.

This book is published in the following electronic formats: ePDFs 9781444394979; Wiley Online Library 9781444395006; ePub 9781444394993

Set in 10.5/13.5pt Palatino by SPi Publisher Services, Pondicherry, India
Printed in Malaysia by Ho Printing (M) Sdn Bhd

1   2011

Table of Contents

Aims and Acknowledgements

A Short History of Early Modern England: British Literature in Context has a very simple purpose: to provide a survey of the backgrounds necessary to study the literature produced in early modern England. While editing two volumes for the Modern Language Association's *Approaches to Teaching* series, I came across numerous complaints that students arrive in our classrooms innocent of the basic facts of the Tudor–Stuart era, a phenomenon backed up by much anecdotal evidence and studies illustrating the generally parlous state of historical knowledge. This book aims to help remedy this problem by providing a clear narrative of the period's political history along with explanations of the age's religious conflicts. *A Short History of Early Modern England: British Literature in Context* aims to answer such basic questions as who ruled when, what was the English Reformation, what exactly are the differences between Catholicism and Protestantism and between the various subdivisions among Protestants, what are the Wars of the Roses, why were the Elizabethans so obsessed with it, what happened between 1640 and 1660, and why does this period go by so many names? While any number of studies and guides place early modern literature in its historical contexts, these books all assume a fair amount of background knowledge on the reader's part.

A Short History of Early Modern England: British Literature in Context aims to provide that knowledge.

I have tried to stick to the facts, balancing narrative with quotations from primary sources. When I depart from convention, such as my decision to eschew the term, "Puritan," I have made my decisions explicit. I also give brief explanations of the controversies among historians and why they are relevant to students of literature. Periodization is always tricky, since history does not proceed in easily definable segments, and I have been guided by what I hope would be most useful to a literature student. Consequently, the book begins with the deposition of Richard II and the consequences following that act (i.e. the Wars of the Roses), both because the events of this period are so important to the Tudor–Stuart era, and because they are dramatized by William Shakespeare in some of his most popular plays. I have chosen the publication of Milton's final poetic works in 1674 as the endpoint, since that is when most classes in early modern literature conclude.

One point, however, deserves to be explained before going further: this book is largely "history from above" rather than "history from below." My reason for this approach is not that I disagree with the latter or consider the history of working or illiterate people less worthy of note than the doings of kings and parliaments. Rather, I base my approach on my sense that wherever one rests on the social ladder, the monarch constituted the center of the political universe. When, for example, the Elizabethan pamphleteer and proto-novelist, Thomas Deloney, challenges the fundamental social organization of England, he does not imagine doing away with the monarchy altogether, but by having the monarch recognize the superiority of working people over the aristocracy. For a relatively brief period, the Interregnum (1649–60), a few tried to imagine England without a monarchy, but ultimately the experiment failed, and it failed even before the Restoration because Cromwell had to fend off numerous attempts to make him king. To write "history from below" without first taking into account the basic facts of "history from above" would, I think, lead to a warped view of the period's literature.

Three tools have aided the research for this book immeasurably. First, *Early English Books Online* allows students access to nearly every book, pamphlet, proclamation, and newsbook printed in England between 1485 and 1700. Whenever possible, I have gone back to the original sources rather than relying on quotations in contemporary historians. Second, as a cursory glance at my notes will quickly indicate, I have relied heavily on *The Oxford Dictionary of National Biography*, an extraordinary resource whose articles provide up-to-date, deeply scholarly, and yet entirely accessible biographies that are essential reading for anyone seeking to understand British history. The third source came as a surprise: Google Books and Archive.org. As most people know, Google decided some years ago to try to create a universal library by scanning I do not know how many out-of-print volumes from the major research libraries in North America. Consequently, such essential primary source resources such as Sir John Harington's *Nugae Antiquae* (1804), and John Rushworth's *Historical Collections of Private Passages of State* (1689) are now available to everyone with a web connection.

Finally, I have personal debts that I eagerly and gratefully acknowledge. Heidi Brayman Hackel, Anne Lake Prescott, and Johann P. Sommerville answered what must have seemed like a never-ending stream of queries with patience and learning. Peter Platt, Elizabeth Sauer, and Ronald Simon read and commented on each chapter as I finished it. I am also exceedingly grateful to the advice, enthusiasm, and patience provided by Emma Bennett, Isobel Bainton, and Ben Thatcher. Gillian Andrews was the ideal copy-editor. Finally, I gratefully thank the College of Arts and Letters at San Diego State University for a grant that helped pay for the illustrations. If this book has any merit, they deserve the praise. I gladly accept the blame.

Quoting from Early Modern Texts

Every book we read today comes with page numbers, and it seems self-evident that this is how books were organized. If you want to find a particular topic, go to page 32. Or 64. Or 102. But the technology for creating printed books in the early modern period demanded a different organization. Books in this period were printed by a hand press, and a single large sheet of paper would be imprinted on each side with 2, 4, 8 or even more pages of type, depending on the intended size of the book (which roughly correlated with the book's cost). These pages would then be folded in half for a folio, twice for a quarto, four times for an octavo, and so on, and then collected with the other sheets to form a book. To keep track of the correct order of sheets and folds, the print shop identified each fold with a letter of the alphabet, and if the book went beyond the 26th letter, they started over again, using double letters, then triple letters, etc. These are called *signatures*. Because numerical pagination is notoriously unreliable in this period, the convention is to refer to the signature number (the contraction is "sig.") rather than the page number, and to identify the left or right side of the page by adding a "v" for *verso* (the left) or an "r" for *recto* (the right). Consequently, in the notes, readers will find references to such signature numbers as "A2v" or "B4r."

For greater comprehension, I have modernized all quotations, regardless of whether they come from early modern or contemporary editions or books.

Illustrations

England's Rulers
From Richard II to Charles II

Richard II	1377–99
Henry IV	1399–1413
Henry V	1413–22
Henry VI	1422–61 (deposed); 1470–71
Edward IV	1461–1470 (deposed); 1471–83
Richard III	1483–85
Henry VII	1485–1509
Henry VIII	1509–47
Edward VI	1547–1553
Lady Jane Gray	July 10–19, 1553
Mary Tudor	1553–1558
Elizabeth I	1558–1603
James VI/I	1603–25
Charles I	1625–49
Parliament (the Commonwealth)	1649–1654
Oliver Cromwell (Lord Protector)	1654–58
Richard Cromwell (Lord Protector)	1658–59
Charles II	1660–85

Timeline of Key Events

1377	**Death of Edward III; accession of Richard II**
1381	Peasant's Revolt
1399	Richard resigns the crown to Henry Bolingbroke, who becomes Henry IV
1415	October 25, Battle of Agincourt
1422	Henry VI becomes king after father dies
1440s	Disorder caused by Henry VI's poor rule
1450	Jack Cade Rebellion
1453	Henry VI incapacitated by madness
1455	1st battle of St. Albans, start of War of the Roses
1461	**Henry VI deposed by Edward of York (Edward IV)**
1470	**Edward IV briefly deposed**
1471	**Edward IV re-deposes Henry VI**; 4 May, Battle of Tewkesbury, end of Lancastrian line

1483   Richard, Duke of Gloucester murders Edward IV's
              children, crowned on July 6

1485   Henry Tudor defeats Richard III on 22 August, the
              Battle of Bosworth Field, becomes Henry VII and
              begins the Tudor dynasty

1509   Death of Henry VII, accession of Henry VIII

1530   Fall of Cardinal Thomas Wolsey

1533   Henry VIII divorces Katherine of Aragon, marries
              Anne Boleyn; Act in Restraint of Appeals passed

1534   Act of Supremacy designating Henry VIII (and all
              future English monarchs) "Supreme Head" of the
              Church of England

1535   Execution of Sir Thomas More

1536   Act for dissolution of smaller monasteries; Henry VIII
              beheads Anne Boleyn, marries Jane Seymour, who
              dies giving birth to Edward IV; execution of William
              Tyndale

1536–37   Pilgrimage of Grace

1539   Act of the Six Articles; Act for dissolution of larger
              monasteries; parishes required to purchase and
              display "Great Bible"

1540   Henry VIII marries Anna of Cleves, marriage
              annulled; then marries Catherine Howard; execution
              of Thomas Cromwell

1542   Catherine Howard beheaded

1543   Henry VIII marries Katherine Parr

1547   **Henry VIII dies, Edward VI crowned**

1549   Kett's Rebellion; first Book of Common Prayer

1552	Execution of Thomas Seymour; John Dudley, Duke of Northumberland becomes Lord Protector; revised Book of Common Prayer
1553	**Edward VI dies, Protestant Lady Jane Grey queen for nine days; Catholic Mary Tudor becomes queen of England;** England shifts from Protestantism to Catholicism
1554	Royal Supremacy repealed; revival of heresy Acts
1555	Protestant "heretics" burned at stake
1558	**Death of Queen Mary, accession of Elizabeth I;** England shifts back to Protestantism
1559	Act of Uniformity, Queen Elizabeth "Supreme Governor" of Church of England
1563	Thirty-Nine Articles (doctrinal formulary for the Elizabethan Settlement)
1562	John Hawkins and Francis Drake start English trade in slaves
1562–98	French wars of Religion
1567–98	Dutch revolt against Spanish rule
1568	Mary, Queen of Scots flees to England
1586	Mary, Queen of Scots executed
1588	Defeat of Spanish Armada
1594–98	Major crop failures, "Crisis of the 1590s"
1598–1603	O'Neill rebellion in Ireland
1601	Essex conspiracy
1603	**Death of Elizabeth I; accession of James VI/I (sixth of that name to rule Scotland; first to rule England)**
1604	Hampton Court Conference

1605	Gunpowder Plot
1606	Bate's Case
1610	Whitehall Speech declaring monarchy the "supremest thing on earth"
1611	King James Bible
1612	Death of Prince Henry, Charles now heir to the throne
1613	Princess Elizabeth marries Frederick, Elector Palatine; Overbury scandal
1614	"Addled" Parliament
1615	Rise of George Villiers, eventually Duke of Buckingham, starts
1618–48	Thirty Years War
1619	Death of James's wife, Anna of Denmark
1620	*Mayflower* sails to New World
1622–23	Charles and Buckingham travel to Spain
1624	England declares war on Spain
1625	**Death of James VI/I; Charles I ascends to throne**
1626–29	War with France, failed naval expeditions
1627	Five Knights' Case
1628	Petition of Right; Buckingham assassinated August 23
1629	Charles dissolves third Parliament, 12 years of "personal rule"; peace with France (1629), peace with Spain (1630)
1633	William Laud made Archbishop of Canterbury
1634	Ship Money imposed

1637	Ship Money Case
1638	Attempt to impose Laudian Protestantism in Scotland; National Covenant in Scotland
1638–39	First Bishop's War
1640	Second Bishop's War; Short Parliament
1640	Long Parliament convenes April 13 (will meet until 1653); Root and Branch petition to end episcopacy; imprisonment of Laud; end of licensing; George Thomason starts collecting books, pamphlets, and newsbooks
1641	Grand Remonstrance; rebellion in Ireland, Protestant settlers slaughtered; impeachment and execution of Strafford
1642	Attempt to arrest Pym; March, Militia Ordinance; August 22, Charles raises standard at Nottingham, Civil Wars begin (Battle of Edgehill); closing of the public theatres
1643	Parliament aligns with Scots (Solemn League and Covenant); Charles I allies with Irish
1644	Royalist defeat at Marston Moor means Charles I lost; Self-Denying Ordinance proposed
1645	Laud executed; New Model Army formed; Parliamentary victory at Naseby
1646	Charles surrenders to Scots; end of First Civil War
1647	Charles delivered to Parliament by Scots; Putney Debates
1648	No Further Addresses to King; Second Civil War; Pride's Purge (remainder of Long Parliament now "The Rump")

1649	Charles I executed; Cromwell goes to Ireland, massacres in Drogheda and Wexford; Digger colonies established
1650	Cromwell returns from Ireland; defeats Scots at Battle of Dunbar; Blasphemy Act
1651	Charles II goes into exile
1652	1st Anglo-Dutch war
1653	Cromwell forcibly dissolves Rump; April–December, Nominated Assembly or "Barbebone's Parliament"; Instrument of Government installs Cromwell as Lord Protector
1655	Penruddick's Rising; rule of Major-Generals; readmission of the Jews
1657	Cromwell offered crown and refuses
1658	Cromwell dies, succeeded by son, Richard
1659	Political chaos
1660	April, declaration of Breda and Restoration of Charles II; theaters re-open; Royal Society established
1661–65	"Clarendon Code" legislation against nonconformists passed
1665	2nd Anglo-Dutch War begins; Great Plague in London
1666	Great Fire of London
1667	2nd Anglo-Dutch War concluded

Map 0.1 The Countries of England and Wales before 1972.

1

An Overview of Early Modern England

Before we begin, the two terms in the above chapter title require definition. First, why **"early modern"** as opposed to **"Renaissance"**? Literary scholars and historians have come to prefer the former term because it is more capacious. "Renaissance," with its emphasis on the rebirth of classical learning and culture, necessarily privileges high culture, whereas there is increasing attention to non-elite cultural products and history, which "early modern" can encompass.[1] Second, "early modern" has the advantage of greater accuracy, because the world we live in at the start of the twenty-first century – the "modern" world – has its beginnings in the sixteenth and seventeenth centuries. This period witnessed the rise of the nation state, the transformation of government into a professional bureaucracy, the establishment of the modern economy, including empires, world trade and stock markets, and the development of science. This period also witnessed less happy events, such as wars of religion, a revolution, the execution of a

A Short History of Early Modern England: British Literature in Context, First Edition.
Peter C. Herman.
© 2011 Peter C. Herman. Published 2011 by Blackwell Publishing Ltd.

king, and regular outbreaks of the plague. Nearly all (the exception being disease) were greatly enabled by one invention: **the printing press,** brought into England in the late fifteenth century by William Caxton (c. 1414–92), who became England's first printer and book retailer. The early version of modernity, including the adoption of new technologies of communication (the printed word), can be traced back to the Tudor–Stuart era, and so literary scholars and historians have tended toward replacing "Renaissance" with "early modern."

Second, what do we mean when we talk about **"England"**? The island of Britain (largest of the British Isles) contains two kingdoms and one principality. First, there is the kingdom of **England**, which takes up roughly three fourths of the island. The most fertile and wealthiest part of the country is in the southeast, not coincidentally the part closest to Europe, and includes London, Oxford, and Cambridge. The principality of **Wales**, located on the western part of the island, joined England under King Edward I (1239–1307), but Wales retained its own language and identity throughout the sixteenth and seventeenth centuries. To the far north (beyond Cumberland and Northumberland), lies **Scotland**, independent of the English crown since the Treaty of Edinburgh of 1328, and sometimes England's friend, sometimes England's enemy. Despite the efforts of King James (1566–1625), the sixth king of Scotland and the first of that name to rule England, Scotland would remain its own entity until the Act of Union in 1707. The fourth component is **Ireland**, once called the graveyard of English reputations, and colonized by England since Norman times. By 1485, direct English authority was restricted to a small area around Dublin, known as **"the Pale."** Rebellions against English rule, sparked by resentment against the English presence, Tudor and Stuart attempts to impose Protestantism on the Catholic population, and the second-class status of the native Irish, were brutally repressed. "England" in the Tudor-Stuart era was neither homogeneous nor entirely harmonious, but rather a patchwork of restive, independent and semi-independent political and ethnic identities.

Population Size, Family Life, and Life Expectancy

England's population steadily grew over the course of the Tudor–Stuart era. In 1485, approximately 2.2 million people lived in England and Wales. By 1660, that number had risen to 5.5 million. Progress, however, was not steady. Outbreaks of the plague and bad harvests, especially the disastrous years 1594–97, significantly increased mortality and halted growth. Overall, the population increased, as did the size of the cities, especially London, which rose from approximately 40,000 inhabitants in 1500 to over 200,000 by 1600. By the end of the seventeenth century, London's population may have reached 600,000. By way of contrast, the next largest cities were Norwich (15,000), and York and Bristol (12,000 each). While London would grow to be the largest city in Europe, most people lived in rural England.

People got married in this period later than we commonly think. Childhood marriage very occasionally happened at the highest levels of the aristocracy, and even there, only rarely. **Robert Cecil, Lord Burghley**, Elizabeth I's right-hand man, refused a possible suitor – the son of an earl, no less – for his daughter because

> I have determined (notwithstanding I have been very honourably offered matches) not to treat of marrying of her, if I may live so long, until she be above fifteen or sixteen; and if I were of more likelihood myself to live longer than I look to do, she should not, with my liking, be married before she were near eighteen or twenty.[2]

Burghley's preferences are backed up by archival evidence. Studies of parish records show that the average age for marriage among non-aristocratic couples was 25 for the period 1550–99, rising to 26 between 1600 and 1650.[3] But while the period's literature abounds in close relations between parents and children, family life in the early modern period was fundamentally different than today. Childhood as we know it did not exist, and most adolescents, rich or poor, were sent to live, work, and serve in other households. The identification with the household exhibited by Capulet's servants ("The quarrel is between our masters, and us their men" [*Romeo and Juliet* 1.1.20]) would have been very familiar to Shakespeare's audience.[4]

The life expectancy for England's growing population varied, as one might expect, according to the wealth of the population, members of the elite enjoying a better chance at survival than those who lived in more crowded, less healthy circumstances. But even in the best of circumstances, childbirth, infancy, and childhood were fraught with danger. The chances of mothers dying in childbirth were just under 10 deaths per 1000 births, jumping upward to 16 per 1000 in the later seventeenth century (nobody quite knows why). But rates in London were 30 to 50% higher than in rural England (again, nobody is quite sure why, but crowded and unsanitary conditions in the city likely played a part). By way of contrast, the rate of maternal mortality in the industrialized West today is six to eight maternal deaths per 100,000 births. What this means is that "most people approaching a child-birth of their own or within their immediate family would have known someone who had died in childbirth within very recent memory."[5] Women necessarily looked forward to birth with trepidation, but also piety. In a diary entry from 1689, one Mrs. Witton recorded that she considered pregnancy "a means to keep me on my watch and so make me ready for life or death."[6] Mortality rates for infants and children were also by modern standards appallingly high – approximately 20%.

However, once one reached adulthood, the chances were relatively good for survival until one's fifties or sixties. Shakespeare, for example, died at age 52; Michael Drayton at 68; and John Milton at 66. There are rare cases of people reaching their eighties and nineties. **Jane Shore**, for example, who was **Edward IV's** mistress and featured prominently in **Thomas More's** history of Richard III (also mentioned in Shakespeare's *Richard III*), lived to the ripe age of 82, and the political philosopher, **Thomas Hobbes**, author of *Leviathan* (1651), lived to 91! But one needs the qualification of "relatively" because of the omnipresent threat of death from one of the many outbreaks of bubonic plague, or "the black death" (which was transmitted by rats) in the sixteenth and seventeenth centuries, or such diseases as dysentery, known at the time as "the bloody flux," which killed **Henry V**.

Printing, Scribal Circulation, and Literacy

The latter years of **Edward IV's** rule witnessed one of the most consequential developments ever in Western culture: the invention of
the printing press and its importation into England. **Johannes
Gutenberg** (c. 1398–1468) combined movable type, oil-based ink,
and the use of a screw press to create the printing press, and the technology spread very rapidly, with presses set up in Cologne (1466),
Rome (1467), Venice (1469), Paris (1470), and Cracow (1473). **William
Caxton** (c. 1415–92) brought the printing press to England in 1475 or
1476, and the first book he published was *The History of Troy* (c. 1476).
Caxton's second great contribution was to focus on works by native
English writers, including John Lydgate and Geoffrey Chaucer (his
edition of *The Canterbury Tales* appeared in 1477). One cannot overes-
timate the importance of the print revolution. Books and the ideas
contained within them (sometimes revolutionary ideas) started to
become widely available, and, while universal literacy was a long
way off, the printing press enabled the steady spread of reading from
the monastic and aristocratic elites down the social ladder, with
corrosive effects on the hegemony of ideas.

> Even as print came to serve the interests of authority, it equally came
> to serve the interests of those who would resist that authority, allow-
> ing dissident ideas to circulate and coalesce, in many cases allowing
> new communities to form through the lineaments of a book trade.[7]

Printing, it has been rightly said, made possible the Protestant
Reformation by allowing a much larger distribution of the Bible
than was previously possible. Every literate person could now
access the central texts of Christianity, which in turn further encouraged the spread of literacy. The printing press would also play a
shaping role in the dissemination of radical ideas during the 1640s
and 1650s.

   The authorities were quite aware of the power of the press, and in
1538 Henry VIII instituted press licensing as a way of trying to suppress debate on doctrinal matters. Except for a brief period during

Edward VI's reign, when licensing was suspended, all books in the Tudor–Stuart era needed to be submitted to the government for approval. But it would be a mistake to think that Tudor–Stuart press censorship was unified and monolithic, equivalent to censorship in contemporary tyrannies. Censorship "proceeded ad hoc rather than by unifying principle," and while one can find occasional spectacular instances of censorship, such Elizabeth I's 1589 order for the destruction of the Marprelate tracts and the Archbishop of Canterbury's 1599 banning of satires, epigrams, unlicensed histories and plays, overall authors and printers seem to have been granted an amazing amount of latitude.[8] Nor was it hard to evade the censors. **Thomas Deloney's** proto-novels of the late 1590s, such as *Jack of Newbury*, were likely published without a license, yet were so popular that the initial editions were literally read out of existence, and Elizabeth's government could never shut down the Marprelate press.

The invention and subsequent growth of the book trade in England, however, did not mean that **scribal circulation**, meaning writing fiction and poetry by hand and then circulating the manuscript among a small group, some of whom might make further copies for themselves or others, came to halt. Quite the opposite. Throughout the early modern period, manuscript transmission and circulation thrived, and we know (or suspect) that some of the most important pieces of early modern literature, such as Sir Philip Sidney's *Arcadia*, the poetry of Sir Thomas Wyatt and John Donne, and William Shakespeare's sonnets, began life in manuscript and only later appeared in print. Sometimes class would play a role in preferring manuscript to print (publishing a book for cash might seem below a gentleman's dignity), but sometimes "scribal circulation might also be chosen for the speed with which texts could be put into circulation."[9] It was quicker to copy an important speech in Parliament, for example, than wait for the cumbersome process of print publication. Scribal and print circulation, in other words, happily co-existed in the early modern period.

The existence of words on the page of course assumes the ability to decipher them, and while it is superficially evident that literacy increased as the years went by, — historians agree that the Tudor–Stuart era was an age of "increasing literacy, education, and book ownership"[10] — determining the precise level of literacy in the early modern period faces serious difficulties. First, the term resists easy definition: does "literate" mean reading *and* writing? Or reading alone? Also, literacy rates (however defined) varied according to geography and one's place on the social ladder. London was more literate than the provinces, and the aristocracy was almost universally literate, whereas not everyone among the middle and lower rungs of society could read, although those numbers continued to rise, especially after the midpoint of the sixteenth century. While more non-aristocratic men could read than women, non-aristocratic female literacy was far from uncommon. In Thomas Dekker's wonderful play, *The Shoemaker's Holiday* (1599), Hammon, a suitor, presents Jane, the wife of a shoemaker, a letter containing the names of everyone who has died fighting in France (her husband was pressed into service at the play's start). He asks her, "Cannot you read?", and when Jane replies "I can," he gives her the letter (sc.12.88–91).[11] While Hammon does not think that female literacy can be assumed, neither is he particularly shocked or surprised by Jane's positive response, and as further evidence, many books of various sorts, ranging from devotional works to a compendium of laws pertaining to women, were published explicitly aimed at a female audience.

Literacy became more widespread in part because schooling became more widespread. While Oxford and Cambridge remained the two sources of higher education, and the various Inns of Court provided legal training (although many attended without either graduating or becoming lawyers), the sixteenth century witnessed a significant increase in parish or "petty" (meaning small, not petulant) schools that were often run by highly educated teachers, thanks to the numbers of Oxford and Cambridge graduates who could not find other employment. Children also often arrived at these schools already knowing how to read. In addition, many, including girls, were taught by private tutors in the home, and that is how women were educated. While women were banned from careers and college degrees, extremely learned women were far from uncommon in early modern England. **Elizabeth I**, fluent in several modern and ancient languages and a more than competent poet, represents perhaps the best example, but far from the only one.

Religion

Despite the common perception that the so-called "Middle Ages" were religious and the Renaissance secular, the early modern period was an intensely religious as well as secular period. There was no separation between church and state as there is in the contemporary United States of America (John Milton, in *A Treatise of Civil Power* [1659], would be among the first to argue for this concept), and from Henry VIII onward, England's monarch was at least in title also the head of the Anglican Church. However, to say that there was little agreement about doctrine is a vast understatement. In addition to the division between English Protestants and English Catholics, also called **recusants**, Protestantism itself, both inside and outside of England, was from the start riven by divisions and furious controversies. Adding to this combustible mix is the fact that in the early modern era, politics and religion are only artificially separable, and people fully realized that seemingly arid debates about church government had very serious political consequences. Faced with arguments against bishops, **King James VI/I** responded, "If bishops were put out of power, I know what would come of my supremacy. No bishop, no king."[12] The God-centric focus of early modern culture is also evident from the huge number of sermons and devotional manuals crowding early modern bookshops. Indeed, the period's runaway bestseller was the metrical translation of the psalms by Sternhold and Hopkins (more than 200 editions between 1550 and 1640). Religion and religious controversies also permeated the literature of the period (e.g., John Bale's *King Johan* [1538], Edmund Spenser's epic, *The Faerie Queene* [1590; 1596]; and George Herbert's *The Temple* [1633]), and we will deal extensively with this topic in subsequent chapters.

And yet, there are other sides to this story. While from 1558 onward, church attendance was mandatory, that did not mean that everyone was equally pious, and there are many instances of people taking religion less than seriously. The 1572 *Admonition to Parliament*, for example, criticizes those who come to church only to socialize: "The people some standing, some walking, some talking some reading, some praying by themselves, attend not to the minister."[13] The *Second Admonition* complained that there is "no such praying as should touch the heart"; instead, you have people going through the motions:

> One he kneeleth on his knees, and this way he looketh, and that way he looketh, another he kneeleth himself asleep, another kneeleth with such devotion that he is so far in talk that he forgetteth to arise till his knee ache, or his talk endeth, or service is done .... [A]nother hath so little feeling of the common prayer that he bringeth a book of his own, and though he sit when they sit, stand when they stand, kneel when they kneel, he may pause sometime also, but most of all he intendeth his own book. Is this praying?[14]

Some had serious doubts about religion and the nature, even the existence, of God. "Of this sort of murmurers," one divine wrote in 1592, "there are too many at this day among us, who in the time of scarcity ... do more like Pagans than Christians begin to murmur against God .... These murmurers by their grudging seek to make a trial whether God be among them or no ...."[15] This skepticism found its way into the period's literature (e.g., the anonymous play, *Selimus, Emperor of the Turks* [1594]; Shakespeare's *King Lear* [1605]; Milton's *Paradise Lost* [1667; second edition 1674]; and *Samson Agonistes* [1671]).

Government: Absolutism versus the Ancient Constitution

Turning to the question of secular government, early modern England was ruled by a monarch and parliament – the important exception being the **Interregnum**, the period in between the execution of

Charles I in 1649 and the restoration of the monarchy in 1660. Parliament itself is divided into two parts, the **House of Lords**, consisting of nobles and bishops, and the **House of Commons**, comprising 296 elected members. Then as today, laws are made by the monarch signing off on legislation created by both houses. By the Elizabethan era, the **House of Commons** had developed a strong sense of its own identity and insisted, sometimes successfully, sometimes not, on its own "liberties" or privileges, including freedom of speech. However, the relative importance of the English parliament was contested just as the relative powers of the Crown were contested. The overall question concerned what sort of monarchy most effectively served early modern government: **absolutism** or **constitutionalist** or **mixed monarchy**.

Under absolutism, sometimes called "**the divine right of kings**," the monarch is not accountable to anyone other than God, his or her commands are to be obeyed without reservation, and rebellion is never, under any circumstances, justified or allowed. One finds this doctrine stated explicitly in *An Homily against Disobedience and Willful Rebellion"* (1570):

> As in reading of the Holy Scriptures we shall find in very many and almost infinite places, as well of the Old Testament as of the New, that Kings and princes, as well the evil as the good, do reign by God's ordinance, and that subjects are bound to obey them; that God does give princes wisdom, great power and authority; that God defends them against their enemies and destroys their enemies horribly; that the anger and displeasure of the prince is as the roaring of a lion, and the very messenger of death; and that the subject that provokes him to displeasure sings against his own soul.[16]

The Stuart kings, **James VI/I** and his son **Charles I** (1600–49), especially championed this political philosophy. In *The True Law of Free Monarchies* (1598; rpt. 1603, 1616), James asserted that the people should consider the monarch:

> God's lieutenant in earth, obeying his commands in all things, except directly against God, as the commands of God's minister,

acknowledging him a Judge set by God over them, having power to judge them, but to be judged only by God, whom to only he must give [ac]count of his judgment; fearing him as their judge, loving him as their father, praying for him as their protector, for his continuance, if he be good, for his amendment if he be wicked, following and obeying his lawful commands, eschewing and flying his fury in his unlawful, without resistance, but by sobs and tears to God ....[17]

In *Richard II*, Shakespeare's John of Gaunt refuses to take any action against the king who probably had his brother murdered because he endorses absolutism: "God's is the quarrel, for God's substitute, / His deputy anointed in His sight, / Hath caus'd his death, the which if wrongfully, / Let heaven revenge, for I may never lift / An angry arm against His minister" (1.1.37–41).

However, it would be a great mistake to assume that these views, while widespread, reflected unanimously shared assumptions about English politics. Far from an absolute monarchy, England enjoyed a mixed or constitutionalist monarchy that was shaped by **the Ancient Constitution**, a phrase that started circulating in the seventeenth century to connote the unwritten rules governing the relative powers of the monarch and the people, as represented by parliament. According to this theory of government, the monarch is subject to the law, not above the law, and the monarch cannot unilaterally make law. Rather, laws are made by the monarch in concert with parliament (hence the term "mixed"), and both parliament and individual subjects have "ancient liberties," to use a frequently invoked phrase, that cannot be infringed.

The primary exponent of **the Ancient Constitution** is the fifteenth-century jurist and chief justice, **Sir John Fortescue** (1395–1477). In his influential and frequently reprinted book, *In Praise of the Laws of England*, Fortescue distinguishes between "royal" government, by which he means absolutism, and "political" government, meaning, constitutionalism. In England, he declares, the king

is not able to change laws of his kingdom at pleasure, for he rules his people with a government not only royal but also political. If he were to rule over them with a power only royal, he would be able to change the laws of his realm and also impose on them tallages [taxes] and other burdens without consulting them; this is the sort of dominion which the civil laws indicate when they state that "What pleased the prince has the force of law." But it is far otherwise with the king ruling his people politically, because he himself is not able to change the laws without the assent of his subjects nor to burden an unwilling people with strange impositions, so that, ruled by laws that they themselves desire, they freely enjoy their goods, and are despoiled neither by their own king nor any other.[18]

Fortescue is very aware of absolutism, and he rejects it without qualification:

> among the civil laws there is a famous sentence, maxim or rule, which runs like this, "What pleased the prince has the force of law." The laws of England do not sanction any such maxim, since the king of that land rules his people not only royally but also politically, and so he is bound by oath at his coronation to the observance of his law.[19]

To return to Shakespeare, Henry Bolingbroke justifies his returning from exile after he hears that Richard II has confiscated his inheritance: "I am a subject," Henry exclaims, "And I challenge law" (2.3.133–4).

The difference between **absolutism** and **the Ancient Constitution** can be seen in the opposite interpretations King James and Fortescue make of the body politic metaphor, which compares the state to the various parts of the human body. The question is: what part, if any, dominates? In his first speech to parliament after becoming king of England, James invoked corporeal imagery to describe the relationship between the monarch and his subjects:

> I am Head and governor of all the people in my dominion who are my natural vassals and subjects, considering them in numbers and distinct ranks; So if we will take the whole people as one body and mass, then as the head is ordained for the body and not the body for the head, so must a righteous king know himself to be ordained for his people, and not his people for him.[20]

Fortescue also employs the body politic metaphor, but whereas James argues that the head is the indisputable ruler of the body, Fortescue construes the metaphor in the opposite direction:

> And just as the head of the physical body is unable to change its sinews, or to deny its members proper strength and due nourishment of blood, so a king who is head of the body politic is unable to change the laws of that body, or to deprive that same people of their own substance uninvited or against their wills.[21]

While many in early modern England adhered to the absolutist or divine right theory of kingship, many others did not, and often those people were in positions of significant authority. They were part of the mainstream establishment, not marginal figures with little to no actual influence. For example, after King James finished his speech, the Speaker of the House, Sir Edward Phelips, delivered a polite but pointed rebuttal of his new monarch:

> And as, by the disbranching of any one particular from the natural body, the perfection of the whole is dissolved; so, by the dismembering from the politic body of any one of the four politic parts, the glory of the whole is disrooted. This politic head now is ... Your most honoured and best deserving Self; this body politic now is, and still desire to be, your loyal and faithful subjects; this politic life now is, and so well deserves to be, your Highness's common and positive laws; this politic soul now is, and so of necessity must be, your absolute justice in the true distribution of the same. And as the natural head of the one ... cannot be supported without his natural body, nor the natural body without his natural life, nor the natural life breathe without the soul; no more can the politic head of the other (although the supreme and commanding part) stand secure without his subjects ....[22]

Whereas James regards the head, i.e. the monarchy, as supreme, Phelips sees law, monarchy, subjects, and justice as inter-related and inter-dependent, all equally important, all equally essential, none predominating.

Nor was Phelips alone is regarding absolutism with deep suspicion. **Sir Thomas Smith** (1513–77), for example, in *De Republica Anglorum: The Manner of Government or Policy of the Realm of England* (1579), granted that in times of war the monarch could act without restraint, but "in time of peace, [absolute administration] is very dangerous, as well to him that doth use it, and much more to the people upon whom it is used."[23] Power, Smith writes, does not inhere in the monarch; rather, "The most high and absolute power of the realm of England is in the Parliament,"[24] and Smith was no wild-eyed, bearded radical: he was Queen Elizabeth I's ambassador to France when he wrote this book. Even so, absolutism certainly had its adherents, and a great deal of the political history of early modern England consists of the "endless tugging," as **John Milton** (1608–74) termed it in *The Ready and Easy Way to Establish a Free Commonwealth* (1660), between absolutism and the Ancient Constitution.[25]

At times, however, the "tugging" went considerably beyond squabbles in Parliament or litigation, which raises the question of whether rebellion was ever justified. As we have seen, according to absolutist thinking, the answer is an unqualified no. But the reality is more complicated. During the 1550s, a group of Protestant exiles wrote a series of books proposing that it is entirely lawful to depose, as **John Ponet** (1514–56) writes in *A Short Treatise of Politic Power*, "an evil governor and a tyrant."[26] However, while resistance theorists framed their works in the context of the Catholic Mary Tudor's persecution of Protestants, the concept of monarchic accountability is very much part of English political history, as obedience to the crown was always conditional upon the monarch respecting the people's liberties and the rule of law. In 1399, for example, Richard II was deposed (an event we will return to in the next chapter) not through armed revolution but by an act of Parliament, and one of the articles proving that he was "worthy to be deposed" claimed that Richard "said that the laws of the realm were in his head, and sometime in his breast, by reason of which fantastical opinion, he destroyed noble men and impoverished the poor commons."[27] The lawyer and antiquarian, John Selden (1584–1654), also agreed that deposition, even rebellion, has always been an option, if an unofficial one, in English history. In answer to the question, "What law is there to take up arms against the prince in case he breaks his Covenant?" Selden replied: "Though there be no written law for it, yet there is custom, which is the best law of the kingdom; for in England they have always done it."[28] Indeed, between 1327 and 1485, there were no fewer than five depositions of English monarchs.

This "tugging" between the monarch's authority and the "ancient rights and liberties," to use a commonly invoked phrase, of parliament's authority equally describes other aspects of English life. Cities, towns and ports also had their "ancient liberties." **Magna Carta** (1215), for example, included a provision reconfirming all of London's "old liberties" as well as those held by "all other cities, boroughs, towns, and … ports."[29] So did the church, both before and after the Reformation. While in 1485, England belonged to the Catholic – meaning "universal" – Church, that institution also constituted a separate site of authority in early modern England, as recognized by the coronation oath. In addition to swearing to uphold the laws of England, the monarch also pledged to "keep and maintain the right and liberties of the Holy Church of old time granted by the righteous Christian kings of England."[30]

Consequently, England's political and religious structure does not consist of a single line of authority, but rather, of various competing and overlapping sites of authority. Royal, parliamentary, civic, and religious authorities all vied for prominence, a situation that will get even more complicated after Henry VIII split off from Rome in 1533 to create the Church of England. This event ushered in the English Reformation, when the supposed unity of the Catholic Church will fracture into any number of competing versions of Christianity. Not only does one have the main division in England between **Catholicism** and **Protestantism**, but Protestantism itself will continuously subdivide (much more on this in subsequent chapters).

Social Organization

The same complexity and tension applies to England's social organization. On the one hand, the hierarchy of the Church and absolutism seems to have found its analogue in the ladder of English society, at least, according to the official versions of the social order. According to the "Homily on Obedience" (1547):

> Almighty God hath created and appointed all things in heaven, earth and waters in a most excellent and perfect order. In heaven he hath appointed distinct orders and states of archangels and angels. On earth he hath assigned kings, princes, with other governors under them, all in good and necessary order .... Every degree of people in their vocation, calling and office, hath appointed to them their duty and order. Some are in high degree, some in low; some kings and princes; some inferior and subjects, priests and laymen, masters and servants, fathers and children, husbands and wives, rich and poor, and every one have need of other so that in all things is to be lauded and praised the goodly order of God, without the which, no house, no city, no commonwealth, can continue and endure, for where there is no right order, there reigneth all abuse, carnal liberty, enormity, sin, and Babylonical confusion.[31]

God is to creation, in other words, as monarch is to subject, male to female, aristocrat to subject, those of high degree to low, and parent to child. While the overall picture is of an organic, interdependent society ("every one have need of other"), yet it is a society based on deference: subjects defer to the monarch, children defer to parents, and women defer to men. This order is divinely ordained, and therefore, stable.

The sixteenth-century historian, **William Harrison** (1535–93), also reproduces the official view of England's social order. The land is governed by "three sorts of persons."[32] First, "the prince, monarch, and head governor, which is called the King or (if the crown fall to the woman) the Queen"; second, "the gentlemen," or what we would call the aristocracy; and third, "the yeomanry," or wealthy, landed citizens who do not belong to the aristocracy.[33] At the very bottom one finds "the fourth and last sort of people," as Harrison calls them, who consist of "day laborers, poor husbandmen, and some retailers [traders] (which have no free land,) copyholders, and all artificers, as tailors, shoemakers, carpenters, brickmakers, masons etc."[34] These people "have neither voice nor authority in the commonwealth, but are to be ruled and not to rule other."[35] Those at the top of the hierarchy, the landowners with most of the wealth and power, constituted approximately one half of one percent of England's population.

Yet it would be a mistake to assume that this vision of a stable, hierarchical society in which everyone accepts the place God gave them enjoyed universal and unquestioned acceptance. Despite the assertion in the Homily on Obedience that each "have need of other," the massive inequality between the "fourth sort" and those with land and power did not go unnoticed or unchallenged, and periodically, fury against the "haves" would explode. "[L]et the rich churls pay, for they may well," cried the poor Londoners in 1522 after Henry VIII imposed yet more taxes to subsidize his French wars.[36] In 1595, enraged by the indifference of the wealthy to the suffering of the poor on account of the disastrous harvests, an anonymous libeler in Norfolk threatened that "some barbarous and unmerciful soldier shall lay open your hedges, reap your fields, rifle your coffers, and level your houses to the ground."[37] In 1649, the same year that **Charles I** would be executed, a Digger manifesto (the Diggers were one of the many radical groups to arise in the wake of **the Civil Wars**) called property "a bloody and subtle thievery."[38] The Homily's vision of everyone marching in mutual, well-beseeming ranks seems more wishful thinking than accurate reportage.

Economics

England's economic development contributed to this underlying sense of stress and instability. The growth in population after a century and a half of decline meant that prices also rose, and the Tudor–Stuart era witnessed a sustained period of inflation. Wages doubled, but prices increased by a factor of between five and seven times the original price in 1500. The harvest failures in 1519–21, the 1550s, the 1590s, and the 1630s also caused prices to spike, although good harvests would somewhat ease inflationary pressures. Agriculture provided the main industry in this period. First wool, then cloth, provided the main export commodity, and the price for raw wool went up accordingly. A key consequence (according to sixteenth-century commentators) of this rise was **the enclosure movement**, meaning, the "enclosing" or fencing off of previously unrestricted, or common, fields for raising sheep because the animals offered more profits than corn. In fact, the enclosure movement had been going on since the fourteenth century, but for a variety of reasons, it was widely considered to have reached crisis proportions in the first half of the sixteenth century. Because sheep take much less manpower to raise than corn, enclosing fields by greedy landlords contributed to depopulation, unemployment, abject poverty, and social unrest, a fact noted by **Thomas More** (1478–1535) in *Utopia* (1516): "Your sheep," says Hythlodaeus (More's chief exponent of the Utopian way of life and chief critic of European and English society), "which are usually so tame and so cheaply fed, begin now, according to report, to be so greedy and wild that they devour human beings themselves and devastate and depopulate fields, houses, and towns."[39] The problem eased by 1550s, but not before causing the 1549 insurrection, the largest in the sixteenth century, led by **Robert Kett** of Norfolk (see Chapter 4). While the discovery of the New World and the early English attempts at colonization had an incalculable intellectual impact on early modern England, their economic impact would become significant only after the Restoration.

While in one sense England's economy in the sixteenth and seventeenth centuries encouraged the stratification of society, in that the rich generally got richer while the poor got poorer, the ranks of the aristocracy and the wealthy merchants were in constant flux in this period. "Social mobility, upwards and downwards, was occurring at an unprecedented rate," as one distinguished historian writes, and the Jacobean poet and playwright, **Ben Jonson**

(1572–1637) is reported to have remarked, "the most worthy men have been rocked in mean cradles." Yet the porosity of supposedly fixed boundaries between the divisions in society caused terrific anxiety in some quarters.[40] Elizabeth's government tried to fix the problem through sumptuary laws (rules governing who can wear what), but these statutes were a dead letter from the moment of their publication. The result, as the Elizabethan pamphleteer, Phillip Stubbes, wrote in his diatribe against contemporary mores, the *Anatomy of Abuses* (1583),

> is such a confuse[d] mingle-mangle of apparel in Ailgna [England], and such preposterous excess thereof, as every one is permitted to flaunt it out, in what apparel he lust himself [he wants], or can get by any means. So that it is very hard to know who is noble, who is worshipful, who is a gentleman, who is not.[41]

Yet while some, like Stubbes, mourned the loss of old certainties, the growth of trade also led to the development of an increasingly powerful merchant class, people whose wealth was not always grounded in land (although as merchants acquired capital, many purchased the land that aristocrats, caught in a financial bind by a combination of extravagant spending and inflation, had to sell). This group developed its own identity, its own politics, and they demanded their own literature. Shakespeare, whose father was a glover, and Ben Jonson, whose stepfather was a brick-layer, belonged to the **middling sort**, the term historians often use for this group, and the public theater catered to their tastes. Francis Beaumont's *The Knight of the Burning Pestle* (1607), a clear precursor to Monty Python, explicitly lampoons the middling sort's desire for a literature of its own.

Even so, one's position in society did not always determine one's politics. Stubbes belonged to the merchant class, yet he opposed social mobility. Similarly, when in 1525, Thomas Howard, the third Duke of Norfolk, was sent to quell an insurrection in Suffolk, he sympathized with the rebels because he understood that their complaints of economic hardship were "true."[42] **Edward Seymour**

(King Edward VI's Lord Protector, see Chapter 4) also took the side of those protesting the enclosure movement. However, those who opposed absolutism were not necessarily in favor of the disenfranchised. Even as **Sir Thomas Smith** denounces absolutism as fundamentally un-English, he is the source for William Harrison's comments about the "fourth sort of men which do not rule."[43] Politics in the early modern era was messy and, often to our eyes, inconsistent or contradictory.

Gender

The same applies to the problem of gender. As with politics, here again one has to recognize the multiplicity of ideas, some contradictory, circulating throughout early modern England, sometimes within the same texts. Certainly, many believed that women should occupy a subordinate position in early modern society. Like the view of class and social structure in the Homily on Obedience, the notion that women are fundamentally inferior to men has a Biblical warrant, in particular, Eve's creation after Adam in the second creation story (Genesis 2:18–25)[44] and the Fall (Genesis 3:1–24), one result being women's subjection to men: "thy desire shall be to thy husband, and he shall rule over thee" (Gen. 3:16). This passage was elaborated in the New Testament. In his epistle to the Corinthians, for example, Paul insists that the man does not have to cover his head when praying, but women do, because "he is the image and glory of God: but the woman is the glory of the man. For the man is not of the woman; but the woman of the man. Neither was the man created for the woman; but the woman for the man" (I Cor. 7–9). This view received official sanction in the "Homily on the State of Matrimony:" (1563): For thus doth Saint Peter preach to them:

> "You wives, be you in subjection to obey your own husbands" [1 Peter 3:1]. To obey is another thing than to control or command, which yet they may do to their children, and to their family; but as for their husbands, them must they obey, and cease from commanding, and perform subjection.[45]

20

Women were not only subordinate to men, they were widely considered fundamentally inferior. To again quote the Homily on Matrimony:

> For the woman is a weak creature, not endued [endowed] with like strength and constancy of mind, therefore, they be the sooner disquieted, and they be the more prone to all weak affections and dispositions of mind, more than men be; and lighter they be, and more vain in their fantasies and opinions.[46]

This position had severe practical consequences in early modern England. Women could not, for example, attend Oxford or Cambridge; they could not pursue a career in law or medicine, and when married, all their property became their husband's. According to *The Law's Resolutions of Women's Rights* (1632), written by one "T. E.," the status of women was almost exactly analogous to that of the "fourth sort": because of Eve's punishment after the Fall,

> women have no voice in Parliament; they make no laws; they consent to none; they abrogate none. All of them are understood either married or to be married, and their desires subject to their husband …. The Common Law here shaketh hand[s] with Divinity.[47]

At the same time, the status of women in early modern culture was both officially and unofficially more complex. Despite the injunctions mandating female subservience and fulminations about female inferiority, England was ruled by a woman for over half a century (first Mary Tudor, then Elizabeth I). Contemporary descriptions of England's political structure fully accept that the monarch may be a "King or Queen," and that a queen's powers are identical to a king's.[48] To return to the question of marriage, women had more agency in choosing their partners than was often thought. When Lord Burleigh declined the marriage offer, he does not say, presumably because it would be assumed, that his daughter would have veto power over the match. While marriage manuals and other texts on domestic affairs often insisted that children needed to consult their parents before marrying, these texts evidence a long, vociferous tradition deploring forced marriage and warning of its consequences.[49] Furthermore, a sizable minority of women did not get married at all.

Despite the lack of access to formal education, literacy became increasingly common among both elite and non-elite women. (T. E., for example, writes at the conclusion of *The Law's Resolutions* [1632] that his work is "chiefly addressed to women."[50]) The same applies to paid labor and the law. Even though women were supposed to restrict themselves to the home and parenthood, it was not unusual for married women to have shops, and widows were granted the right to practice their late husband's craft. While the law clearly favored men in property disputes, during Elizabeth's reign, the court of Chancery "developed procedures to protect and enforce the property rights of wealthy married women," and the common law courts held that "a husband could not dispose of a wife's property or her dower as he wished."[51] While misogyny and the secondary status of women were facts of life in this period, there is strong evidence that many thought otherwise, and they acted out their lives accordingly. T. E., for example, may declare that the "Common Law here shaketh hand[s] with Divinity" in authorizing the inferior status of women, but that does not mean he is happy about it, and he recognizes that theory and practice conflict with each other for at least some: "I know no remedy, though some women can shift it well enough."[52]

Indeed, there is a fascinating awareness of the costs of being a woman in early modern culture even among those insisting upon that cost. The Homilist, for example, grants women "must especially feel the grief and pains of their matrimony, in that they relinquish the liberty of their own rule, in the pain of their travailing [giving birth], in the bringing up of their children. In which offices they be in great perils, and be grieved with great afflictions, which they might be without, if they lived out of matrimony."[53] T. E. also illustrates how misogyny and a consciousness of the injustice of misogyny could co-exist. In his section on widowhood, T. E. first claims that the death of the husband means that the wife's "head is cut off, her intellectual part is gone, the very faculties of her soul are, I will not say clean taken away, but they are all benumbed, dimmed and dazzled."[54] T. E. then offers to provide comfort, but he does not suggest that the widow restore her soul by remarrying. Rather, he reminds the widow that for the first time in her life, she is free: "Why mourn you so, you that be widows? Consider how long you have been in subjection under the predominance of parents, of your husbands; now you be free in liberty ... at your own law."[55] T. E.'s emphasis on newfound liberty reflects social reality, as those widows lucky enough to inherit their husband's business were often reluctant to remarry.

* * *

Early modern England, therefore, is a study of contrasts, contradictions, and contending forces. For every position on monarchy, social organization, or gender, there is a counter position. Absolutism is answered by the Ancient Constitution; a view of the social order as hierarchical, stable, and divinely instituted is complemented by social mobility and more than occasional vitriolic outbursts against inequality; the one true church must contend with the competing claims of many churches; and Biblically sanctioned misogyny is answered by decades of female rule and a keen awareness of the price women pay for the accident of their gender. The key is not to privilege one view over another, but to try to comprehend England's multiple and competing discourses and ideologies.

Notes

1 For an excellent introduction to the differences between these two terms, see David Loewenstein and Janel Mueller, "Introduction," *The Cambridge History of Early Modern English Literature*, ed. David Loewenstein and Janel Mueller (Cambridge: Cambridge University Press, 2003), 4–7.

2 *Illustrations of British History, Biography, and Manners in the Reigns of Henry VIII, Edward VI, Mary, Elizabeth and James I*, ed. Edmund Lodge (London: John Chidley, 1838), vol. 2, 52–3.

3   D. M. Palliser, *The Age of Elizabeth: England under the later Tudors 1547– 1603* (London: Longman, 1983), 40–1.

4   All references to Shakespeare's plays will be to the Riverside edition.

5   The information from this paragraph is taken from Louis Schwartz, *Milton and Maternal Mortality* (Cambridge: Cambridge University Press, 2009), 37–40.

6   Quoted in Sara Mendelson and Patricia Crawford, *Women in Early Modern England: 1550–1720* (Oxford: Oxford University Press, 1998), 152.

7   David Scott Kastan, "Print, Literary Culture, and the Book Trade," *Cambridge History of Early Modern Literature*, ed. David Loewenstein and Janel Mueller, 82.

8   Cyndia Susan Clegg, *Press Censorship in Elizabethan England* (Cambridge: Cambridge University Press, 1997), 75. With her two subsequent books, *Press Censorship in Jacobean England* (Cambridge: Cambridge University Press, 2001) and *Press Censorship in Caroline England* (Cambridge: Cambridge University Press, 2008), Clegg has written the definitive history of the subject.

9   Harold Love and Arthur F. Marotti, "Manuscript Transmission and Circulation," *Cambridge History of Early Modern Literature*, ed. David Loewenstein and Janel Mueller, 57.

10 D. M. Palliser, *The Age of Elizabeth: England under the Later Tudors 1547– 1603* (New York: London, 1983), 365.

11 Thomas Dekker, *The Shoemaker's Holiday*, in *English Renaissance Drama: A Norton Anthology*, ed. David Bevington *et al.* (New York: Norton, 2002).

12 Quoted in David Harris Willson, *King James VI & I* (London: Jonathan Cape, 1956), 207.

13 *An Admonition to Parliament,* in *Puritan Manifestoes: A Study of the Origin of the Puritan Revolt*, ed. W. H. Frere and C. E. Douglas (rpt. New York: Burt Franklin, 1972), 29.

14 *Admonition to Parliament*, 115.

15 Thomas Tymme, *A Plain Discovery of Ten English Lepers* (1592), sig. M1v.

16 *An Homily against Disobedience and Willful Rebellion* was printed in the aftermath of the Northern Rebellion, and the text consists of not one, but six connected homilies on the evils of rebellion. I have used the abridged version in *Divine Right and Democracy: An Anthology of Political*

Writing in Stuart England, ed. David Wootton (London: Penguin, 1986), 95–6.

17 *The True Law of Free Monarchies*, in *King James VI and I: Political Writings*, ed. Johann P. Sommerville (Cambridge: Cambridge University Press, 1994), 72.

18 Sir John Fortescue, *In Praise of the Laws of England*, in *On the Laws and Governance of England*, ed. Shelley Lockwood (Cambridge: Cambridge University Press, 1997), 17.

19 Fortescue, *In Praise of the Laws of England*, 48.

20 *King James VI and I: Political Writings*, ed. Sommerville, 143.

21 Fortescue, *In Praise of the Laws of England*, 21.

22 *Journals of the House of Commons* (London: House of Commons, 1803), 147.

23 Smith, *De Republica Anglorum*, ed. Mary Dewar (Cambridge: Cambridge University Press, 1982), 54.

24 Smith, *De Republica Anglorum*, 78.

25 *The Ready and Easy Way to Establish a Free Commonwealth*, in *The Complete Poetry and Essential Prose of John Milton*, ed. William Kerrigan, John Rumrich, and Stephen M. Fallon (New York: Modern Library, 2007), 1128. Unless otherwise noted, all further references to Milton's poetry and prose will be to this edition.

26 John Ponet, *A Short Treatise of Politic Power* (Strasbourg, 1556), sig. Gii.

27 Edward Hall, *Hall's Chronicle*, ed. Sir Henry Ellis (London: J. Johnson et al., 1809), 10.

28 Selden, *Table Talk of John Selden*, ed. Frederick Pollock (London: Selden Society, 1927), 137.

29 *The Boke of Magna Carta and all Other Statutes* (London, 1534), sig. Aiiii. It was common in this period for collections of statutes to begin with Magna Carta.

30 *English Coronation Records*, ed. Leopold G. Wickham (Westminster: Archibald Constable, 1901), 240–1.

31 "The Exhortation concerning Good Order and Obedience to Rulers and Magistrates," in *Certain Sermons or Homilies* (London, 1547), sigs. Riir–Riiiv. Faced with the problem of an uneducated clergy, Thomas Cranmer (1489–1556), Archbishop of Canterbury, proposed writing a book of model sermons or homilies. The first book of homilies was officially issued in 1547, during the reign of Edward VI. It was repressed during the reign of the Catholic Mary Tudor, but reissued by Elizabeth I

in 1559. A second book of homilies, with twenty one additional sermons, came out in 1563.

32   William Harrison, *The Description of England*, ed. Georges Edelen (Ithaca: Cornell University Press, 1968), 120.
33   Harrison, *Description of England*, 120.
34   Harrison, *Description of England*, 118.
35   Harrison, *Description of England*, 118.
36   *Hall's Chronicle*, 642.
37   *Historical Manuscripts Commission: Calendar of the Manuscripts of the Marquis of Salisbury*, ed. E. Salisbury (London: HMSO, 1915), ser. 9, vol. 13, 168–9.
38   *The True Leveller's Standard Advanced*, in *Puritanism and Liberty*, ed. A. S. P. Woodhouse (Chicago: University of Chicago Press, 1951), 382.
39   Thomas More, *Utopia*, ed. Edward Surtz (New Haven: Yale University Press, 1964), 24.
40   Laurence Stone, *The Crisis of the Aristocracy: 1558–1641* (New York: Oxford University Press, 1967), 23. John Aubrey, *Aubrey's Brief Lives*, ed. Oliver L. Dick (New York: Godine, 1999), xxiii. I am grateful to Robin Hamilton for his help with this quotation.
41   Stubbes, *The Anatomy of Abuses* (London, 1583), sig. C2v.
42   The incident is recounted in Hall, *Hall's Chronicle*, 699–700.
43   Smith, *De Republica Anglorum*, 76.
44   The first creation story can be found in Genesis 1:1–2:3. Generally, early modern interpreters conflated the two stories. I have used the King James translation.
45   *The Second Tome of Homilies* (London, 1563), sig. Lll.5v-r.
46   *The Second Tome of Homilies*, sig. Lll.4v.
47   T. E., *The Law's Resolutions of Women's Rights* (London, 1632), sig. B4v.
48   Smith, *De Republica Anglorum*, 85. See also Harrison in note 52.
49   Alan McFarlane, *Marriage and Love in England: Modes of Reproduction 1300–1840* (Oxford: Blackwell, 1986), 134.
50   T. E., *The Law's Resolutions*, sig. Dd2r.
51   Mendelson and Crawford, *Women in Early Modern England: 1550–1720*, 40, 41.
52   T. E., *The Law's Resolutions*, sig. B4v.
53   "Homily on the State of Matrimony," sig. Lll.6v.
54   T. E., *The Law's Resolutions*, sig. Q5v.
55   T. E., *The Law's Resolutions*, sig. Q5v.

2

The Back-Story of the Tudor Dynasty: From Richard II to Henry VII

The story of the Tudor–Stuart dynasty does not begin with the accession of Henry VII in 1485 (which in any event was less an "accession" and more of a coup). Rather, we need to begin with the reign of Richard II, as his deposition in 1399 and assassination the following year would lead directly to Henry Tudor's becoming king of England almost a century later. This understanding of history, it is important to note, is not a product of contemporary scholars, but how sixteenth- and seventeenth-century writers viewed these events. Furthermore, it would not be an overstatement to say that the early modern period was obsessed with history. Richard's deposition, the various kings of the fifteenth century, and the Wars of the Roses provided a constant source of inspiration for chroniclers, poets, and playwrights. In addition to Shakespeare's history plays (the three parts of *Henry VI* [1589–91], *Richard III* [1592–93], *Richard II* [1595], the two parts of *Henry IV* [1596–97, 1598] and *Henry V* [1599]), other examples include Hall's

A Short History of Early Modern England: British Literature in Context, First Edition.
Peter C. Herman.
© 2011 Peter C. Herman. Published 2011 by Blackwell Publishing Ltd.

Chronicle (1548), *Holinshed's Chronicles* (1577; 1586), Thomas Heywood's drama, *Edward the Fourth* (1599), and Samuel Daniel's long poem, *The Civil Wars* (1609).

The Wars of the Roses

While the Lancastrians, the Yorkists, and the Tudors included the rose among their emblems, Sir Walter Scott coined the phrase "The Wars of the Roses" at the start of the nineteenth century.

The politics of the late-fourteenth and fifteenth centuries also provided a sharp analogue for contemporary events. Confronted with a performance of Shakespeare's play sponsored by supporters of the Earl of Essex, Elizabeth I said to William Lambarde, "I am Richard II. Know ye not that?"[1] This period was sufficiently incendiary that writing its history could put one into mortal danger. In 1599, the lawyer John Hayward published *The Life and Reign of King Henry IV*, a book focused much more on Richard II's deposition than on the life of the man who succeeded him, and for his pains he was arrested for treason. One of Hayward's prosecutors demanded to know: "What was the true cause of setting forth this single story?"[2] Early modern writers believed that the political events of the late fourteenth and fifteenth centuries provided much more than a parallel for their own times. They believed, rightly, that this period formed the Tudor–Stuart polity in much the same way that many today argue that the American Civil War shapes the contemporary United States of America. However, in recounting the back-story of the Tudor dynasty, one has to distinguish between what actually happened (or at least, the evidence given by contemporary chroniclers and documents), how those events were interpreted by Tudor–Stuart writers, and how those interpretations were interpreted by contemporary literary critics and historians.

Two caveats before we begin: First, while I will occasionally animate the record by referring to Shakespeare's immensely influential history plays, students need to resist the gravitational pull of assuming that these dramas reflect what actually happened. They do not. While these plays are "based on true events," as the phrase goes, Shakespeare had no qualms about altering characters, events, and chronology if that made his works dramatically more effective. The portrayal of Henry IV's son, Prince Hal, indulging in highway robbery and hanging out with lowlifes in taverns has no basis in reality, and the marvelous character of Sir John Falstaff originates entirely in Shakespeare's imagination. Shakespeare's plays, as well as other history plays, may bring history alive, and they offer many keen insights into politics, but for what actually transpired we must try to stick with the archives.

Second, this chapter will largely concern the dynastic history of the Tudor dynasty. It is "history from above," not "history from below," and while I will pay some attention to the experiences of the non-elite in this period, in particular, the Jack Cade Rebellion, they are not the primary focus. My approach in this chapter arises from the fact that dynastic history was supremely important to people living in the sixteenth and seventeenth centuries. Claims to political power were based on lineage and seemingly abstruse family relationships. For example, in Shakespeare's *I Henry VI*, just before he dies, Mortimer gives a long speech (32 lines) rehearsing the dynastic history that justifies (in his view) his claim to the throne (2.5.61–92), and in *2 Henry VI*, Richard, Duke of York, rehearses the family tree justifying *his* claim: "The third son, Duke of Clarence, from whose line / I claim the crown, had issue, Philippe, a daughter / Who married Edmund Mortimer, Earl of March; / Edmund had issue, Roger Earl of March; / Roger had issue, Edmund, Anne, and Eleanor" (2.2.34–8). These speeches did not put the audience to sleep (in fact, the *Henry VI* plays were wildly popular) because this information *mattered* to early modern audiences and readers in ways that contemporaries, whose eyes tend to glaze over when confronted with long passages filled with who had issue by whom, need to recover if we are to fully understand this period's literature. For example, the legitimacy of King James VI's claim to be Elizabeth I's heir rested in his descending from Henry VIII's sister, Margaret, who married King James IV of Scotland in 1503. Consequently, James's claim to the throne rested in the female line, not the male, which (switching to literature) gives a tremendous boost to Caliban's claim to sovereignty in *The Tempest*: "This island's mine by Sycorax my mother" (1.2.331). Given that Caliban's claim to legitimacy mirrors that of King James, a Jacobean audience could not, or should not, easily dismiss it, and therefore, we are invited to reconsider both Caliban and Prospero's claims to sovereignty and moral probity. To understand the full extent of Shakespeare's treatment of Caliban, we need a basic knowledge of England's dynastic history. That is what this chapter hopes to provide.

Titles and Names of the Nobility

A *duke* is a hereditary rank of nobility, ranking just below that of the monarch or prince. Under Richard II, the rank was gradually extended beyond the royal family. An *earl* is a step below a *duke*, and the title implies the governorship of a county.

The names of medieval and early modern nobles can be very confusing as the same person can be referred to in a variety of ways. Generally, each person has a Christian or a first name (e.g., "Thomas," "Richard," "Henry") and a territorial name, either his most prestigious or wealthiest holding (e.g., "Norfolk" or "Lancaster") or the place where he was born. For example, Henry V was born at Monmouth Castle, and so he is sometimes known as "Henry of Monmouth" or even "King Henry of Monmouth." In *1 Henry VI*, Mortimer will refer to Henry V as "Henry Monmouth" (2.5.33).

Sometimes a person can be known by both their lands and their birth place. For example, Richard II's uncle, Thomas, born in the town of Woodstock, was made Duke of Gloucester in 1384, and so he is called either "Woodstock" or "Gloucester."

Plantagenet is the surname of all the kings of England from Henry II to Richard III.

The history of the English monarchy in the fifteenth century is very much a family affair in which two rival branches of the Plantagenet family vied for the crown. In 1362, **Edward III** (1312–77) told Parliament that he felt blessed "in many ways and especially in the engendering of sons who are come to manhood,"[3] and indeed that was the case, although Edward III's actuarial good fortune did not redound to England's benefit. His sons, along with their important progeny, are as follows:

- **Edward, the Black Prince** (1330–76), so-called because of his armor's color, **Edward III**'s eldest son and heir to the throne, father of **Richard II** (1367–1400).
- **Lionel, Duke of Clarence** (1338–68). He died while **Richard II** was a baby, and his grandson, **Roger Mortimer, Earl of March** (1328–60) would be Richard's legitimate heir. Lionel's great-grand-daughter would become the mother of **Richard, Duke of York** (1411–60), who would die in battle trying to depose **Henry VI** (1421–71), thus starting the conflict between the **house of Lancaster** and the **house of York** later known as the "**Wars of the Roses**."
- **John of Gaunt, Duke of Lancaster** (1340–99), father of **Henry of Bolingbroke** (1366–1414), later **Henry IV.** His descendants constitute the **house of Lancaster**.
- **Edmund of Langley, Duke of York** (1341–1402). His grandson would be **Richard, Duke of York**, whose mother descended from **Lionel, Duke of Clarence** (see above). The "Wars of the Roses" is a conflict between his descendants (the **house of York**) and his brother's, **John of Gaunt, the Duke of Lancaster (the house of Lancaster)**.
- **Thomas of Woodstock, Duke of Gloucester** (1355–97).

The course of Richard II's life was determined by the early death of his father and the subsequent demise of his grandfather. The death of Edward III's heir, **Edward, the Black Prince**, in 1376, made the young Richard next in line for the throne, and when his grandfather, **Edward III**, succumbed the following year, 1377, Richard became king of England at age ten.

The most important event of Richard's early reign was the **Peasants' Revolt** of 1381 (Richard was 14 at the time). Successive outbreaks of the bubonic plague had greatly reduced England's workforce, leading those remaining in a position to demand more money; the Statute of Laborers (1351) tried to limit their bargaining power by specifying wages and limiting mobility. Increasing taxation exacerbated tensions to the point that laborers in Essex and Kent rioted. Led by **Wat Tyler** (d. 1381), the rebels marched on London, where they stormed the Tower, killing the Archbishop of Canterbury, among others, and destroying John of Gaunt's palace (the rebels did not, however, loot it, suggesting that they were not a wild mob). In addition to economic grievances, the rebels were also motivated by a fiery brand of radical egalitarianism that would resurface during the English Civil Wars. At the beginning of the rebellion, **John Ball** (d. 1381) preached a sermon based on the proverb, "When Adam delved and Eve spun, / Who was then a gentleman?" Richard met with the rebels and defused the violence by promising a pardon if they dispersed, a promise that he initially fulfilled but, on July 2, formally revoked.

The king's courageous demeanor over the course of these events demonstrated that he was no longer a child (although subsequent events would show that neither was he quite an adult), and Richard demanded more independence in the formation and maintenance of his court. As one might expect, giving a teenager free rein did not end well. As Anthony Tucker puts it, the king's spending on his courtiers and friends was "lavish to the point of foolishness,"[4] especially since the continuing war with France (known as the "Hundred Years War") also required significant financing, and parliament had to step in to restore financial order and stop Richard's extravagant spending. The Commons also demanded that Richard sack his chancellor, Michael de la Pole (1330–89), thus raising the key issue of the king's prerogative to appoint and dismiss ministers as he pleased. Richard refused, escalating the problem into a major crisis that was momentarily resolved only with Richard's agreeing to the dismissal and imprisonment of de la Pole and the imposition of a commission to examine and control royal finances. Richard's powerful uncles,

Thomas of Woodstock and **John of Gaunt**, sided with the Commons in their demands.

Richard responded to what he considered an affront to his royal prerogative with a two-pronged strategy. First, in 1387, in order to shore up his legal position, Richard submitted a series of questions to his judges, and they responded that the commission on royal finances imposed by the Commons had infringed upon the king's "prerogative and the liberties of the crown." The most inflammatory determination, however, was the judges' opinion that the sponsors of this commission should be punished as traitors.[5] Second, he went on a progress whose real purpose was to gather a force loyal only to him. When Parliament met in 1388 (the "Merciless Parliament"), a group of lords, known as the **Lords Appellant**, presented an indictment of treason against the king's favorites, and this group comprised of **Thomas of Woodstock**, Richard Fitzalan, Earl of Arundel, Thomas Beauchamp, Earl of Warwick, **Henry Bolingbroke**, Earl of Derby and son of **John of Gaunt**, and **Thomas Mowbray, Earl of Nottingham**. One of those accused of treason, Robert de Vere, Earl of Oxford, raised an army to support Richard, but they were soundly defeated at Radcot Bridge in Oxfordshire on December 20. Richard's friends and supporters were either executed or exiled (including the judges who had unconditionally supported Richard's expansive view of royal power). Richard was now essentially powerless, and some chroniclers suggest he was actually deposed for a few days, but the Lords Appellant could not decide on a replacement.

In 1389, when he turned 21, Richard claimed, and the Lords Appellant agreed, that he was entitled to assume sole responsibility for ruling, and for the next seven years, all remained relatively calm. Richard did not seek revenge for the executions and banishments of his friends, and he pursued a rapprochement with France, which had the important effect of significantly lowering the level of taxation. In the early 1390s, Richard's court also became a center of artistic and literary patronage (the frontispiece to a manuscript of *Troilus and Crisyde* shows Chaucer before Richard's court[6]). More ominously, Richard's inordinate love of authority continued to develop. One chronicler recounts this weird scene:

After this, on solemn festivals when, by custom, [Richard] performed kingly rituals, he would order a throne to be prepared for him in his chamber on which he liked to sit ostentatiously from after dinner until vespers, talking to no one but watching everyone; and when his eye fell on anyone, regardless of rank, that person had to bend his knee towards the king ....[7]

In 1397, for reasons that remain obscure, Richard decided to strike back against the Lords Appellant and to restore what he considered his full authority. The king summoned a parliament, and, in what was almost certainly a deliberate echo of 1388, the speaker of the house charged **Thomas of Woodstock** along with the Earls of Arundel and Warwick with treason because, as a chronicler writes, they "compelled you [the king] to concede a commission touching the government and state of your kingdom, which was to the prejudice of your regality and majesty, whereby they did you great injury."[8] **Thomas of Woodstock** was delivered to **Thomas Mowbray**, the captain of the French port of Calais, where he died under mysterious circumstances. (In Shakespeare's *Richard II,* Mowbray asserts that he "slew him not," mysteriously adding "but to my own disgrace / Neglected my sworn duty in that case" [1.1.133–4]). For Richard, the victory seemed complete. The estates of the Lords Appellant were confiscated, his enemies declared traitors, and his expansive view of royal power confirmed. The latter was so important to him that the epitaph he composed for himself began "He threw down all who violated the royal prerogative ...."[9]

But Richard would soon be forcefully reminded that even a robust view of royal power has its limits. For the next few years, Richard ruled in an oppressive, tyrannical manner. He forced the inhabitants of London, among others, to sign blank charters, essentially allowing the king to confiscate their goods at will, and anyone who protested was hauled into court, where, according to the indictment against Richard presented to parliament, they "were not permitted to enter any response except that they were not guilty, nor to defend themselves otherwise ...."[10] If Richard intended these measures to assure his safety, they had the exact opposite effect, and the period's literature testifies to the growing dissatisfaction with his rule. In his short poem, "O Deus

Immense" (c. 1399), John Gower warned that "When the people's voice does not dare to speak out loud, / They speak their mind more darkly in murmurs" (23–4), and while Gower casts most of the poem in generalities (e.g., "A king who reckons gold greater than the hearts of his people / Immediately falls from the people's mind" [21–2]), at the end, he explicitly warns Richard about his behavior. No longer speaking about "*a* king," Gower concludes, "Therefore let *the king* see how he travels in his chariot, / And take care lest he lose a wheel and suffer a fall" [101–2; my emphasis]).[11] Another chronicler recorded "the harsh bondage to which the whole community was being subjected," and there was at least one serious popular uprising against Richard.[12] Even so, his hold on the throne remained secure. Or so it seemed.

Richard finally went over the line in his dealings with **Henry Bolingbroke** and **Thomas Mowbray**, both of whom, we should recall, were junior members of the Lords Appellant, and Mowbray was likely implicated in Thomas of Woodstock's death. The precise cause of the quarrel between these two remains unclear, but it seems that Mowbray spoke to Henry about their precarious position at court, but rather than making common cause with Mowbray, Henry decided to accuse him of treason, perhaps thinking that this action would make him safer. Somewhat inexplicably, both laid their accusations before Richard, who ordered the matter settled by trial by combat. Thanks to Shakespeare's *Richard II*, the denouement is famous: Richard interrupted the duel ("Stay, the King hath thrown his warder down" [1.3.118]) and exiled both: Mowbray for life (he died in Venice the next year), and Bolingbroke for six years. However, Shakespeare leaves out how the actual Richard II granted Henry Bolingbroke full rights to his inheritance if Bolingbroke's father, John of Gaunt, died before his exile ended. Equally famously, this is exactly what happened. Gaunt died on February 3, 1399, but rather than allowing Bolingbroke to inherit the wealthy and vast duchy of Lancaster, Richard disinherited him and confiscated the lands and their revenue. This action precipitated Henry's return from exile and Richard's deposition.

Why was this act so important? Why does Shakespeare's York warn Richard that if he seizes Bolingbroke's inheritance, "you pluck a thousand dangers on your head / You lose a thousand well-disposed hearts, And prick my tender patience to those thoughts / Which honor and allegiance cannot think" (2.1.205–8). Why does York say that Richard risks rebellion?

As we learned in Chapter 1, there were two theories of monarchy current in early modern England, absolutism (the monarch is above the law), and the Ancient Constitution (the monarch is bound by the law). While the two are largely opposite in their means, they share a common end: the preservation of private property. The 1547 Homily on Obedience declared that without the social hierarchy, "no man shall keep his wife, children, and possessions in quietness, all things shall be common";[13] similarly, Sir John Fortescue asserts that because the monarch cannot change the laws of England at his pleasure, the people "freely enjoy their goods, and are despoiled neither by their own king nor any other."[14] By seizing **Henry Bolingbroke's** inheritance without any legal cause, **Richard II** violated the central tenet of England's political system: the sanctity of private property. While Richard's other tyrannies were directed at particular individuals, this act affected everyone: if Richard "could thus contrive to steal Lancaster, he could steal any inheritance in the land."[15] Richard then made another error. A new outbreak of violence in Ireland broke out in 1398, and the king left England to put down the rebellion. Given the personal nature of royal authority in the fifteenth century, Richard's absenting himself from England after thoroughly antagonizing the landowning classes was a fatal mistake.

Henry Bolingbroke, however, did not simply capture Richard after he returned from his (successful) campaign in Ireland, kill him, and then declare himself king. Rather, Bolingbroke was very careful to proceed by law rather than exclusively by force. Thus, Bolingbroke turned to parliament to give legal sanction to both Richard's deposition and his acceptance of the crown. In 1399, **Richard II**, willingly or unwillingly (the chronicles give conflicting versions), resigned the crown, and the articles against Richard were announced in parliament. While the charges singled out Richard's treatment of the Lords Appellant, they also focused on Richard's conception of monarchy. For example, item sixteen reads (in Edward Hall's translation): "he said that the laws of England were in his head, and sometime[s] in his breast, by reason of which fantastical opinion, he destroyed noble men and impoverished the poor commons."[16] After the charges were read, **Henry Bolingbroke** rose and claimed the throne "through that right that God of his grace hath sent me."[17] When he had done, according to the parliamentary records, "the lords spiritual and temporal and all the estates there present, singly and in common, were asked how they felt about this claim and vindication [and the] same estates with all the people without any difficulty or delay unanimously consented ... that the aforesaid duke should reign over them."[18] Thus began the reign of **Henry IV**.

As for Richard, the details of his fate remain uncertain. One chronicler wrote that Sir Piers Exton killed him at the new king's behest (while Shakespeare dramatizes this version, it is almost certainly not true). Others say Richard was starved to death while still more claim that Richard starved himself to death. The only point of agreement is the date that Richard died: February 14, 1400. While Henry IV had Richard entombed at the royal manor of Kings Langley, Henry IV's son, **Henry V**, had him reburied in Westminster Abbey in 1413 in an attempt to heal political wounds.

In the table of contents prepared for Edward Hall's chronicle (Hall died the year before its publication in 1548), the next two chapters are called "The Unquiet Time of King Henry the Fourth" and "The Victorious Acts of King Henry V," which may seem contrived but actually provides a reasonably accurate description of their reigns.

Henry IV's time on the throne (1399–1413) was indeed "unquiet," or at least, for the first eight years the king was beset by an ongoing series of rebellions. Even though Henry proceeded by law (or by color of law), not everyone accepted the legitimacy of Richard's deposition. From Henry II (1154–89) onward, the English crown had passed from father to son, and Henry Bolingbroke broke that chain. Consequently, the taint of usurpation hung over the majority of Henry's reign. Overall, **Henry IV** faced three major and several less threatening challenges to his rule.

First, continuing Scots raids across the northern border along with Scots king, Robert III's refusal to recognize Henry's title led Henry IV to lead an army into Scotland. Apparently, appearances were sufficient to pacify the Scots, as there was no resistance, and the English army also showed restraint in not wasting the countryside. But on the way back from Scotland in 1400, Henry IV learned of a much more serious and tenacious threat: **Owain Glyn Dŵr (Owen Glendower)** (c. 1359–c. 1416), a Welsh nobleman, had proclaimed himself Prince of Wales and raided various English towns in north Wales and Shropshire. Every summer (the "campaign season" since bad weather, planting, and harvesting prevented warfare at other times) for eight years, **Henry IV** and his son, also named Henry but better known by his nickname, **Hal,** fought Glendower's rebel forces.

In Shakespeare, Glendower's claims that at his birth "the earth did shake" and that he can call spirits from the "vasty deep" (*1 Henry IV* 2.4.20, 52) make him hard to take seriously, but the actual Glendower posed a very significant threat. Not only did the Welsh rebellion deprive Henry of income from those lands (money was always scarce during his reign), but in 1405, **Glendower** invaded western England with reinforcements from France. Fortunately for Henry IV, the assault foundered, France withdrew its support in 1406, and the rebellion petered out. Even so, from 1403 onward **Henry IV** devolved primary responsibility for defeating Glendower to **Prince Hal**, which is why the legends of a youth misspent in drunk revelry and petty theft are so fanciful. He "must have squeezed a great deal of self-indulgence into his winter trips to the capital. During the campaign season he was otherwise occupied."[19]

The second challenge came from the **Percy** family, including **Henry Percy, Earl of Northumberland** (1341–1408), and his son, also named Henry (the repetition of names is a constant source of confusion) but like Henry IV's son, better known by his nickname, **Hotspur** (1364–1403). This family ranked among the most powerful of the northern earls, and their advice and military support was essential in Henry Bolingbroke's campaign against Richard II. It was, for example, Northumberland who captured **Richard II** in July, 1399. Determining the precise reasons for the Percy rebellion against the man they did so much to help remains difficult because chroniclers depict their motivations differently, according to their bias.

Those sympathetic to the Henry IV and the Lancastrians accuse the Percies of ingratitude and pride; those sympathetic to the Yorkist cause view them as rightfully opposing an unlawful king whom they never intended to put on the throne.[20] In a sense, the question comes down to what Henry Bolingbroke said or did not say when he landed at Ravenspur in July 1399. When in 1403 their quarrel with the new king descended into armed conflict, the Percies claimed, and many chroniclers repeat the claim, that Bolingbroke swore – in public – that he had come only to recover his inheritance. However, their protests of ignorance about Bolingbroke's true intentions may have been more strategic than actual as these were hardly naïve men, and everyone understood both the stakes and the consequences of backing Bolingbroke rather than Richard II.

The actual reasons seem to be a combination of money issues and dynastic ambition. The Percies complained, with some justification, that Henry IV was far too slow in paying them for defending the realm (lack of money was a constant concern for Henry IV), and the king gave lands to a rival that had been promised to them. As a result of these financial squabbles, **Hotspur** refused to hand over to the king certain valuable Scots prisoners on the grounds that Henry IV owed them money. Henry IV also refused to ransom **Sir Edmund Mortimer**, Hotspur's brother-in-law, after he had been captured by the Welsh rebels. The king was all too glad to have Mortimer out of the way because Mortimer arguably had an equally good if not better claim to the throne: just as **Henry IV** could claim royal blood through being the grandson of Edward III's third son, John of Gaunt, Sir Edmund Mortimer could claim that he was the progeny of Edward III's *second* son, Lionel (birth order counts in these matters). The key difference is that while Henry IV's claim descended through the father (John of Gaunt), Edmund Mortimer's claim descended through his mother, **Philippa**, Lionel's daughter, and inheritance was not supposed to pass through the maternal line.

The Percies may have rebelled because they wanted to install Edmund on the throne, which would make them the most powerful family in England, since they would have been kingmakers twice over. But it was not to be. **Henry IV** defeated the rebels at the **Battle**

of Shrewsbury on July 21, 1403 (the battle that ends Shakespeare's *1 Henry IV*), in which Hotspur was killed. While Northumberland managed to avoid being charged for treason, he did not stop scheming against Henry IV, and in 1405, he entered into an alliance with Owen Glendower and Sir Edmund Mortimer, creating a plan to divide the kingdom among them and place Mortimer on the throne (Shakespeare alters the chronology by moving the plot to before the Battle of Shrewsbury). This plot also failed, and Northumberland was essentially on the run until finally killed in 1408.

In 1403, **Henry IV** also faced another, probably unrelated rebellion led by **Richard Scrope, Archbishop of York** (1327–1403) who decided to take up arms against Henry IV in reaction to the king's excessive taxation of the laity and other crimes against good government.[21] Henry IV easily crushed Scrope's uprising, and he had him executed after a legally dubious proceeding. The king suffered his first attack of ill-health, which immobilized him for a week. Henry IV's enemies moralized his illness as divine vengeance for the execution of a bishop. The end of the Scrope rebellion and the collapse of Northumberland's plots meant the end of any meaningful resistance to Lancastrian rule, and the next eight years were blissfully uneventful in terms of outward events. This lengthy period of peace had the effect of maturing **Henry IV**'s claim to the throne, so that when he died in 1413, the crown passed to his son, Hal, now **Henry V** (1386–1422) without incident or protest.

Three aspects of **Henry V**'s reign that are especially notable. First, almost nobody rebelled against him. Indeed, with the sole exception of one feeble conspiracy that was easily defeated, **Henry V** is the first monarch in a very long time to occupy the throne without any internal resistance to Lancastrian rule. For Henry V, the problems of legitimacy that plagued his father no longer existed. While Henry IV died, to use a distinguished historian's description of two later monarchs, "uneasily grasping a crown that was his by force rather than right," Henry V came to the throne "in secure, relaxed and supremely rightful possession."[22] Or as Shakespeare's Prince Hal says to his dying father in *2 Henry IV*, "You won it, wore it, kept it, gave it me; / Then plain and right must my possession be"

(4.4.221–2). Furthermore, few monarchs came to the throne as well prepared as he did. Until 1408, Prince Henry participated in suppressing the rebellion in Wales. Once that was done, from 1408 to 1412, he actively participated in Henry IV's council, and was instrumental in reforming the king's finances. In sum, **Prince Henry** became king after extensive experience in politics, administration, and warfare. **Henry V**'s expertise in government, along with his military exploits and genuine piety would make him a hero at the time and a model for future monarchs, Henry VIII in particular.

Second, domestic calm coupled with the disarray of French politics (the king, Charles VI, suffered from an incapacitating mental illness, and the country was deeply divided along factional lines) gave **Henry V** the opportunity to press the English claims to French territories established by the Treaty of Brétigny (1360). After capturing Harfleur, Henry and his army, now reduced by hunger and disease, finally confronted the French army at the **Battle of Agincourt** (October 25, 1415 – St. Crispen and St. Crispian's Day). The myth, developed by fifteenth-century English chroniclers and embroidered by later poets, balladeers and playwrights, such as the anonymous author of the *Famous Victories of Henry the Fifth* (1598) and Shakespeare, who places the Battle of Agincourt at the heart of *Henry V* (1599), is that the vastly outnumbered English forces miraculously defeated the vastly overconfident French. More recent historians, however, using contemporary pay records and other primary sources, have proposed that the battle was much more evenly matched.[23] Even so, the English victory resulted from a combination of very smart military tactics (longbow archers proving superior to knights on horseback) and pure luck – rain the previous night turned the recently ploughed field to mud, making it extremely difficult for the French chivalry, burdened by heavy armor, to maneuver. Both the sources and Shakespeare's play have Henry attributing the victory to divine assistance (according to Hall, Henry declares that the English victory "hath not been obtained by us nor our power, but only by the sufferance of God"[24]). Yet Henry's victory did not mean that he had conquered France, even though he and his army received a hero's welcome when they returned to England and, more substantively, pledges of financial support by Parliament. Several more years of diplomacy and two more military campaigns would pass before the treaty of Troyes (1420) would be signed, giving England significant lands in France, making **Henry V** heir to the French throne. To unite the two crowns, **Henry V** married Catherine of Valois, daughter of the French king, Charles VI, on June 2, 1420.

Ironically, the achievement for which Henry would earn such fame – the conquest of France – would also lead directly to its undoing. The treaty of Troyes did not mean the end of French resistance, and during his final campaign, Henry would contract dysentery and die on August 31, 1422. Queen Catherine would give Henry V an heir, soon to be **Henry VI** (1421–71), but the combination of the king's incompetence along with the loss of the French territories conquered by Henry V would plunge England into dynastic strife and civil war. (The events of **Henry VI**'s reign would also provide Shakespeare with the material for his first three history plays.)

Henry VI was not a bad person or a tyrant. He did not murder his way to the throne, nor did he greedily steal his subjects' lands and money. By all accounts, he was a decent, pious, intelligent man whose most lasting achievements were the founding of Eton College and King's College, Cambridge in the 1440s. Henry of Windsor (he was born in Windsor Castle) would have made an excellent cleric or don (although his simplicity might not have served him well in the sometimes vicious world of academic politics). But fate placed him in the one position for which he was manifestly unsuited: king of England. While it is true that monarchs were subject to the law, a strong monarch was nonetheless necessary for preventing factionalism and ensuring the delivery of fair, impartial justice. A weak king, as Henry VI's example demonstrates, almost guaranteed political and economic chaos. While personal ambition doubtless played an important role in the uproars of the fifteenth century, as would vengeance, it would be a mistake to underestimate the desire for competent government as a causal factor in the Wars of the Roses.

This was not the first time that England had an infant for a king, and the traditional arrangements were quickly implemented.

Humphrey, Duke of Gloucester (1390–1447) was nominated Henry VI's guardian and chief councilor. A great patron of the arts and learning, Gloucester was responsible for England's welfare during the king's minority, while Henry V's brother **John, Duke of Bedford** (1389–1445) got responsibility for France. The third major player in the subsequent drama was **Henry Beaufort, Bishop of Winchester** (1375?–1447). (A fourth uncle, **Thomas Beaufort, Duke of Exeter** [1377–1426], played a lesser role.) A similar situation obtained during the first years of Richard II's reign. But Richard's uncles, somewhat surprisingly, behaved themselves during this period, whereas relations among infant Henry VI's were marked by intense quarrels over policy and precedence. Their rivalries would mark Henry's reign from its beginning until their deaths in the 1440s.

In 1429, two events occurred that would have momentous repercussions for Henry VI's reign and for English history. The first was the marriage of Henry V's widow, **Catherine of Valois**, to the Welsh courtier, **Owen Tudor** (1400?–1461), who in time would become the grandfather of **Henry Tudor**, later **Henry VII**, founder of the Tudor dynasty. The second had more immediate consequences: the rise of **Joan of Arc**. While Joan, after several notable successes, would be captured by the Duke of Burgundy, sold to the English and executed, her resistance marked the beginning of the end of the English occupation of France.

Jeanne d'Arc (1412–31)

Jeanne (in English, Joan), a French peasant, claimed that she had visions from God telling her to expel the English conquerors from France. Charles VII (not yet crowned king of France) sent her to relieve the siege at Orléans, which she did in only nine days. Several more victories led to Charles VII's coronation. In 1430, Philip, Duke of Burgundy, an English ally at the time, captured her, and the Duke then sold her to the English. To his discredit, Charles VII failed to ransom Joan, and the

English tried her for heresy. Found guilty, she was burnt at the stake on May 30, 1431. Joan figures prominently in Shakespeare's *1 Henry VI*, where she is called "Joan de Pucelle" and "Joan of Aire." Joan was beatified in 1909 and canonized in 1920.

The worsening situation (from the English perspective) in France exacerbated the political tensions at home. The "political bitterness, even personal hatred," between Gloucester and Beaufort poisoned the atmosphere at court, while the populace openly hated the king's chief advisers, especially **William de la Pole, Duke of Suffolk** (1396–1450).[25] As part of an attempt to pacify France, Henry VI married **Margaret of Anjou** (1430–82) on April 23, 1445, but the match, while personally successful (the couple were quite close), neither stopped the fighting in France nor buttressed Henry's authority at home, especially since it was rumored that giving up French territory (the province of Maine) was part of the price France exacted for the match. It did not help that her own father, Duke René, served with the French army that sought to liberate Normandy from English occupation.

It is possible that even if Henry VI had inherited his father's military ability, England could not hold on to its conquered territories, but the growing domestic chaos, the complete breakdown of the mechanisms for maintaining law and order, during the 1440s clearly arose from the king's inability to rule effectively. The Commons blamed Suffolk, as the king's closest adviser, for the losses in France, the parlous financial condition of the monarchy, and the perversions of justice, and Henry VI tried to save his friend's life by banishing him. Unfortunately, the ship taking him across the channel was intercepted by a ship belonging to the Duke of Exeter, Constable of the Tower of London. The captain of this vessel, as Hall writes, recognized Suffolk, had him beheaded "on the one side of a cock boat ... and left his body with the head upon the sands of Dover."[26] Nor was he the only one of Henry VI's ministers to suffer such an ignominious end: Bishop Moleyns of Chichester was lynched by his own soldiers.

At the end of May 1450, **John (Jack) Cade** (d. 1450) led an insurrection from Kent. In *2 Henry VI*, Shakespeare portrays the rebels as illiterate boors who kill the learned because they are learned. When they find a law clerk, Cade tells his followers to "Hang him with his pen and inkhorn about his neck" (4.2.109–10). But the real Cade and his actual followers consisted of lesser gentry and gentlemen, landed, educated people, driven to violence by the breakdown of order at home and the loss of territories abroad. Even though Cade claimed that he belonged to the Mortimer family (thus giving him dynastic airs), he did not seek to depose Henry. Instead, the protests focused on the king's advisers, who, as one of the extant bills of complaint says, undermined the very foundation of the commonwealth through by corrupting the law (suggesting why Shakespeare has one rebel propose "The first thing we do, let's kill all the lawyers" [*2 Henry VI* 3.4.76]). These men, the complaint states (echoing the charges against Richard II), held "that our sovereign is above his law and that the law is made to his pleasure, and that he may make [or] break it as ofte as him [he] list without distinction"; equally bad, the law serves nothing "else in this day for to do wrong which for no thing almost is sped but false matters by colour of the law for mede [reward], dread, or favor, and no remedy is had in the Court ...." In sum, the king's "merchandise is lost, his commons destroyed, the sea is lost, France is lost."[27] Unlike **Richard II**, **Henry VI** caved in the face of rebellion, withdrawing from London to Kenilworth, thus leaving his treasurer, Lord Say, to be dragged from the Tower and killed. Eventually, Londoners threw the rebels out of the city, and the king's council offered them a pardon if they would disperse. Most did so, but Cade did not. He tried to escape but was hunted down and killed.

It is at this point that **Henry VI's** chief antagonist in the **Wars of the Roses**, **Richard, Duke of York** (1411–60), enters the story, when he returned from Ireland and added his voice to the choir demanding that the corrupt councilors surrounding Henry VI be tried as traitors. While York's precise motivations remain uncertain, it is clear that in 1450 he did not intend to depose Henry VI, nor would he until ten years later. The conflict between the Duke of York and the Lancastrian Henry VI, really **Queen Margaret**, since the king was largely passive, was not a fight between the houses of York and Lancaster for the crown until the very end. When York returned in 1450, he issued a series of bills and public letters joining the chorus of complaint against Henry VI's councilors, but his offers to help were politely declined. When parliament met in November 1450, York arrived with an army at his back, demanding that **Edmund Beaufort, Duke of Somerset** (c. 1406–55; the equally corrupt, equally hated man who took Suffolk's place) be tried. York's effort failed, and he had to swear allegiance.

There matters might have stood had three events not occurred in 1453: further defeats in France, **Henry VI's** falling into incommunicative, unresponsive stupor, and the birth of his and Margaret's son, **Edward** (1453–71), known as Edward of Westminster, Prince of Wales. A group of councilors turned to **York** for help, and he was appointed Protector on March 27, 1454. York acquitted himself well, but the birth of an heir now meant that **Margaret of Anjou** had good reason (she believed) to find herself and her regency threatened by York, given his strong claim to the throne and notwithstanding his disinterest in asserting that claim. **Henry VI** recovered his wits at Christmas 1454, York was removed from office shortly thereafter, and a government overtly hostile to York had formed. The two sides met for the first battle of the Wars of the Roses at **St. Albans** on May 22, 1455. While the Yorkists won, **Richard** still had no interest in deposing Henry VI. Instead, he submitted to the king so long as the king submitted to a second protectorate, one that deprived Henry VI of any true authority. Despite **Henry VI's** attempt at a "loveday" settlement in 1458, Margaret nurtured a fanatically anti-York faction, one that "included the sons of those lords who had fallen at St. Albans .... A passion for revenge without quarter had entered English politics."[28]

The two forces met again at **Ludford Bridge** on October 12, 1459. This time, York and his allies were defeated, and the Duke along with his second son, Edmund, fled to Ireland. When York returned in 1460, this time he asserted his claim to the throne. Yet despite the

Yorkist victory at the **Battle of Northampton** on July 10, 1460, the Duke once again vacillated, perhaps because he understood that most of his supporters wanted to reform Henry VI's government, not replace the king. In concert with parliament, the two sides worked out an agreement that would leave Henry VI on the throne while settling the succession on York and his sons (by disinheriting Henry VI's son, **Edward, Prince of Wales,** this compromise guaranteed future strife). At the height of his success, however, **Richard, Duke of York's** career, suddenly halted when on December 30, 1460 he was attacked at **Wakefield** by Lancastrian forces and killed along with his second son, Edmund.

York, however, had two remaining sons: **Edward, Earl of March** (soon to be **Edward IV;** 1442–83), and **Richard** (1452–85; eventually **Duke of Gloucester** and later, **Richard III**), and while their father may have died, they remained very much alive, as did the Yorkist cause.[29] The Lancastrian forces, led by **Queen Margaret**, defeated the Yorkists at the second battle of **St. Albans** (November 30, 1461), but her victory proved only a temporary setback. London refused to allow **Margaret** entry, fearing that her army would plunder the city, and **Edward, Earl of March** defeated a Lancastrian army led by **Owen Tudor** at the battle of **Mortimer's Cross**. According to legend, before the combat started Edward saw three suns that "suddenly joined all together in one."[30] He took this meteorological phenomenon as a sign "That we, the sons of brave Plantagenet, / Each one already blazing by our meeds [merits], / Should notwithstanding join our lights together, / And over-shine the earth as this world" (*3 Henry VI* 1.4.35–8).

The decisive confrontation, however took place at **Towton** on March 29, 1461), the largest and bloodiest confrontation of the Wars of the Roses. For early modern writers, this battle emblematized the horrors of civil strife. *Holinshed's Chronicles* reports that the river was so clogged with bodies that "men alive" walked over "dead carcasses" to get to the other side.[31] Hall said that "this conflict was in manner unnatural, for in it the son fought against the father, the brother against the brother, the nephew against the uncle, and the tenant against his lord …."[32] Shakespeare dramatizes the laments of "a son that hath kill'd his father" and "a father that hath kill'd his son" (*3 Henry VI*; stage directions 2.5); he also depicts Henry VI immobilized by self-pity as the slaughter takes place around him (2.5.1–54). The Yorkist forces triumphed and the royal family absconded to Scotland. **Margaret** and her son, **Edward, Prince of Wales**, returned to France to negotiate help from her father and Louis XI, but Henry VI was captured in July 1465, and conveyed to the Tower of London, where he stayed until 1470.

Edward, Duke of York was crowned **Edward IV** in March 1461, and while his reign would last 22 years, the central issues of his reign demonstrate how for a monarch, the personal does not exist. The problems began with Edward's announcing his surprise marriage in May 1464 to the widow, **Elizabeth Woodville** (c. 1437–92; also known as **Elizabeth Grey**) while **Richard Neville, Earl of Warwick** (1428–71), Edward's chief ally and the man known as the "kingmaker," was in France negotiating a more diplomatically advantageous match. There are several reasons why this match would prove so troublesome. First, Edward married beneath his station, and Elizabeth came from a large family that took as much advantage as they could of their new proximity to the source of power and patronage. Contemporaries did not know what to make of Edward's actions. Some thought he was bewitched, others that he was sexually infatuated with Elizabeth, and she made herself available on condition of marriage. Given that they had a long and happy life together, that hypothesis seems unlikely.

Edward IV's motivations, however, in this case matter less than the consequences of his actions, the most important being **Warwick**'s transformation from friend to enemy. **Warwick** joined with Edward's brother, **George, Duke of Clarence** (1449–78; the "false, fleeting perjur'd Clarence" of Shakespeare's *Richard III* [1.4.55]), in capturing the king. Warwick tried to rule in Edward's name in much the same way that Richard, Duke of York sought to rule in Henry VI's, and with equal success. Edward IV bided his time until April 1470, when he declared both Warwick and his brother traitors. Warwick fled to France, where he switched sides and allied himself with Henry VI's wife, **Queen Margaret**. Together, they returned with an army and this time it was Edward who had to flee the kingdom. Henry VI emerged from the Tower and was reinstalled on the throne (Henry's "re-adeption"). But his restoration did not last long. In March 1471 **Edward IV** returned, and at the **Battle of Tewkesbury** (May 4, 1471) defeated the Lancastrian forces once and for all. The Lancastrian heir, **Edward, Prince of Wales**, died at that battle, and both Henry VI and Margaret were brought back to London as prisoners. **Henry VI** died shortly thereafter, undoubtedly at **Edward IV's** behest, and **Margaret** returned to France (Louis XI ransomed her) four years later. She died in 1482.

The rest of Edward IV's reign was blessedly uneventful. At the time of his death, "this realm was in quiet and prosperous estate: no fear of outward enemies, no war in hand, nor none toward [impending]," in Thomas More's words.[33] But trouble can come, as More continues, where "no man can look for,"[34] and in this case it would come from one of the most maligned figures in English history, certainly, in early modern English historical writing, Edward IV's brother, **Richard, Duke of Gloucester**, whom Shakespeare calls a "bottled spider" (*Richard III* 1.3.241). One needs to take the many lurid tales about **Richard** with a grain of salt: given that **Henry VII** would gain the throne by killing **Richard III**, apologists for the Tudor dynasty had every reason to paint as black a picture as humanly possible, and much of what was said is patently untrue. The actual **Richard III** was not a hunchback, nor was he fundamentally evil from the start, as Shakespeare and others claim. In fact, nothing in his life suggested that he would commit the crimes that he did. Unlike his brother, **George, Duke of Clarence**, Richard remained loyal to Edward IV, and as a reward, inherited Warwick's offices, which allowed both Richard and the king to assert royal authority in the troublesome north. After Edward IV had disposed of Henry VI, Richard acted as the constable and admiral of England, and he did well in both capacities. Indeed, Richard "was a man who had won universal respect for his probity and loyalty to his brother, as well as his piety, courage and chivalric zeal."[35] Consequently, when **Edward IV** died on April 9, 1483, no one had any reason to assume that Richard would not serve his brother's eldest child as he did the child's father. But that is not what happened. The late king's elder son was declared **King Edward V** on April 11, 1483. Yet **Richard, Duke of Gloucester** was crowned **King Richard III** on July 6, 1483. What happened?

There is little doubt that the hostility displayed toward him by **Edward V**'s mother, **Queen Elizabeth Woodville**, in good part motivated Richard. In a letter dated June 10, 1483, the Duke asked for military help against Queen Elizabeth and her associates because they "intended and daily doth intend to murder and utterly destroy us."[36] But Richard may have been exaggerating the danger. There also remains the possibility that, with the example of Henry VI in mind, Richard believed that an extended protectorate was not in the nation's interest, and that he was the best man for the job of king. Ultimately, we do not know. But we do know that Richard arrested Earl Rivers, Lord Richard Grey, and Thomas Vaughan, Edward V's chamberlain, and then seized the young king himself. Queen Elizabeth and her younger son (also named Richard) immediately took sanctuary in Westminster. After declaring himself Lord Protector, Richard's coup proceeded apace. He executed William, Lord Hastings, arrested Lord Stanley and John Morton, Bishop of Ely (who figures prominently in Thomas More's *History of King Richard III*), somehow persuaded Queen Elizabeth to exit sanctuary and surrender her younger son, cancelled the parliament, and on June 22 declared himself king on the grounds that Elizabeth's children were illegitimate. Significantly, it was Edward's private failings that gave Richard this opportunity. **Edward IV's** "fleshly wantonness," as More writes, may not have "greatly grieved the people," but this personal failing allowed Richard to have Edward IV's children declared bastards, and therefore not in line for the throne, because Edward supposedly had pre-contracted marriage with another woman.[37] With **Edward V** already in hand, **Richard** convinced **Queen Elizabeth** to give up her younger son to the Lord Protector. The princes were sent to the Tower of London, and they were never seen or heard from again.

Richard III, however, did not enjoy the throne for very long. The fact that he deposed a king who did not deserve deposition meant that he had no legitimacy, even though he was far from a bad ruler. Forces of resistance started to center around **Henry Tudor**, who had fled to Brittany in 1471. He landed in Wales on August 7, 1485 and the two armies met on August 22 at **Bosworth Field**. **Henry Tudor** won, becoming **Henry VII**, and the founder of the **Tudor dynasty**. With his marriage to **Elizabeth of York**, the Wars of the Roses were officially over.

Historians disagree over the scale of the Wars of the Roses and its overall effect on fifteenth-century English society.[38] The tendency of Tudor chroniclers to depict England swimming in blood with half the population killed has led some twentieth-century writers to minimize the effects of the Wars. Certainly, life continued as the elite battled it out for who would sit on the throne, as suggested by Shakespeare's rural Justice Shallow and his musings about how much "a good yoke of bullocks" would cost at the Stamford fair (*2 Henry IV*, 3.2.38). Animals must be husbanded, crops sown and harvested regardless of factional struggles. Furthermore, the Wars of the Roses were fought mainly by the nobility and their retainers, not the general population, who were largely spared the suffering civil wars entail.[39] That does not mean, however, that they were spared other forms of suffering. Thanks to the Black Death of the fourteenth century, England's population severely declined, and while historians still debate the causes, there is no doubt that by the middle of the fifteenth century England had entered "one of the deepest, most pervasive, and enduring of all depressions."[40] Broadcloth and wool exports plunged, as did imports of wine and other commodities. The decline in overseas trade ran parallel to an equally steep deterioration in the agricultural economy. Prices for wheat were lower in the 1440s than they had been for over a century, and the decline in prices did not originate from bountiful harvests, but lack of demand.[41] Finally, the movement by landlords to convert cultivated land into sheep pastures started about 1440, lasting through the early sixteenth century, and would cause much complaint and social unrest.[42] **Thomas More's** graphic description of the devastation wrought by the enclosure movement in *Utopia* (Hythlodaeus tells Cardinal Morton that England's sheep now "devour human beings"[43]) applies to the fifteenth as well as the six-teenth centuries. While the Wars of the Roses and England's parlous condition seem to run in parallel lines, the two would intersect when it served someone's interest. In 1459–60, Yorkists appealed to the res-tive people of Kent (the origin of Jack Cade's rebellion) to gain popu-lar support for their cause, and in 1469, Warwick and Edward IV's brother, Clarence, "turned popular disappointment at Edward IVs failure to restore 'good government' to their own account."[44]

* * *

What did the Tudors and Stuarts make of these events? How did they understand them? An earlier generation of scholars, whose works are still influential among both literary critics and histori-ans, proposed the existence of "the Tudor myth": understanding that he had a weak claim to the throne, Henry VII decided to but-tress his authority through ideological means rather than exclu-sively by force.[45] He thus promoted a view of history that was both teleological (events move toward a particular conclusion) and providential (God guides these events). According to the "Tudor myth," Henry IV's deposition of Richard II was a crime against both man and God because Richard was an anointed monarch, and thus "God's lieutenant" on earth. As punishment, God plunged England into civil war and strife, culminating in the horrible reign of Richard III. The advent of Henry Tudor, however, meant that God had forgiven England, and sent Henry to bind up the coun-try's wounds, as evidenced by his decision to marry Elizabeth of York, thus combining the two warring houses. The advantage of this scheme is that it created a highly effective means of undermin-ing the opposition's credibility. For a Yorkist to oppose a Lancastrian (or vice versa) constitutes factionalism; opposing Henry Tudor, on the other hand, means opposing the will of God. While most con-temporary critics assume that Shakespeare and other Tudor–Stuart writers take a more skeptical approach to the "Tudor myth," most do not question its existence in the first place. And yet, there are good reasons for doubting whether the "Tudor myth" ever existed in the form that E. M. W. Tillyard and others (even those who question its assumptions) assume.

First, there was nothing particularly original in the claim for divine appointment to the throne. Henry IV was considered a king "chosen [electus] by God," who sanctioned his rule and by implication, Richard II's deposition.[46] Similarly, Edward IV claimed that he derived his title from God, and the commons "thanked God for His decision" to place a king on the throne who rules "by God's law, man's law, and the law of nature."[47] Even Richard III would make this claim: the petition entered into the *Roll of Parliament* asserted that God wanted Richard to be king, not the progeny of the adulterous Edward IV.[48] Each of the kings who deposed another king argued that God approved of their actions. Furthermore, if the claim of providential approval seemed to have been conventional, it is remarkable how the Tudor chroniclers leave such claims out of their narratives. Hall, for example, writes that during Henry Tudor's progress to London, the common people gladly tried "to touch and kiss that victorious hands [sic] which had overcome so monstrous and cruel a tyrant," and they thank God for the man "by whose meane and industry the commonwealth of the realm was preserved."[49] Henry Tudor gets the credit, and there is no sense that Henry Tudor is God's instrument. Rather, he succeeded because he was a man gifted with "the ingenious forecast of the subtle serpent."[50]

If the "Tudor myth" of providential history and a divinely appointed dynasty did not hold much water, how then did Tudor–Stuart writers understand England's history? First, it is important to stress that there is no one understanding of history in the Tudor–Stuart era (or any other, for that matter). And clearly, some Tudor–Stuart writers were phobic about rebellion. Edward Hall, for instance, begins his chronicle with a series of rhetorical questions: "What mischief hath insurged in realms by intestine division, what depopulation hath ensued in countries by civil dissention, what detestable murder hath been committed in cities by separate factions and what calamity hath ensued in famous regions by domestical discord and unnatural controversy?"[51]

However, some of the strongest denunciations of rebellion concern class as much as politics. Richard, Duke of York's complaints about Henry VI were not very different from Jack Cade's, but he was received very differently, by both his contemporaries and Tudor-Stuart writers, because of his social station. In literature, the Elizabethan courtier, poet, and prose fiction writer, Sir Philip Sidney (1554–86), may allude in his eclogue, "On Ister Bank," to his mentor, Hubert Languet, who argued for the right of subjects to rise against a tyrant, but Sidney's treatment of peasant rebellion in his romance, the *Arcadia* (written c. 1579) is utterly vicious.[52] The elite may depose, but not those belonging to "the fourth and last sort of people."[53] Also, it is not accidental that some of the strongest arguments for the divine origin of the social order, such as the *"Homily on Obedience"* (1547) and the *Homily against Disobedience and Willful Rebellion"* (1570), come from government pens, and written in response to an insurrection.

That being said, it seems that the events described in this chapter were generally understood by early modern minds in *constitutional* terms.[54] That is to say, early modern writers of both fiction and non-fiction largely understood the serial depositions of the late fourteenth and fifteenth centuries as evidence for the contractual nature of early modern monarchy and the legitimacy of taking action against a monarch who oversteps his bounds. If a monarch has an overly broad view of his authority (i.e. Richard II's belief that the laws of England are in his head) or if a monarch is incompetent (i.e. Henry VI, although significantly his councilors were accused of believing that the monarch was not subject to the law), then he could be deposed legitimately and by process of law. This helps explain the interest among Tudor–Stuart chroniclers in providing primary sources, such as the list of charges against Richard II and Richard, Duke of York's complaints to Henry VI, that demonstrate how the opposition to these monarchs was rooted in law, not factionalism or desire for power. This principle will return in many ways and in different forms, both secular and religious, over the course of the Tudor–Stuart era and the early Restoration period.

Notes

1 Quoted in E. K. Chambers, *William Shakespeare: A Study of Facts and Problems* (Oxford: Clarendon Press, 1930), vol. 2, 236.
2 John J. Manning, "Introduction," *The Life and Raigne of King Henrie IIII*, ed. John J. Manning (London: Royal Historical Society, 1991), 27.
3 Quoted in David Starkey, *Henry: Virtuous Prince* (London: Harper Press, 2008), 22.
4 Anthony Tuck, "Richard II (1367–1400)," *Oxford Dictionary of National Biography*, Oxford University Press, Sept 2004; online edn., January 2009. http://www.oxforddnb.com/view/article/23499, accessed July 14, 2009.
5 William Huse Dunham, Jr. and Charles T. Wood, "The Right to Rule in England: Depositions and the Kingdom's Authority, 1327–1485," *The American Historical Review* 81.4 (1976), 743.
6 Corpus Christi College, Cambridge, MS 61. I am grateful to my late colleague, Laurel Amtower, for identifying this manuscript.
7 *Continuatio Eluogii*, in *Chronicles of the Revolution 1397–1400: The Reign of Richard II*, ed. and trans. Chris Given-Wilson (Manchester: Manchester University Press, 1993), 68.
8 *Vita Ricardi Secundi*, in *Chronicles of the Revolution*, 55.
9 Quoted in Tuck, "Richard II."
10 "The Record and Process," in *Chronicles of the Revolution*, 180–1.
11 John Gower, "O Deus Immense," ed. and trans. R. F. Yeager. TEAMS Middle English Texts. University of Rochester. Accessed July 14, 2009. http://www.lib.rochester.edu/camelot/teams/ryfrm4.htm.
12 The Dieulacres Chronicler, quoted in Nigel Saul, *Richard II* (New Haven: Yale University Press, 1997), 390. On the uprising, see Saul, 389–90.
13 "The Exhortation concerning Good Order and Obedience to Rulers and Magistrates," in *Certain Sermons or Homilies*, sig. R2v.
14 Sir John Fortescue, *In Praise of the Laws of England*, in *On the Laws and Governance of England*, ed. Shelley Lockwood (Cambridge: Cambridge University Press, 1997), 17.
15 Peter Saccio, *Shakespeare's English Kings: History, Chronicle, and Drama* (London and New York: Oxford University Press, 1977), 27.
16 Edward Hall, *Chronicle* (1548), 10.

17 Quoted in A. L. Brown and Henry Summerson, "Henry IV (1366–1413)," *Oxford Dictionary of National Biography*, Oxford University Press, September 2004; online edn., January 2008. http://www.oxforddnb.com/view/article/12951, accessed July 14, 2009.

18 Quoted in Dunham and Wood, "The Right to Rule in England," 748.

19 Saccio, *Shakespeare's English Kings*, 47.

20 Saccio, *Shakespeare's English Kings*, 41.

21 See Peter McNiven, "Scrope, Richard (*c.* 1350–1405)," *Oxford Dictionary of National Biography*, Oxford University Press, September 2004; online edn., May 2008. http://www.oxforddnb.com/view/article/24964, accessed July 15, 2009.

22 Starkey, *Henry*, 308.

23 See Anne Curry, *Agincourt: A New History* (Stroud, Gloucestershire: Tempus, 2006); Curry, *The Battle of Agincourt: Sources and Interpretations* (Woodbridge, Suffolk: Boydell Press, 2000); and James Glanz, "Historians Reassess Battle of Agincourt," *New York Times*, 24 October 2009.

24 *Hall's Chronicle*, 70.

25 R. A. Griffiths, "Henry VI (1421–1471)," *Oxford Dictionary of National Biography*, Oxford University Press, September 2004; online edn., January 2008. http://www.oxforddnb.com/view/article/12953, accessed August 22, 2009.

26 *Hall's Chronicle*, 219.

27 Quoted in I. M. W. Harvey, *Jack Cade's Rebellion of 1450* (Oxford: Clarendon Press, 1991), 189. See also R. A. Griffiths, *The Reign of King Henry VI: The Exercise of Regal Authority, 1422–1461* (Berkeley: University of California Press, 1981), 635–7.

28 Saccio, *Shakespeare's English Kings*, 134.

29 Even so, Shakespeare alters history when he makes Edward's son, Richard part of the final battles of the Wars of the Roses. He was born in 1452, and so was only 8 or 9 when these events occurred.

30 *Hall's Chronicle*, 251.

31 *Holinshed's Chronicles of England, Scotland and Ireland*, ed. Sir Henry Ellis (London: J. Johnson *et al.*, 1808), vol. 3, 278. Raphael Holinshed was not the author of this massive compendium, but its original editor. It is not clear who wrote the material on Henry VI.

32 *Hall's Chronicles*, 256.

33 Thomas More, *The History of King Richard III*, ed. Richard S. Sylvester (New Haven: Yale University Press, 1978), 5.

34 More, *History of King Richard III*, 5.
35 A. J. Pollard, *The Wars of the Roses* (Basingstoke: Macmillan, 1988), 34.
36 Quoted in Rosemary Horrox, "Richard III (1452–1485)," *Oxford Dictionary of National Biography*, Oxford University Press, 2004. http:// www.oxforddnb.com/view/article/23500, accessed August 26, 2009.
37 More, *History of King Richard III*, 5.
38 Pollard, *Wars of the Roses*, 74.
39 Pollard, *Wars of the Roses*, 85–90.
40 John Hatcher, "The Great Slump of the Mid-Fifteenth Century," *Progress and Problems in Medieval England*, ed. Richard Britnell and John Hatcher (Cambridge: Cambridge University Press, 1996), 270.
41 Hatcher, "The Great Slump," 241–3, 245–8.
42 Leonard Martin Cantor, *The Changing English Countryside* (London: Routledge & Kegan Paul, 1987), 28–9.
43 More, *Utopia*, 24.
44 Pollard, *Wars of the Roses*, 85.
45 The locus classicus for the "Tudor myth" is E. M. W. Tillyard, *Shakespeare's History Plays* (rpt. London: Chatto & Windus, 1974). This book was originally published in 1944.
46 Quoted in Dunham and Wood, "The Right to Rule in England," 748.
47 Dunham and Wood, "The Right to Rule in England," 752, 752–3.
48 Dunham and Wood, "The Right to Rule in England," 757.
49 *Hall's Chronicle*, 423.
50 *Hall's Chronicle*, 422.
51 *Hall's Chronicle*, 1.
52 On "Ister Bank," see Blair Worden, *The Sound of Virtue: Philip Sidney's "Arcadia" and Elizabethan Politics* (New Haven: Yale University Press, 1996); on Sidney's treatment of peasants, see Stephen Greenblatt, "Murdering Peasants: Status, Genre, and the Representation of Rebellion," *Representing the Renaissance*, ed. Stephen Greenblatt (Berkeley: University of California Press, 1988), 1–30.
53 On this term and the social hierarchy, see Chapter 1, 16–17.
54 The views of contemporary historians about this period have undergone significant shifts. The "Whig" version of history (which imposes a narrative of a steady progression toward greater liberty and enlightenment) and the interest in long-term causes have been displaced by an emphasis on individual decisions: "We must try to explain what

they did and how the justified it to themselves and to each other" (Christine Carpenter, *The Wars of the Roses: Politics and the Constitution in England, c. 1437–1509* [Cambridge: Cambridge University Press, 25]). On the historiography of this period, see Carpenter, *Wars of the Roses*, 4–26 and A. J. Pollard, *Late Medieval England 1399–1509* (Harlow: Longman, 2000), 1–16.

3

Henry VII, Henry VIII, and the Henrician Era (1509–47)

Henry VII

According to the "Tudor myth," **Henry VII's** decision to marry Edward IV's daughter, **Elizabeth of York**, signaled the providential nature of Henry's victory over King Richard III on Bosworth. By knitting together the red rose of Lancaster and the white rose of York, Henry VII was supposed to usher in a golden age of peace and comity. As the report in *Holinshed's Chronicles* puts it, "By reason of which marriage, peace was thought to descend out of heaven into England," and to a certain extent, legend has its basis in fact.[1] Henry VII successfully held the throne from 1485 to 1509, when he died in his bed of natural causes, and his second son would become **Henry VIII**. But as so often happens, legend and fact do not quite coincide.

First, **Henry VII** did not succeed because God wanted him to be king of England, but because Henry possessed superior political skills. Rather than attacking every enemy and potential opponent,

A Short History of Early Modern England: British Literature in Context, First Edition.
Peter C. Herman.
© 2011 Peter C. Herman. Published 2011 by Blackwell Publishing Ltd.

Figure 3.1 King Henry VIII; King Henry VII by Hans Holbein the Younger, c. 1536–37. © National Portrait Gallery, London.

Henry Tudor prosecuted only the greatest of the Yorkist peers while offering opportunities and favor to the lesser fry. He thus avoided a bloodbath (which likely would have only weakened his hold on power) while depriving his enemies of both manpower and reasons for replacing him. In 1495, he signed into law an act exempting from prosecution anyone who followed the orders of an English king. "The idea was to reassure old Yorkists that he had no intention of pursuing them further for past actions, while encouraging the loyalty of his own followers as well by promising indemnity from the resentment of some future ruler."[2]

Even so, **Henry VII** would face Yorkist challenges throughout his reign, and because all of the legitimate Yorkists' heirs were either too young or deceased, the new king had to deal with no fewer than four pretenders to the throne. "In 1487, the son of a baker, one **Lambert Simnel**, tried to impersonate as Edward, styled Earl of Warwick (1475–99), son of George, Duke of Clarence, and imprisoned by Henry VII since 1485 because of his legitimacy as Richard III's heir."[3] The rebellion centered in Ireland, and was quickly defeated. **Henry VII** showed off both his mercy and his sense of humor by making Simnel a kitchen servant. In 1493, Henry VII would have Simnel serve wine to some of his erstwhile Irish supporters, and upon seeing their embarrassment, the king mordantly remarked, "My lords of Ireland, you will crown apes at last."[4] Another pretender, **Perkin Warbeck** (c. 1474–99), took on the identity of Richard, Duke of York, one of the princes Richard III had murdered in the Tower of London, and would prove more troublesome. The rulers of France, Scotland, and the Holy Roman Empire, all for their own reasons, supported Warbeck, who used Scotland as a base for staging invasions in 1495 and 1496. In 1497, Warbeck invaded a third time, trying to join an unrelated rebellion in Cornwall against high taxes. He was captured and, like Simnel, initially pardoned. But evidence of continued plotting brought about his execution two years later. A third pretender, one Ralph Wilford, also claimed to be the Earl of Warwick, and was duly executed. The final threat, and in some ways the most potent because the man actually had a legitimate claim to the throne, arose when **Edmund de la Pole, Earl of Suffolk** (1472–1513) began in 1502 to plan an invasion of England. While the plot fizzled, and while Suffolk would eventually become Henry VII's prisoner, the first Tudor's political underpinnings were considerably shakier than proponents of the "Tudor myth" allow. An informant's report written in 1506 about the state of opinion in Calais underscores the fragility of Henry VII's support. While the treasurer, Sir Hugh Conway, professes loyalty to the present king, yet, according to Henry's spy, he also said that "it hath be seen in times past that change of worlds hath caused change of mind."[5]

Amid this turmoil, **Queen Elizabeth** helped assure dynastic stability by providing children. All told, Elizabeth and Henry VII had eight, one died in infancy, two others within their first year, and one at three years old. The fates of three, however, were uncommonly important. First, **Arthur Tudor's** birth in September 19, 1486 (d. 1502) provided Henry VII with a male heir (his name symbolized both the Tudor Welsh heritage and English mythology, promising a return to the golden age of King Arthur and the knights of the Round Table). Next, **Margaret** was born in November 1489 (d. 1541) and, finally, **Henry**, eventually **Henry VIII**, arrived on June 28, 1491. Faced with internal strife fueled by foreign support, **Henry VII** sought to nullify his Yorkist enemies by creating marriage alliances, assuming that foreign powers would be less likely to support pretenders to the English throne if their children were wedded to the Tudors. Thus, in his greatest diplomatic coup, **Henry VII** arranged for the marriage of Arthur to **Katherine of Aragon**, daughter of the Spanish king, **Ferdinand**. The couple officially joined in 1500. Next, **Princess Margaret** was married to **King James IV** of Scotland on January 29, 1502.[6] In addition to making it more difficult for Scotland to support Henry VII's enemies, the progeny of this marriage would inherit the English throne after the death of Queen Elizabeth I.

The year 1502, however, marked a turning point in Henry VII's personal fortunes. The precipitating event was the sudden and premature death of **Arthur**. According to witnesses, Henry and Elizabeth grieved terribly, but they comforted each other with the prospect of having more children. Even so, when Elizabeth returned to her chamber, according to a contemporary account, the "natural and motherly remembrance of that great loss smote her so sorrowful to the heart that those about her were fain to send for the king to comfort her."[7] A daughter, Catherine, was born on February 2, 1503, but she died after a few days, and **Elizabeth of York** died shortly after. All reports agree that Henry VII was shattered by his wife's death. One chronicler reported that after he found out, Henry VII "privily departed to a solitary place and would no man should resort unto him."[8]

While he would live six years more, **Henry VII's** health started to decline, but despite his personal troubles, the King did not abandon politics, and he turned his attention to grooming his second son, **Prince Henry**, to succeed him. The younger Henry "was not to come to the throne untrained and untested, as the conventional wisdom assumes; instead he was more conscientiously prepared for kingship than most of his predecessors."[9] As part of that preparation, both **Henry VII** and **Ferdinand of Aragon** decided that the Anglo-Spanish alliance required a marriage, and so negotiations began (with somewhat unseemly haste) for **Katherine** to marry **Prince Henry**. After waiting for a papal dispensation – the Pope had to resolve the contradictory biblical injunctions concerning such a match, "the most fateful wedding in English history took place in June 1509."[10] **Prince Henry** was 18; **Katherine**, 25.

Over the course of the latter years of **Henry VII's** reign, the ground was laid for the momentous changes and events of **Henry VIII's** reign. This period was marked by a fiscal tyranny that went beyond the king's legendary parsimoniousness. Henry and his councilors, Edmund Dudley and Sir Richard Empson in particular, squeezed every possible source of income while taking personal control of the nation's finances. **Henry VII's** financial exactions, however, were also a means of controlling a nobility whom the king did not trust, and who did not trust the king, by forcing them into his debt and remitting payment so long as they behaved themselves. **Henry VII's** poor reputation would constitute the backdrop for the ecstatic celebrations over his son's accession.

Also, the tectonic shift in England's intellectual culture toward **humanism** started to gather increasing momentum. This term has come to be used as shorthand for an intellectual movement that emerged in late thirteenth-century Italy and gradually moved northward.

Like the phrase, "the Wars of the Roses," the term **"humanism"** was not used in the early modern period, but coined in the early nineteenth century.[11] According to *The Oxford English Dictionary*, "humanism" made its way into English around the middle of the 1800s. The term originates in the Latin "humanitas," used by Cicero and others to connote the sort of cultural values we today associate with a liberal arts education. The Italian "umanista" describes a teacher or professor of classical literature, and the English equivalent, "humanist," appears in the late sixteenth century.

While nobody agreed, either in the early modern period or today, on the precise definition of humanism, the overall shape and intent of this movement remain clear enough. Broadly speaking, humanism concerned itself with the study and recovery of ancient Roman, and, to a lesser extent, Greek culture. This project involved recovering and re-editing ancient texts, purging later editions of Latin and Greek authors of the textual corruptions that accrued over centuries of transmission. Humanism arose in opposition to late medieval scholasticism, and while humanism hardly presented a united front, overall, proponents of the "New Learning" accused scholastic philosophy of narrow sterility (e.g., trying to determine how many angels could dance on the head of a pin), and they considered medieval Latin barbarous. Consequently, they sought to replace the scholastic curriculum of logic, theology, and the "quadrivium" (arithmetic, geometry, astronomy, and music) with a program focusing on the more "humane" topics of grammar, rhetoric, poetry, history, and moral philosophy.[12] The key figures for Italian humanism are **Francesco Petrarca** (in English, "Petrarch"; 1304–74), who wrote many works in Latin and Italian in addition to a vernacular sonnet sequence, the *Rime Sparse* or "Scattered Rhymes," **Giovanni Boccaccio** (1313–75), **Collucio Salutati** (1331–1406), **Marsilio Ficino** (1433–99), and **Giovanni Pico della Mirandola** (1463–94).

While it is true that some humanist projects focused on personal interiority (Petrarch's *Rime Sparse*) and human capabilities (Pico's *Oration on the Dignity of Man* [1486]), not to mention **Niccolo Machiavelli's** (1469–1527) utterly secular (and accurate) recipe for achieving and maintaining political power in *The Prince* (1513), it is not true that the early modern period was secular and "man-centric," as opposed to the religious and "God-centric" medieval period. While much in the early modern period was distinctly secular, the period was also intensely religious, as evidenced by the Reformation (see later in this chapter). In fact, the humanist project of "purifying" Latin and recovering the original editions of ancient texts by finding the earliest manuscripts contributed significantly to the development of Protestantism, since many of the same principles and assumptions would be applied to Christian doctrine and the Bible, although it is important to note that not all humanists sided with Luther and the other Protestants. **Sir Thomas More** (1478–1535), for example, wrote numerous tracts at Henry VIII's behest viciously attacking Luther, and he prosecuted Lutherans as heretics.

Humanism filtered into England gradually over the course of the fifteenth century. A few English scholars visited Italy, and a few Italians made their way into England. But England was hardly an intellectual's paradise. For example, Poggio Bracciolini (1380–1459), who, among other accomplishments, had uncovered several lost treatises by Cicero moldering in a monastic library in Cluny, joined Cardinal Henry Beaufort's household in 1418 but left four unhappy years later, complaining about the dearth of like-minded intellectuals and books.[13] By 1490, however, the humanist movement in England began to gather steam. **William Grocyn** (1449?–1519) started lecturing on Greek at Exeter College, and the great Dutch humanist, **Desiderius Erasmus** (1466?–1536), visited England for the first time in 1499. An anecdote included in a letter Erasmus wrote in 1523 captures both the clubbiness of English humanists as well as their access to the highest levels of English society.

In the summer of 1499, **Erasmus** stayed at the Greenwich country house of his former pupil and present patron, **William Blount, Lord Mountjoy**, who, not coincidentally, was Prince Henry's "*socius studiorum*," his "companion in studies" or study partner. One day, **Thomas More** dropped by and invited his friend to take a walk to the nearby village of Eltham. Without first warning Erasmus, More led his friend to Eltham Palace, which served as the royal nursery. Because **Prince Arthur** happened to be in Wales, everyone's attention focused on the eight-year-old **Prince Henry, Duke of York**. More, who had prepared for the occasion by bringing a small literary gift, bowed to the young prince and presented his offering. Erasmus, caught entirely unawares and not a little peeved at More for this surprise, mumbled his excuses and promised to remedy the omission another time. However, during the meal Erasmus received a note from Henry "challenging something from his pen," and the eminent humanist complied several days later with an exceedingly tedious panegyric to the prince, the prince's father, England in general, and a great deal else besides.[14]

Henry's tutor at this time was **John Skelton** (1460–1529), whose verses would later become a thorn in **Cardinal Thomas Wolsey's** side and who would later defend himself in verse by proudly reminding his enemies that he was King Henry VIII's first teacher: "The honor of England I learned to spell / ... / I gave him drink of the sugared well / Of Helicon's waters crystalline, / Acquainting him with the Muses nine" (ll. 95, 98–100).[15] Skelton, however, was firmly rooted in older intellectual traditions, and he would vituperate in verse against the New Learning. It is likely that Skelton urged his young charge to send the note to Erasmus in order to embarrass the visiting scholar, but if that is the case, his plot backfired. In 1503, however, Skelton was let go, and replaced by More's friend, John Holt (d. 1504), who wrote an innovative grammar for teaching children Latin (More also wrote commendatory verses for this book). Humanists would now educate the young prince, and they hoped he would reciprocate once he became king. Humanists wanted access to the court in good part because they wanted the patronage only the court could provide. But their motivations also included a genuine desire to contribute, for by the time humanism had entered England it had taken on a more practical, less abstract cast. Humanists proposed that if the prince or monarch absorbed the lessons of classical literature, if his or her counselors would offer advice based on those lessons, then the commonwealth would thrive. In Thomas More's *Utopia* (1516), for example, the eponymous speaker, More, urges Hythlodaeus to apply the wealth of learning acquired through his travels to the betterment of the state. You should, More says, "attach yourself to some king [for the purpose of] furnishing him with examples and of assisting him with counsel."[16] Or as Sir Philip Sidney would put it in the *Apology for Poetry* (c. 1579), "the ending end of all virtuous learning [is]virtuous action."[17]

Henry VIII

On April 21, 1509, Henry VII breathed his last, and on June 24, 1509, Prince Henry was crowned **King Henry VIII** to overwhelming public celebrations. "Heaven and earth rejoices," wrote **Mountjoy** to **Erasmus**, "everything is full of milk and honey and nectar. Avarice has fled the country. Our king is not after gold, or gems, or precious metals, but virtue, glory, immortality."[18] Certainly, one reason for the outpouring of joy at Henry's coronation was the sense that a hated king had finally gone to meet his maker. While some of the late Henry VII's servants mourned, the chronicler Edward Hall recalled, "the joy that was made for his death, by such as were troubled by rigor of his law" was tremendous.[19] Compared to the avaricious, crabby old man his father had become in his latter years, Henry seemed like "a prodigy, a sun-king, a *stupor mundi*."[20] A gifted athlete, an accomplished musician and composer, an intellectual, a poet, a generous patron, Henry spent the first months of his reign in what seemed like an unbroken stream of festivities. Hall records that the new king exercised "himself daily in shooting, singing, dancing, wrestling, casting of the bar, paying at the recorder, flute, virginals and in setting of songs and making of ballads."[21] It seemed as though England was poised to enter a new Golden Age, and this sense of possibility animates **Sir Thomas More's** thought experiment, *Utopia*, in which he speculates, as the title page says, about "the best state of a commonwealth."[22]

The opening days of Henry's reign also presaged darker events. On his second day as king, Henry VIII had two of his father's tax collectors, Edmund Dudley and Sir Richard Empson, imprisoned and eventually executed. While many vigorously approved, especially, as Hall writes, those who "were by them grieved," their arrest was also "needlessly cruel, arbitrary, and utterly disloyal to two faithful Crown servants," and Henry VIII's casting into eternity two people who served his father well but whose deaths served the new king's interests more anticipated his judicial murder of "two queens, three cardinals, numerous peers and clergymen, and nearly every principal minister who ever served him."[23] As the distinguished literary critic (and co-inventor of the New Historicism), Stephen J. Greenblatt, once mordantly observed, "the survival rate of those closest to Henry VIII roughly resembles the actuarial record of the First Politburo."[24] But all that remained in the future, and two intertwined developments mark the first decade of the Henrician era: Henry's decision to seek military glory for himself (and England) by attempting to restart the Hundred Years War in France, and the rise of **Thomas Wolsey** (1473?–1530), who would become **Cardinal Wolsey** in 1515 and before his fall, the most powerful man in England, besides the king.

Henry VIII decided almost immediately after his accession to the throne that he would revive England's past glories by emulating **Henry V** and seeking military glory on the continent. The king also commissioned the translation into English of a biography of his role-model. This shift in policy away from his father's pacifism did not go without notice or criticism. On Good Friday, 1513, the distinguished humanist, **John Colet**, preached a sermon against war before Henry and his court. After the service, Henry appeared unexpectedly at Colet's house, dismissed everyone, and said "I have come to discharge my conscience, not to distract you from your studies." They then entered into a private conference, and while nobody knows exactly what transpired, after their conversation Henry emerged with his arm around Colet, called for wine, and gave this toast: "Let every man have his own doctor. This is mine." Colet of course changed his mind and blessed Henry's war.[25] **Sir Thomas More** also understood the king's character and the limitations of his devotion to humanist studies. Before More entered Henry VIII's service, the king would visit him regularly, and after dinner, according to More's son-in-law and biographer, William Roper, Henry and More would walk in the garden "holding his arm about his neck."[26] When Roper congratulated his father-in-law on attaining such favor, More replied (presciently) that he had no cause for pride, "for if my head could win him a castle in France … it should not fail to go."[27]

At the time, two rival powers dominated Europe: France and the Holy Roman Empire (made up of what is today central Europe), and for the next decade, England's foreign policy consisted of sending troops to support whichever power Henry VIII had allied with at the time. Between 1511 and 1514, England joined with several other countries, including Spain (Ferdinand being Henry VIII's father-in-law) to keep the French out of Italy. This period marked the high point of English fortunes. The French encouraged the Scots to invade England, resulting in a crushing defeat for Scotland, and England captured the town of Tournai in France. But this high point was not, truth be told, very high, although the Scots defeat at the Battle of Flodden Field did eliminate that threat for two generations. Tournai was not a particularly valuable prize, the campaigns wiped out Henry VII's savings, and Henry's allies were not at all reliable. For example, Ferdinand neglected to tell Henry that he had made a separate peace with France, and when Henry's army of 10,000 soldiers arrived in northeast Spain, nobody had any idea they were coming:

> The Biscaynes that brought vitaile [food] to the army, said to the soldiers: Sirs you be arrived here in trust that the king of Aragon will help you with ordinance and carriages, we hear no preparation that he maketh, nor never sent us word to prepare for your coming, of the which we marvel much.[28]

Undaunted, the English decided to buy their own supplies, which allowed the Spanish to cheat them blind: "one sir John Stile, an Englishman, caused to bought [mules] of such price as the Spaniards gained greatly"; even worse the animals were useless: "when they were put to carry, they would neither bear nor draw, for they were beasts which were not exercised [before]."[29]

Over the next five years (1515–20), the older rulers of France and the Holy Roman Empire died and were replaced by **François I** (1494–1547) and **Charles V** (1400–1558) respectively, and Wolsey occupied himself by trying to secure peace through a series of treaties and summits, culminating in the **Field of the Cloth of Gold** in 1520, which involved a phenomenal amount of pomp, tournaments, and a wrestling match between the kings of England and France (Henry lost). Despite the good feelings, **Henry VIII** allied with **Charles V** against France, and after landing another army, promptly ran out of money, forcing another humiliating return home. But between 1525 and 1528, Henry and Wolsey, stung by Charles V's indifference to English interests, decided to switch sides and ally *with* France *against* the Holy Roman Empire. Fatefully (we will see why shortly), in 1527, Charles V's troops sacked Rome and captured the Pope.

Henry VIII, however, lacked his father's interest in details, preferring leisure to work, and that character flaw gave **Thomas Wolsey** his opportunity to flourish. Wolsey came from humble beginnings – according to a biography written by his servant, George Cavendish, Wolsey was "an honest poor man's son," possibly a butcher, who "was very apt to learning," brought to Oxford and earned a degree at "fifteen years of age, which was a rare thing and seldom seen."[30] Wolsey quickly rose through the ranks, becoming in 1509 the new king's almoner (he distributed the king's charity). Wolsey understood that the way to power ran through the king's nature. **Henry VIII** did not like the dull minutiae of ruling, and **Wolsey** used that trait to his advantage. He recognized that "the King was young and lusty, disposed all to mirth and pleasure and to follow his desire and appetite, nothing minding to travail [work] in the busy affairs of the realm."[31] Therefore:

> [Wolsey] took upon him therefore to disburden the king of so weighty a charge and troublesome business, putting the King in comfort that he shall not need to spare any time of his pleasure for any business that should necessary happen in the council, as long as he, being there, having the King's authority and commandment, doubted not to see all thing sufficiently furnished and perfected.[32]

In other words, the king could play while Wolsey took care of business. The royal almoner, however, took care not to usurp Henry's final authority: he would "first make the King privy of all such matters ... before he would proceed to the finishing or determining of the same, whose mind and pleasure he would fulfill and follow to the uttermost."[33] But **Henry VIII's** delegation of so much authority to **Wolsey**, who in 1515 became both a cardinal and the Lord Chancellor, effectively eclipsed the role of the council and made him the king's chief minister. Nothing happened without his permission, and without his taking payment.

It would be easy to say that Wolsey took advantage of the king to enrich himself beyond all measure, and he certainly spent lavishly on his houses and on maintaining his magnificence. Yet he did not use his authority or his money strictly for self-aggrandizement. Wolsey patronized the arts, funded colleges, and used his position at the top of the legal establishment to enforce "indifferent" justice. As a judge in the Star Chamber, Wolsey "spared neither high nor low, but judged every estate according to their merits and deserts."[34] Even so, the concentration of power in his hands made Wolsey the most hated man in England, at least in part because he was thought to have created a rival, entirely corrupt court that superseded the king's. Referring to Wolsey's magnificent great house at Hampton, John Skelton demanded in his 1522 satire, "Why Come ye Not to Court,"

> Why come ye not to court?
> To the king's court?
> Or to Hampton court?
> Nay, to the king's court!
> The king's court should have the excellence;
> But Hampton Court
> Hath the preeminence. (ll. 401–9)

Wolsey also had to contend with the necessary consequence of centralizing authority: when things go wrong, there is no one else to blame, and much started to go wrong, starting with the economic and social havoc caused by the king's foreign ventures. The king's wars needed money, and parliament's grants were not sufficient. Therefore, in 1522, Wolsey called for an "Amicable Grant," really a forced loan, and he rather than the king was blamed for the result. Hall reports that: "All people cursed the Cardinal and his co-adherents as subvertor[s] of the laws and liberties of England. For they said if men should give their goods by a commission, then were it worse than the taxes of France and so England should be bond [bound] and not free."[35] Londoners complained that Wolsey "was the very cause and occasion of this demand" (p. 698), and even after Henry VIII cancelled the grant, meaning Wolsey had failed to secure funding for his monarch's war, "the commons would hear no praise spoken of the Cardinal, they hated him so much."[36]

Lutheranism also started to seep into England over the 1520s, but before going further, it might perhaps be wise to outline some of the history of the **Reformation** and the differences between **Protestantism** and **Roman Catholicism**. The simplicity of both terms masks the inner divisions and arguments among the various warring groups within each division. Protestantism was a house especially divided. Nonetheless, there are broad differences between the two approaches to Christianity. The central difference between the **Catholic** (meaning "universal") **Church** and **Protestantism** lay in their opposing approaches to religious authority, how one gets to Heaven, and church government (a key issue because how one settles this matter will shape how one thinks about secular government). The Catholic Church believed that God's will is to be found in the Bible. However, the Church reserved to itself the right to interpret the Bible for the laity. The thinking was that the stakes are so high – the fate of one's soul – that interpreting Scripture should be left to professionals. Furthermore, the Catholic Church believed that the Bible was not the sole source of religious doctrine. Tradition itself became its own authority, and the writings of various early Church Fathers, such as Augustine and Jerome, were given equal authority to the Gospels. The Catholic Church also organized itself in a strict hierarchy: the Pope sits atop the ladder, then bishops, and so on downward until one reaches the individual believer, who should obey the Church leaders without question. In order to maintain their monopoly on authority, the Catholic Church opposed translating the Bible into the vernacular. As for the question of salvation, Catholicism holds that one can reach Heaven through a variety of means: belief in God, participation in the seven sacraments (baptism, penance, anointing of the sick, Eucharist, confirmation, matrimony, and becoming a monk or nun), and the performance of good works.

Protestantism adopted very different approaches to each of these issues. In place of finding religious authority in a variety of writings, they insisted that Scripture alone ("sola scriptura") was the exclusive basis of religious truth. In place of a hierarchical structure, they proposed a limited hierarchy, or even no hierarchy at all. In place of earning salvation through a combination of faith and good works, faith alone must suffice (later in the sixteenth century, **John Calvin** [1509–64] would propose that God already knows who is saved and who is damned, a doctrine known as "predestination"). And because Protestants believed that believers could come to salvation on their own, they translated the Bible into the vernacular. **Martin Luther's** (1483– 1546) translations of the Bible into German would start appearing in the 1520s, as would **William Tyndale's** (c. 1494–1536) translations of the Gospels into English.

While the **King James Bible** (1611) is the most famous English version of the Scriptures, the history of Biblical translation stretches back to Anglo-Saxon times. The most important early modern English versions include **Tyndale's New Testament** (1526) and **Pentateuch** (1530), the **Coverdale Bible** (1535), the **Great Bible** (1539, authorized by Henry VIII), and the **Geneva Bible** (1560, and the most influential version besides the King James).[37]

The heated dispute over the doctrine of **purgatory** neatly encapsulates the differences between the two sides. For centuries, the Catholic Church held that there were three options for one's soul after death: heaven, hell, or purgatory, the destination for those whose sins were sufficient to not earn entry to Heaven but insufficient to earn eternal damnation. The theory was that one spent a period of time undergoing punishment that would purify one's soul sufficiently to enter Heaven. Performing good works was supposed to lessen the amount of time one spends in purgatory. However, one could also perform works that would lessen the amount of time in purgatory for someone else's soul, and in the middle ages, the Church started selling "indulgences," which forgave a certain amount of time in exchange for a certain amount of cash or works. For **Luther**, indulgences were nothing but extortion and corruption, and their condemnation is the central theme of his **Ninety-Five Theses** (1517), which are generally credited with beginning the Reformation. The debate, however, quickly moved on to the issue of religious authority. For **Sir Thomas More**, defender of Catholic doctrine, the fact that Saints Augustine, Jerome, Ambrose, Gregory, Chrysostom, and Cyprian, indeed, "all the old holy fathers and blessed saints," believed in purgatory is enough to justify its existence.[38] But for the Protestants, hewing to the doctrine of *sola scriptura*, tradition counts for nothing if you cannot find the doctrine (or even the term) in the Bible. In his refutation of More and two other defenders of purgatory, **John Frith** (1503–33) writes that "their words are nothing but even their own imagination, for they cannot confirm their sayings by the Scripture."[39] Echoing Luther, Frith condemns purgatory as a lie and a cheat, a "vain imagination [that] hath of long time but deceived the people and milked them from their money."[40]

The Reformation, it should be stressed, did not start off as a politically revolutionary movement. Luther tried to restrict his critique of hierarchy to the Church itself, and he savagely condemned the Peasant's Revolt (1525). Tyndale also coupled his uncompromising attack on the Catholic Church with overt submission to secular authority. In *Obedience of the Christian Man* (1528), Tyndale declared, "Such obedience unto father and mother, master, husband, emperor and king, lords and rulers requireth God of all nations ... Neither may the inferior person avenge himself upon the superior, or violently resist him, for whatsoever wrong it be."[41] The monarch, while eventually subject to God's judgment, essentially has unlimited power on earth: "the king is, in this world, without law; and may at his lust do right or wrong …."[42] To a certain extent, Tyndale's promotion of secular authority through an attack on the Pope's worked. After **Henry VIII** finished the *Obedience* (given to him by the Protestant-leaning **Anne Boleyn**), he declared: "This is a book for me and for all kings to read."[43] He even told the Imperial ambassador in October 1529 that if Luther had restricted himself to attacking the corruption of the Catholic Church and not challenged the sacraments, he would have defended him.[44]

But **Henry VIII** and **Wolsey** quickly sensed that Lutheranism constituted a heresy they needed to vigorously oppose both because of its doctrinal content and because of the implicit threat to secular authority (early in his reign, **King James VI/I** would sum up the threat in the phrase, "No bishop, no king"), and so, starting in 1520, they tried to extinguish Lutheran ideas in England through a combination of censorship, oppression, and books both defending Catholic doctrine and attacking Luther and his English followers. In 1520, **Henry VIII** published his own volume defending Catholic doctrine, the *Assertion of the Seven Sacraments* (**Thomas More** likely contributed significantly), for which the Pope awarded him the title, "Defender of the Faith" – a title neither Henry nor his heirs ever relinquished – and More himself wrote a series of scabrous polemical works against Luther, Tyndale, and other reformers or "evangelicals," as they were called.

Dynastic issues also occupied Henry VIII's mind, and by the late 1520s, the king had started to think of divorcing **Katherine of Aragon**. The problem was Queen Katherine's difficulty in producing children, male children in particular. While frequently pregnant, only one of her six children survived: **Princess Mary** (1516–58), who would become **Queen Mary I**. All the rest were either stillborn or died shortly after their birth. While queens could and did rule (although England's last queen was a long time ago), the vast preference was for a male to inherit the throne, and **Katherine's** childbearing years were over, or nearly so. Sex or a marriage gone cold was not the issue. Henry and Katherine got on perfectly well after nearly 20 years together, at least partly because she did not object when her husband engaged in adultery, an activity Henry enthusiastically pursued. Within five years of his marriage he had an affair with **Elizabeth Blount** (c. 1500–c. 1541), one of his wife's ladies-in-waiting, which resulted in a son, **Henry Fitzroy** (1519–36).[45] The next mistress we know about was **Mary Boleyn** (also married at the time). After that, of course, came Mary's sister, **Anne Boleyn** (c. 1500–36), whom he probably met in 1526.

Henry VIII's Marital Record

1. Katherine of Aragon: m.1509 – annulled, May, 1533
2. Anne Boleyn: m. June, 1533 – executed for adultery, May 17, 1536
3. Jane Seymour: m. May 30, 1536 – dies after childbirth, October 24, 1537
4. Anne of Cleves: m. January 6, 1540 – annulled, June 1540
5. Katherine Howard: m. July 28, 1540 – executed for adultery, February 13, 1542
6. Katherine Parr: m. July 12, 1543

Henry's marriages can be remembered by this rhyme: "divorced, beheaded, died; divorced, beheaded, survived."

The problem with **Henry's** marriage to **Katherine** originated in her earlier marriage to Henry's brother, the late **Prince Arthur**, and the conflict between two opposing biblical verses. Leviticus 20:21 states "if a man shall take his brother's wife, it is an unclean thing he hath uncovered his brother's nakedness; they shall be childless." Deuteronomy 25:5, on the other hand, mandates that if one brother's wife dies, "her husband's brother shall go in unto her, and take her to him to wife." The contradiction required a papal dispensation for

Henry to marry Katherine. However, Katherine's childbearing difficulties caused Henry to question the validity of both his marriage and the Pope's ruling. While annulments for diplomatic or dynastic reasons were far from uncommon, the central stumbling block was that **Pope Clement VII** had been captured by **Charles V**, **Katherine of Aragon's** nephew, and the Holy Roman Emperor was not inclined to enhance English power by helping assure the continuation of the Tudor dynasty. **Henry VIII** then turned to **Cardinal Wolsey** to bring about the divorce, but **Wolsey**, while supremely powerful in England, had much less influence abroad. In short, he failed, and consequently fell from power.[46]

Five years of diplomatic activity and public debate ensued that also involved courtly factions pro and con. Queen Katherine certainly had powerful allies, including **Sir Thomas More** and **Bishop John Fisher** (1459–1535), both of whom would eventually be executed for opposing the king's will, as well as the combined forces of tradition and resistance to change. On the other side, supporting the divorce and Anne Boleyn's becoming queen, we have the clergymen who supported church reform (the Boleyn family sympathized with Luther and Tyndale), **Thomas Cranmer** (1489–1556), and Wolsey's former servant and successor as the king's chief minister, **Thomas Cromwell** (c. 1485–1540). In between were many who had their doubts about the divorce and Protestantism, but who ultimately acquiesced to the king's will.

The Pope clearly would not grant Henry's request, which meant that Wolsey had failed, and so earned **Anne Boleyn's** enmity. To finally settle the king's "Great Matter," in May 1529, Henry convened a trial at Blackfriar's Hall, but **Queen Katherine** (no fool her) countered by demanding her right to appeal the case to Rome, which as we have noted, would likely not resolve the case in Henry's favor. Therefore, **Henry VIII** started looking for more extreme solutions as well as a scapegoat, and the instrument for Wolsey's defeat ominously anticipated the future. Rather than firing the Cardinal and stripping him of his high offices, **Henry VIII** charged **Wolsey** with violating the **Statute of Praemunire**, the law barring loyalty to anyone other than the king. In other words, **Wolsey** was charged with assuming that someone else's authority could trump the king's. **Henry VIII** would next extend his rejection of that principle to the Church itself. If the Pope would not grant a divorce, then the king would deny the Pope's authority and claim it for himself.

Henry VIII always had a high regard for the scope of royal power. He tried (unsuccessfully) to alter the coronation oath so that he would swear to uphold only those laws that did not limit royal prerogative, and in a 1520 letter he would describe his "absolute power" as "above the laws."[47] Now he would force the Church to submit to his authority; even so, the Reformation had to proceed through a series of acts of parliament. Despite his claims of superiority to the law, **Henry VIII** had to follow the forms of mixed-monarchy, which is exactly what he did. In 1529, the King charged parliament to look into church corruption, and in 1530, **Henry VIII** charged the entire clergy with violating the **Statute of Praemunire**. They submitted, and Henry pardoned them after they paid a huge fine. Significantly, the prologue to the document of submission referred to Henry as the "sole protector and supreme head of the English church and clergy."[48] In 1532, Henry suspended payments to Rome, and in 1533, the penultimate piece of legislation formalizing Henry's break with Rome, **the Act in Restraint of Appeals**, made the English monarch the final court for ecclesiastical disputes. The preamble famously begins:

> Whereby divers sundry old authentic histories and chronicles it is manifestly declared and expressed that this realm of England is an empire, and so hath been accepted in the world, governed by one Supreme Head and King ... unto whom a body politic, compact [made up] of all sorts and degrees of people divided in terms and by names of Spirituality and Temporality, be bounden and owe to bear next to God a natural and humble obedience ....[49]

The Pope no longer had any authority in England; the English monarch was now and henceforth the last arbiter of all matters secular *and* religious.

Shifts in Reformation Historiography

An earlier generation of historians believed that England's population eagerly embraced Henry VIII's and Cromwell's innovations because they were unhappy with a Church they perceived as ignorant and corrupt. More recent historians, however, have argued that most people in 1529 were satisfied with their Church and resisted change. The former group interpreted the Reformation as a grassroots movement; the latter sees it as imposed from above.[50] In recognition of how the Reformation was not a single event that occurred at a distinct point in history, many historians now refer to "Reformations" rather than employing the singular.

Henry VIII and **Anne Boleyn** had good reasons for hurrying things along because by the end of 1532, **Anne** was pregnant. The two secretly married in January, 1533 (Henry did not consider this marriage bigamy because he denied the validity of his union with Katherine). On May 23, Boleyn's protégé, **Archbishop Thomas Cranmer**, following the dictates of the **Act in Restraint of Appeals**, heard the king's "Great Matter" and determined, unsurprisingly, that the marriage to Katherine was null and void. On September 7, 1533, Anne gave birth to a girl, **Elizabeth** (later **Queen Elizabeth I**), and despite legend, there is no evidence that Henry was crushed by his child's gender.[51]

The new queen and the new heir meant that a new **Act of Succession** needed to be passed, and so Parliament declared **Princess Mary** illegitimate and reserved the succession of the Crown to Henry and Anne's issue. **Henry** and **Cromwell's** legislative agenda, however, went much further. In 1534, Parliament passed the final law separating England from Rome, the **Act of Supremacy**, which officially made the king "The only supreme head in earth of the Church of England" (26 Henry VIII, c. 1), and in 1536, as part of the plan to undo the Catholic Church's authority in England, Cromwell also started in on the **dissolution of the monasteries**, claiming their land and property for the Crown and scattering the inhabitants. The reason for this action is twofold: first, monasteries reported directly to Rome, not the English crown, and so this competition to the Crown needed to be eliminated; second, the dissolution of the monasteries provided a solution to the chronic financial problems of the crown. Selling off their lands would make Henry "the richest prince in the world." (As we will shortly see, **Anne Boleyn's** objections to this plan would lead to her downfall.)

Cromwell also shepherded into law a new Treason Act that significantly broadened the definition of this crime. Normally, a crime requires a guilty act to qualify. One has to physically *do* something to be found guilty, and historically, speech did not qualify. The **Treason Act of 1534,** however, made it a capital crime to speak against the succession, the king's title (i.e. leader of the Anglican Church), or to call the king or queen a heretic, usurper, or like term. For the first time in English criminal law, speech alone could convict you. "It were a strange world as words were made treason," said one nobleman tried and condemned on the basis of this statute.[52] Even further, and even more revolutionary, silence could also become treason. Rather than assenting to the submission of the clergy and the stripping of the Pope's power in England, **Sir Thomas More** resigned his position as Lord Chancellor. While **More** never overtly opposed **Henry VIII**, neither would he take the oath of allegiance Henry demanded from everyone, and for his silence **Cromwell** engineered More's trial and execution on July 6, 1535. Nor did Henry VIII restrict himself to executing the powerful. **Elizabeth Barton**, a Benedictine nun otherwise known as the **Holy Maid of Kent**, prophesied that if Henry VIII divorced Katherine and married someone else, "his majesty should not be king of this realm by the space of one month after, and in the [repudiation] of God should not be king one day nor one hour."[53] She and her followers were burned at the stake.

Like his mentor, **Wolsey**, **Cromwell** paradoxically combined utter ruthlessness with a great sense of mission, and the full scope of his achievements as chief minister go well beyond destroying the Catholic Church and promoting royal power. **Cromwell** also dedicated himself to promoting social, economic, and agricultural reform. He sought to restrict the enclosure movement and to promote English cloth exports. **Cromwell's** most important legislation in this area was the Poor Relief Act of 1536, which made parishes responsible for combating local poverty. "Although this statute was far from resolving the problem and soon lapsed, it nevertheless marks the first occasion on which an English government had recognized a responsibility to those on the fringes of society."[54]

But while **Cromwell** may have been inspired by humanist ideals to improve the commonwealth, he had no mercy on his political enemies, as **Anne Boleyn** was about to find out. The commonly accepted version of events is that after two years, Anne and Henry's marriage had gone cold. The final straw was Anne's miscarriage of a male fetus, which proved to the king that their union, like his marriage to Katherine, was an abomination unto God, and therefore no living male children would come of it. But much of this version is simply not true, although Henry's roving eye had already lighted on **Jane Seymour** by 1536. Henry, however, wanted an affair, not a divorce, and while Anne's miscarriage in January 1536 came as a blow, Henry repeatedly made clear his disinterest in leaving the marriage and (despite pressure from court conservatives) the restoration of **Princess Mary** to the succession. The actual story is more sordid, in its way.

What happened is that **Anne Boleyn** got into **Cromwell's** way, and she had to be removed.[55] The Queen threatened Cromwell in two ways. First, **Anne** objected to Cromwell's plan to use the proceeds from the dissolution of monasteries to enrich the king rather than for charitable purposes. Unwisely, Anne instructed one of her chaplains to deliver a sermon to the court comparing Cromwell to Haman, the good Queen Esther's enemy, and accusing the clergy's enemies of masking greed with reform: "nowadays madmen ... rebuke the clergy ... because they would have from the clergy their possessions."[56] Second, Anne threatened to upset the delicate see-saw of England's relations with France and the Holy Roman Empire by interfering with **Cromwell's** desire to move England closer to **Charles V**. Having seen Anne engineer the fall of his patron, **Cardinal Wolsey**, **Cromwell** decided that, to save himself, **Anne** must be destroyed. Cromwell then applied his organizational genius to removing the Queen. Realizing that Henry VIII would not divorce Anne without both good reason and an alternative, Cromwell found the latter in **Jane Seymour** (1508–37) and the former in using Queen Anne's informality and immersion in the language of courtly love against her. Protestations of eternal love and fealty would be twisted into evidence of adultery and adulterous incest with her brother. Ultimately, six people, including Anne, her brother, and four others, would be executed because of these trumped-up charges, and more, including the poet and courtier-diplomat, **Sir Thomas Wyatt** (1503?–1542) would find themselves threatened with death in the Tower of London. Wyatt almost certainly watched **Anne Boleyn's** beheading ("The bell tower showed me such a sight / That in my head sticks day and night"), and he summed up the terror of **Henry VIII's** reign:

> These bloody days have broken my heart,
> My lust, my youth did them depart,
> And blind desire of estate.
> Who hastes to climb seeks to revert.
> Of truth, *circa Regna tonat* [Around the throne, thunder rolls].[57]

Henry VIII married **Jane Seymour** on May 19, 1536, the same day that **Anne Boleyn** lost her head. But their happiness did not last long. Twelve days after giving birth on October 12, 1537 to Henry's longed-for son, **Edward**, who would succeed his father as **Edward VI** (1537–53), the queen died from childbirth complications.

Thunder rolled elsewhere as well, as the enforcement, clarifications and reversals of the new religion caused rebellion, confusion, and a pervasive sense of insecurity, even terror. In the autumn and winter of 1536, a series of uprisings in England's north, known today as the **Pilgrimage of Grace**, collectively protested the king's divorce, his religious policies, especially the suppression of the monasteries, economic hardship, and the enclosure movement. According to Edward Hall, the rebellion was sparked by the government's attempt at clarifying religious matters in the Act of the Ten Articles, but the Act had the opposite effect because it tried to split the difference between the old and new religions. Prayers for the dead were allowed, but not purgatory. Those seeking doctrinal certainty were disappointed. The fuzziness, however, did nothing to blunt popular resentment in England's north. People "made open clamors in every place where opportunity served that [the] Christian religion should be utterly violate despised, and set aside."[58] Because the Act dealt with only three sacraments, Hall records that people said "See friends, now is taken from us four of the seven sacraments and shortly you shall lose the other three also, and thus the faith of holy church shall utterly be suppressed and abolished."[59] **Henry VIII** sent **Thomas Howard, Duke of Norfolk** (1473–1554), coincidentally uncle to both **Anne Boleyn** and Henry's fifth wife, **Katherine Howard**, to defeat the rebels, but when he arrived he realized that the king's army was hopelessly outnumbered. Perhaps also because he had some sympathy for the uprising's demands, **Norfolk** defused the situation by promising to take the rebels' demands to the king. **Henry VIII** rejected this agreement, and when further uprisings occurred in 1537, ruthlessly suppressed them, executing nearly 200 people.

The **Pilgrimage of Grace** only spurred **Cromwell** to press even harder the reform agenda, and in 1538 he sponsored a campaign against images (**iconoclasm**) that resulted in the destruction of much sacred art. More positively, he required that each church obtain a copy of the new English translation of the Tyndale Bible as revised by Miles Coverdale. (In 1535, Tyndale himself had been kidnapped by Henry's agents while in exile in Antwerp, and executed despite Cromwell's pleas.) The tide of opinion, however, ran ahead of the government's ability to control it, and in 1538, Henry's government issued a proclamation (in the Kings name) ordering that nobody "shall reason, dispute, or argue upon" religious matters, on pain of death.[60] Henry tried again the next year with the Act of the Six Articles, but this legislation only increased dissension and oppression:

> In this parliament was an act made which bore this title: *An Act for Abolishing Diversity of Opinions, in Certain Articles concerning Christian religion.* This act established chiefly six articles, whereof among the common people it was called "the act of six articles," and of some it was named "the whip with six strings," and of some other – and that of the most parte – it was named the bloody statute, for of truth it so in short time after scourged a great number in the city of London.[61]

Cromwell's reform agenda also informed his search for a new queen. France and the Holy Roman Empire had signed a peace treaty, and so to keep England from becoming the odd man out, and to further bind England to the evangelical cause, in 1540 Cromwell arranged a match that would ally England with the Lutheran princes of Germany. Henry's new bride was **Anne of Cleves**, but the marriage was a disaster. **Henry** found his new bride so repellent that he could "never in her company be provoked and steered to know her carnally."[62] "I like her not," Henry famously said after meeting her. The marriage was annulled after six months. Rather than facing the humiliation of returning home, having been rejected by her husband, Ann chose to stay in England, and the two actually became good friends.

The failure of Henry's fifth marriage, however, had much larger consequences than personal disappointment. **Henry's** quarrel with the Catholic Church was less about theology and much more about power. He wanted the Pope's authority in England eliminated, and once that happened, his interest in reform largely ended. **Cromwell**, not **Henry VIII**, was the driving force for the evangelical movement in England. The failure of the marriage with **Anne of Cleves** gave **Cromwell's** conservative enemies a huge opportunity to get rid of their antagonist and return England to traditional ways, and they proceeded on two fronts. Using a variety of pretexts, they had Henry's last chief minister arrested for treason in June 1540, and they sought to bind the king to their cause through marriage.

Henry, with his amazing ability to find his next wife among the ladies serving the present one, fell in love (or lust) with **Katherine Howard** (c. 1520–42), the nineteen-year-old niece of the Catholic

Thomas Howard, Duke of Norfolk (the same person Henry sent to crush the **Pilgrimage of Grace**). Henry married her on July 28, 1540, the same day that **Cromwell** was executed, and there is no doubt that the older king was absolutely besotted with his young bride (he was 49; she was 20), and that Katherine took full advantage of the situation. A contemporary Spanish chronicler recorded that "the king had no wife who made him spend so much money in dresses and jewels as she did, and every day some fresh caprice."[63] The conservative triumph, however, did not last because of Katherine's sexual escapades both before and (much more seriously) after her marriage. Of all Henry's wives, the Spanish chronicler observes, she was the "handsomest" but also "the most giddy."[64] Katherine Howard was beheaded on February 13, 1542 along with her lovers. The decline in the king's marital fortunes also meant that **Henry VIII** no longer fully backed the conservative cause (assuming he ever did). In fact, **Henry VIII** had grown equally suspicious of both sides of the religious debate because their quarrel prevented the unity in religion he desired. Consequently, two days after **Cromwell's** execution, **Henry VIII** "ordered the execution of three evangelicals arrested in March, as well as three conservatives loyal to Rome."[65] Henrician tyranny had become equal opportunity.

Henry VIII's final years were spent attempting to impose order at home while waging war abroad. In the summer of 1541, the delicate balance between France and the Holy Roman Empire shifted yet again, and the two restarted their hostilities. **Henry** decided to enter the fray, this time on the side of the Emperor, and to disrupt French influence on England's turf while also pacifying the northern border, **Henry VIII** invaded Scotland in the fall of 1542. In one way, the campaign worked. The Scots were defeated, but the campaign was ruinously expensive, costing over one million pounds. But Henry was not done. In 1544, he decided to invade Scotland yet again, this time over who would marry **Edward**, Henry VIII's son and heir. According to the Treaty of Greenwich (1543), the infant queen of Scotland, **Mary Stuart** (1542–87; better known as Mary, Queen of Scots), daughter of King James V and Mary of Guise, was supposed to marry Edward, but the Scots reneged on the promise. Henry VIII responded with the **"Rough Wooing,"** a war that left both the Scottish Lowlands and English coffers devastated. That same year, despite his many illnesses and debilities (**Henry VIII** was obese and suffered from gout, among other illnesses), the king chose to accompany his army to France, and had to be carried about in a litter because he could barely move. While the campaign netted England the town of Boulogne, it too was horribly expensive, and the monarch's bills ran well ahead of his ability to pay. To help defray the costs, the government had to demand forced loans along with selling off the monastery lands and debasing the currency, but those measures were still not sufficient. In August, 1545, Lord Chancellor Thomas Wriothesley, despairingly wrote to the Council: "this year and last year the King has spent about £1,300,000. His subsidy and benevolence ministering scant £300,000, and the lands being consumed and the plate of the realm molten and coined. I lament the danger of the time to come ... And yet you write to still Pay! Pay! Prepare for this and for that!"[66] The king's final military ventures would wreck royal finances for at least a century and the English economy generally for at least 20 years.[67]

The domestic front was only marginally more peaceful. In July, 1543, **Henry VIII** married **Katherine Parr** (1512–48), an intelligent, attractive, and dignified woman with reformist leanings (she held daily scripture readings in her rooms, and patronized younger reformers at court). Katherine was in the service of Princess Mary (Henry's daughter by Katherine of Aragon), which is how she came to Henry's attention. At the time, Katherine had intended to marry **Sir Thomas Seymour** (1509–49), Queen Jane's brother (we will hear more of him and Katherine as well as **Sir Edward Seymour** in the next chapter), but her reformist family pressured her into accepting the king's attention, asserting that resisting the king was the same as resisting God. She later wrote to Sir Thomas that while at the time she truly wanted him as her husband, "Howbeit, God withstood my will therein most vehemently ... [and] made me to renounce utterly mine own will, and to follow his most willingly."[68] Even so, Queen Katherine made it her business to be a good wife to Henry and to ensure good relations with Henry's children. She especially encouraged **Elizabeth's** and **Edward's** scholarly pursuits. (In 1544, the eleven-year-old Elizabeth translated Marguerite de Navarre's *Le Miroir de l'âme pécheresse [The Mirror of the Sinful Soul]* and presented Katherine with a manuscript copy.[69])

But while Henry's personal life may have settled into calm, his persecution of anybody he thought threatened domestic peace and even more importantly, his son Edward's accession, continued unabated. Henry's last victim was **Henry Howard, Earl of Surrey** (1516–47), the son of **Thomas Howard, Duke of Norfolk**, an arrogant and unstable man who along with his younger contemporary, **Sir Thomas Wyatt**, significantly contributed to the development of English lyric poetry by combining Italian (meaning, Petrarchan) themes with English verse forms. **Surrey** made the fatal error of including royal symbols in his coat of arms, thus asserting his own right to the throne. That was rightly considered treason, and he went to the block on January 19, 1547. While in the Tower, he wrote a paraphrase of Ecclesiastes that portrayed the king as a vicious monster:

> I saw a royal throne whereas that Justice should have sit;
> Instead of whom I saw, with fierce and cruel mood,
> Where wrong was sat, that bloody beast, that drunk the guiltless blood.[70]

Henry VIII followed Surrey nine days later, breathing his last at 2 a.m., January 28, 1547.

Notes

1 *Holinshed's Chronicles*, vol. 3, 482. Note that the author does not unqualifiedly endorse the providential interpretation of Henry VII's marriage. Peace does not descend out of heaven, but *"was thought"* to descend.
2 Robert Bucholz and Newton Key, *Early Modern England 1485–1714: A Narrative History* (Oxford: Blackwell, 2004), 43.
3 When Edward's father, George, Duke of Clarence, was accused of treason by Edward IV, Edward's inheritance of the Warwick earldom

reverted to the crown, and the attainder was never reversed. Consequently, while Edward would occasionally be referred to as the earl of Warwick, he never took possession of his lands. See Christine Carpenter, "Edward, styled earl of Warwick (1475–1499)," *The Oxford Dictionary of National Biography*, Oxford University Press, September 2004; online edn., January 2008. http://www.oxforddnb.com/view/article/8525, accessed September 8, 2009.

4 Quoted in J. R. Lander, *Government and Community: England 1450–1509* (London: Edward Arnold, 1980), 340.

5 *Letters and Papers Illustrative of the Reigns of Richard III and Henry VII*, ed. James Gairdner (London: HMSO, 1857), 233. See also David Starkey, *Henry: Virtuous Prince* (London: Harper Press, 2008), 193–6.

6 Mary (1496–1533), Henry and Elizabeth's third daughter and fifth child, would marry Louis XII of France in 1514, and she was queen of France until Louis's death a year later.

7 Quoted in Rosemary Horrox, "Elizabeth [Elizabeth of York] (1466–1503)," *The Oxford Dictionary of National Biography* (Oxford: Oxford University Press, 2004). http://www.oxforddnb.com/view/article/8635, accessed September14, 2009.

8 Horrox, "Elizabeth."

9 Starkey, *Henry*, 188.

10 Bucholz and Key, *Early Modern England*, 45.

11 Nicholas Mann, "The Origins of Humanism," *The Cambridge Companion to Humanism*, ed. Jill Kraye (Cambridge: Cambridge University Press, 1996), 1.

12 Paul Oskar Kristeller, "Humanism," *The Cambridge History of Renaissance Philosophy*, ed. Charles B. Schmitt *et al.* (Cambridge: Cambridge University Press, 1988), 113.

13 Maria Dowling, *Humanism in the Age of Henry VIII* (London: Croon Helm, 1986), 7.

14 Carolly Erickson, *Great Harry* (New York: Summit Books, 1980), 27. See also Starkey, *Henry*, 175.

15 "Against Garnesche,"in *John Skelton: The Complete Poems*, ed. John Scattergood (New Haven: Yale University Press, 1983), 132.

16 More, *Utopia*, 16.

17 Sidney, *Sir Philip Sidney's "an Apology for Poetry" and "Astrophil and Stella,"* ed. Peter C. Herman (Glen Allen, VA: College Publishing, 2001), 71.

18 Quoted in J. J. Scarisbrick, *Henry VIII* (Berkeley: University of California Press, 1968), 12.

19   Edward Hall, *Chronicle* (1548), 507.

20   Scarisbrick, *Henry VIII*, 20.

21   *Hall's Chronicle*, 515. The importance of Henry VIII's lyrics to the development of early modern, English verse is only now starting to be recognized. See Peter C. Herman, *Royal Poetrie: Monarchic Verse and the Political Imaginary of Early Modern England* (forthcoming, Cornell University Press).

22   More, *Utopia*, 2.

23   *Hall's Chronicle*, 505; Bucholz and Key, *Early Modern England*, 55.

24   Greenblatt, *Renaissance Self-Fashioning: From More to Shakespeare* (Chicago: University of Chicago Press, 1980), 15.

25   This anecdote is recounted in Scarisbrick, *Henry VIII*, 33.

26   William Roper, *The Life of Sir Thomas More*, in *Two Early Tudor Lives*, ed. Richard S. Sylvester and Davis P. Harding (New Haven: Yale University Press, 1962), 208.

27   Roper, *The Life of Sir Thomas More*, 208.

28   *Hall's Chronicle*, 528.

29   *Hall's Chronicle*, 528.

30   George Cavendish, *The Life and Death of Cardinal Wolsey*, in *Two Early Tudor Lives*, 5.

31   Cavendish, *The Life and Death*, 12.

32   Cavendish, *The Life and Death*, 12–13.

33   Cavendish, *The Life and Death*, 12.

34   Cavendish, *The Life and Death*, 25.

35   Cavendish, *The Life and Death*, 696.

36   Cavendish, *The Life and Death*, 698, 701.

37   For an exhaustive and readable history, see David Daniell, *The Bible in English: Its History and Influence* (New Haven: Yale University Press, 2003). See also Adam Nicolson, *God's Secretaries: The Making of the King James Bible* (New York: HarperCollins, 2003).

38   More, *The Supplication of Souls, The Complete Works of St. Thomas More*, ed. Frank Manley *et al.* (New Haven: Yale University Press, 1963), vol. 7, 194–5.

39   Frith, *A Disputation of Purgatory* (Antwerp, 1531), sig. B5v.

40   Frith, *A Disputation*, sig. a5r.

41   William Tyndale, *Obedience of the Christian Man*, in *Doctrinal Treatises and Introductions to Different Portions of the Holy Scriptures*, ed. Henry Walter (Parker Society; Cambridge: University Press, 1848), 177.

42   Tyndale, *Obedience of the Christian Man*, 178.

43 Quoted in Scarisbrick, *Henry VIII*, 247.

44 Susan Brigden, *New Worlds, Lost Worlds: The Rule of the Tudors 1485–1603* (New York: Viking, 2000), 114–15.

45 Henry recognized his son, and letters between them show considerable affection between them. While the king may have considered legitimizing him, Henry never did so, and Henry Fitzroy died young of a pulmonary infection. See Beverley A. Murphy, "Fitzroy, Henry, duke of Richmond and Somerset (1519–1536)," *The Oxford Dictionary of National Biography*, Oxford University Press, September 2004; online edn., January 2008. http://www.oxforddnb.com/view/article/9635, accessed October 3, 2009.

46 Wolsey's fall, the rise of Anne Boleyn and Thomas Cromwell, and their subsequent falls, are brilliantly (and accurately) rendered in Hilary Mantel's Man Booker Prize-winning novel, *Wolf Hall* (New York: Henry Holt, 2009).

47 Quoted in E. W. Ives, "Henry VIII (1491–1547)," *The Oxford Dictionary of National Biography*, Oxford University Press, September 2004; online edn., May 2009.

48 Quoted in Bucholz and Key, *Early Modern England*, 73.

49 *Tudor Constitutional Documents*, ed. J. R. Tanner (Cambridge: Cambridge University Press, 1951), 41.

50 For the "Reformation from Below," see A. G. Dickens, *The English Reformation*, 2nd ed. (London: B.T. Batsford, 1989), and Diarmaid MacCulloch, *The Later Reformation in England, 1547–1603* (London: Macmillan, 1990). For the "Reformation from Above" perspective, see Christopher Haigh, *English Reformations: Religion, Politics, and Society Under the Tudors* (Oxford: Clarendon Press, 1993) and Eamon Duffy, *The Stripping of the Altars: Traditional Religion in England, c. 1400–c. 1580* (New Haven: Yale University Press, 1992). For an excellent survey of developments, see Christopher Haigh, "The Recent Historiography of the English Reformation," *Reformation to Revolution: Politics and Religion in Early Modern England*, ed. Margo Todd (New York: Routledge, 1995), 13–32.

51 See Ives, "Henry VIII."

52 Quoted in Brigden, *New Worlds, Lost Worlds*, 120.

53 Quoted in Diane Watt, "Barton, Elizabeth (*c.* 1506–1534)," *The Oxford Dictionary of National Biography*, Oxford University Press, September

2004; online edn., January 2008. http://www.oxforddnb.com/view/article/1598, accessed October 6, 2009.

54 Howard Leithead, "Cromwell, Thomas, earl of Essex (*b.* in or before 1485, *d.* 1540)," *The Oxford Dictionary of National Biography*, Oxford University Press, September 2004; online edn., May 2009. http://www.oxforddnb.com/view/article/6769, accessed October 7, 2009.

55 For the full story, see Eric Ives, *The Life and Death of Anne Boleyn* (Oxford: Blackwell, 2004), 306–37.

56 Quoted in Ives, *Life and Death*, 307.

57 Wyatt, Poem CXXIII, "Who list his wealth and ease retain," *Sir Thomas Wyatt: The Complete Poems*, ed. Ronald A. Rebholz (New Haven: Yale University Press, 1978), 155.

58 *Hall's Chronicle*, 820.

59 *Hall's Chronicle*, 820.

60 "The King's Most Royal Majesty Being Informed ..." (London, 1538), n. p.

61 *Hall's Chronicle*, 828.

62 Quoted in Bridgen, *New Worlds, Lost Worlds*, 128.

63 *Chronicle of King Henry VIII of England. Being a contemporary record of some of the principal events of the reigns of Henry VIII and Edward VI*, ed. and trans. Martin A. Hume (London: G. Bell and Sons, 1889), 77.

64 *Chronicle of King Henry VIII*, 77.

65 Howard Leithead, "Cromwell, Thomas, earl of Essex (*b.* in or before 1485, *d.* 1540)," *The Oxford Dictionary of National Biography*.

66 Quoted in Roger Lockyer, *Tudor and Stuart Britain: 1471–1714* (Harlow, Essex: Longman, 1985), 82.

67 Bucholz and Key, *Early Modern England*, 96.

68 Quoted in Susan E. James, "Katherine [Katherine Parr] (1512–1548)," *Oxford Dictionary of National Biography*, Oxford University Press, September 2004; online edn., January 2008. http://www.oxforddnb.com/view/article/4893, accessed December 15, 2009.

69 John Bale published Elizabeth's translation in 1548. A reproduction of the manuscript and a contemporary edition of the poem can be found in Marc Shell, *Elizabeth's Glass* (Lincoln: University of Nebraska Press, 1993).

70 Quoted in Brigden, *New Worlds, Lost Worlds*, 139.

4

Edward VI, Lady Jane Grey, and Mary I (1547–53)

In one sense, **Henry VIII's** dream came true: the crown passed to the Tudor male heir, Edward VI, without the slightest hiccup. No pretenders invaded, and nobody challenged Edward's right to the crown. The Tudor dynasty, in other words, had been established beyond all doubt. But **Henry VIII** bequeathed his son a kingdom burdened by massive debt, economic distress, religious controversy, and wars in Scotland, Ireland, and France. All of these crises overlapped. To help pay for the wars, the government debased the currency by reducing the amount of gold or silver in the coin while retaining the original face value. This move caused massive inflation, thus putting the price of bread out of the reach of the poor, which in turn caused deep resentment and anti-government riots. Nor did Henry VIII's demise help calm the turmoil engendered by the late king's religious policies, such as the split from Rome, the dissolution of the monasteries, and the ever-shifting statements of official doctrine. In short, 1547 was not a good year for a child to

A Short History of Early Modern England: British Literature in Context, First Edition.
Peter C. Herman.
© 2011 Peter C. Herman. Published 2011 by Blackwell Publishing Ltd.

become king, and while Edward VI would be crowned without any challenges to his legitimacy, his accession marks the start of possibly the worst decade in early modern English history, one that would be marked by extreme alterations in the official religion, the largest and bloodiest popular uprising in the sixteenth century, and the return of punishing "heretics" by burning them alive.

The Reign of Edward VI

Before **Henry VIII** died, he altered his will in two significant ways. First, he changed the line of succession so that the throne would go first to **Edward**, his son by **Jane Seymour**; then, if he died without issue, to **Mary**, his daughter by **Katherine of Aragon**; and then, if she died without issue, to **Elizabeth**, his daughter by **Anne Boleyn**, who was, officially at least, still considered illegitimate. Both daughters had previously been disinherited, and while Henry obviously did not know it at the time, this change would have momentous consequences for English history. Next, **Henry VIII** tried to avoid the problems associated with a child-king by creating a council of 16 peers who would collectively rule England until Edward reached his eighteenth birthday. With breathtaking idealism and naïveté, Henry intended that all members would be equal and that decisions would be taken by a majority vote.

Within days of his death, however, the will was altered, and possibly forged, by **Edward Seymour** (c. 1500–52; he was made **Earl of Hertford**, at Edward VI's birth, and in 1547, elevated himself to **Duke of Somerset**), the late Queen Jane's elder brother and Edward's uncle. First, an "unfulfilled gifts" clause appeared, in which Henry willed "that all such grants and gifts as we have made, given and promised to any, which be not yet perfected … shall be perfected …."[1] As the will gave no further details, this clause gave Edward's counselors carte blanche to reward themselves according to their desires. And they did. Second, Edward Seymour and Henry's secretary, **Sir William Paget** (1505–63), together agreed that Seymour would become the Lord Protector and essentially England's ruler until Edward reached adulthood. In an astonishing letter written two years later, **Paget** reminded **Seymour** of their plotting while Henry lay dying: "Remember what you promised me in the gallery at Westminster, before the breath was out of the body of the king that dead is. Remember what you promised me immediately after, devising with me concerning the place which you now occupy ...."[2] Not everybody rejoiced at this subverting of the late king's will. Edward's brother, **Sir Thomas Seymour** (1509–49) bitterly complained: "Why was he made Protector? There is no need of a Protector. It was not the King's will that dead is that any one man should have both the Government of the King ... and also the Realm."[3] **Edward Seymour**, however, using the "gifts" clause inserted into Henry VIII's will, bought off the opposition (as well as rewarding himself with a dukedom), and, as Van der Delft, the ambassador for the Holy Roman Empire, observed, **Edward Seymour, Duke of Somerset**, now "governs everything absolutely," and he consulted only with Paget.[4] **Somerset** even adopted the royal "we" in his correspondence.

The memory of the last Lord Protector, **Richard III,** and the fate of his charges, was fresh in everyone's minds, and Somerset's aggrandizement of power and offices did not bode well, but **Somerset** was not interested in power for power's sake. He asked Parliament to repeal the Henrician era's most oppressive legislation, such as the 1534 Treason Act, the Act of the Six Articles (Hall recorded that while many called it "the whip with six strings," most referred to this legislation as the "bloody statute"),[5] and all the restrictions on printing the Bible in English. He also repealed the fifteenth-century Act for the Burning of Heretics. Henry VIII's Treason Act, which made speech a capital crime, may have been "very expedient and necessary," but times had changed, Somerset explained, and so this "very strait, sore extreme and terrible" legislation had to go:

> as in tempest or winter one course and garment is convenient, in calm or warm weather a more liberal race or lighter garment both may and ought to be followed and used, so we have seen divers strait and sore laws made in one parliament, the time so requiring, in a more calm and quiet reign of another prince ... repealed and taken away.[6]

Somerset wanted to make England a better place to live, and ironically, his sympathy for the poor and concern for social justice would spark the largest uprising in the sixteenth century and lead directly to his removal from power.

Somerset's first task, however, concerned trying to assure the future of the Tudor dynasty. He decided to continue Henry VIII's "rough wooing" of Scotland (the attempt to force the Scots into marrying James V's daughter, **Mary Stuart**, to Edward VI). While **Somerset** scored a major military victory over the Scots at the **Battle of Pinkie**, the policy failed dismally because in 1548, the infant Mary was spirited out of Scotland to France, where she would be brought up in the French court and eventually marry Henri II's son, the *dauphin*, François II.[7] To make matters worse, England could not pay for this campaign without further debasing its currency (we will deal with the economic consequences shortly), and the only lasting consequence of this military venture was to re-animate "the auld alliance" between Scotland and France, thus eventually causing Elizabeth I no end of trouble.

The end of the Scots war meant that **Somerset** had to deal with his troublesome brother, **Thomas**, who as noted above was none too pleased with how Edward combined the offices of Lord Protector and governor. **Thomas Seymour** was Katherine Parr's love before she attracted **Henry VIII's** attentions,[8] and after the king's death, he wasted no time renewing his suit. According to one source, he started in the day after Henry VIII's demise.[9] She demurred (if they married quickly and had a child, it would not be clear if Seymour or the late king was the father), but he pressed his suit, even writing a short love poem in one of Parr's religious books. She relented, and the two were secretly married in May or June, 1547, and the match caused much tension between the brothers and the court. Thomas Seymour, who had been sneaking into **King Edward's** chambers and giving him pocket money (the king supposedly complained that his "uncle Somerset dealeth very hardly with me and keepeth me so straight that I can not have money at my will"[10]), managed to ask the king to write a letter to **Somerset** supporting the marriage, but that only further infuriated the Lord Protector, who did not like anyone having a private channel to King Edward. **Katherine Parr** and **Somerset** also tussled over the jewels Henry VIII had purchased for his last wife. **Katherine** thought they were hers – understandably, since Henry VIII had bequeathed them to her in his will – but **Somerset** considered them the property of the state, and she never got them back.[11]

To make matters worse (at least, for his reputation today), **Thomas Seymour** started flirting with **Princess Elizabeth**, who was residing at their household in Chelsea, even while his wife was pregnant. **Katherine Parr's** death from child-birth complications (ironically, the same complications that led to Jane Seymour's premature demise), seems to have unhinged **Seymour**. He started pressing his unwanted attentions on Elizabeth in ways that everyone considered scandalously inappropriate. According to Elizabeth's governess, Thomas would:

> come many mornings into the said Lady Elizabeth's chamber … And if she were up, he would bid her good morrow, and ask how she did, and strike her upon the back, or on the buttocks familiarly …. And if she were in her bed, he would put open the curtains, and bid her good morrow, and make as though would come at her: and she would go further in the bed, so that he could not come at her; and one morning he strove to have kissed her in her bed.[12]

Thomas Seymour's shenanigans extended to plotting to kidnap **King Edward**. On January 16, 1549, he broke into the Privy Garden and made his way to Edward's bedroom, where he was attacked by Edward's dog, which he shot dead. He was immediately arrested and executed on March 19, 1549, defiant to the end. In a sermon, Hugh Latimer would declaim how Seymour "died very dangerously, irksomely, horribly …. He was a man the farthest from the fear of God that I knew or heard of in England."[13] The fall of **Thomas Seymour**, however, was a sideshow to the major events of 1549, although they played their part in loosening Somerset's grip on power, as some accused him of repeating Cain's murder: "Where is thy brother? Lo! His blood crieth against thee unto God from the ground," a "godly and honorable woman" exclaimed to him.[14]

While Thomas Seymour needed to be reined in, many thought that **Somerset** acted with unseemly coldness, and his reputation suffered accordingly.

Somerset's great project was to carry forward the stalled reformation of religion. In his last days, **Henry VIII's** commitment to evangelical Protestantism wavered, as the late king worried more about political stability than theology. Consequently, both religious conservatives and reformers found themselves repressed if they made too much noise (or any noise at all). The Lord Protector, however, unambiguously adhered to the Protestant cause, and while **Edward VI** may have been very young, he too was committed to reform. As a result, **Edward VI's** reign and **Somerset's** ascendency marked a significant intensification in promoting the Reformation in England, which also meant destroying Catholicism, both symbolically and physically.

Edward VI's reign is not generally known for its literature, but several key publications came out during this period. The historian, Richard Grafton, published the late Edward Hall's *The Union of the Two Noble and Illustre Families of Lancaster and York* (1548), better known as *Hall's Chronicle*. The literary critic, John N. King, has demonstrated how a distinctly Protestant literary tradition, characterized by religious themes and a plain style, flourished during Edward's reign and would deeply influence such later writers as Edmund Spenser, John Donne, and John Milton.[15] Authors include Richard Crowley, John Bale, and William Baldwin, whose 1553 prose fiction, *Beware the Cat*, may be the first English novel.

Somerset tried to proceed cautiously. On July 31, 1547, the government issued a set of injunctions warning against the abuse of images, enjoining the local clergy to remind everyone that "images serve for no other purpose but to be a remembrance whereby men may be admonished of the holy lives and conversation of them that the said images do represent";[16] the *Injunctions* also mandated that each church purchase "the whole Bible, of the largest volume in English" and that nobody should be discouraged "from the reading of any part of the Bible either in Latin or in English."[17] **Archbishop of Canterbury, Thomas Cranmer** (1489–1556) had published the first **Book of Common Prayer** at the end of 1548, but while the prayers are all in English, the book was fundamentally an attempt at compromise: "Indeed it is none other but the old," Cranmer explained, "the self-same words in English which were in Latin, saving a few things taken out."[18] Other government actions were less conciliatory. **The Chantries Act of 1549** not only abolished all chantries – endowments set up for the purpose of masses to shorten one's time in purgatory – but denounced "vain opinions of purgatory and masses."[19] The Act further reduced the institutional presence of the "old religion" in people's lives by closing down almshouses, schools, hospitals and other charitable institutions, essentially, all institutions that provided competition or an alternative to the village church, which was becoming thoroughly "Protestant-ized." In 1549 the **Act of Uniformity** mandated the use of the first **Book of Common Prayer** and allowed priests to marry (about one in ten did so).[20]

Attempts by Somerset's government to control the pace of religious reform, however, failed in both directions. On the Protestant end, Henry VIII's death and the *Injunctions* inspired a wave of iconoclasm throughout the country. The more radical evangelicals did not note the distinction in the *Injunctions* between the proper use and "abuse" of images; in their view, all images merited destruction. Consequently, "images in churches [were] smashed and medieval wall paintings white-washed over and replaced with the text of the Ten Commandments. At Shrewsbury they made a bonfire of images in the market place, whilst in Much Wenlock, Shropshire, they burnt the local saint's bones. In Durham the royal commissioner went as far as to smash up images with his own hands, jumping up and down upon them."[21]

But not everyone enthusiastically embraced the Reformation, as became evident in June 1549. Deep resistance to changes in religion, along with underlying economic tensions, resulted in a massive uprising known as **the Western Rebellion** that started in Cornwall and soon spread to the rest of the West Country. According to a list of demands probably drawn up as the rebels surrounded Exeter,[22] they wanted restored the religious formulary set out in Henry VIII's Act of the Six Articles, the Latin mass, and purgatory. They also demanded the return of abbey and chantry lands, and they denounced the new service, set out in the 1548 Book of Common Prayer, as a "Christmas game," insisting that "we will have our old service of Matins, mass, evensong and procession in Latin, not in English, as it was before." Bluntly put, "we the Cornishmen … utterly refuse this new English."[23] To be sure, the **Western Rising** had local causes. Cornwall, isolated on the Western tip of England, retained its own language (an offshoot of Gaelic), and because, as the rebel demands admitted, "certain of us understand no English," the replacement of Latin with English meant that many would no longer understand Christian services.[24] The government agent, William Body, had no local ties (a major disadvantage in such an insular culture) and no diplomatic skills. The local clergy resented his attempt to enact the Edwardian Injunctions both because of their content and because these changes were imposed by what must have seemed like a foreign power, one to which they felt little connection or loyalty. Add to this mix resentment against the new tax on sheep and cloth (see later in this chapter).[25] But while the **Western Rebellion** arose, as most such events do, from a variety of causes, the sudden shifts in religion constituted the primary motivation: people took up arms "to keep the old and ancient religion as their forefathers before them had done and as King Henry the eight by his last will and testament had taken order that no alteration of religion should be made until king Edward his son were come to his full age."[26]

If the government's imposition of radical religious change largely motivated the **Western Rebellion**, economic issues, mainly the enclosure movement, caused the massive uprising in Norfolk (the eastern part of England) known as **Kett's Rebellion** in July 1549.

It was **Somerset's** bad fortune to make himself Lord Protector at a time when England faced major economic turmoil. The population's continuing rise contributed to unemployment because there were insufficient jobs to absorb the new members of the workforce. Landowners exacerbated unemployment by continuing the more profitable practice of enclosure (shifting arable land from crops or cattle to raising sheep for wool). **Henry VIII's** massive debt and policy of debasing the currency, continued by **Somerset**, contributed to sharply rising inflation, as did a series of bad harvests. Eight years of wars with Scotland and France, as William Paget told Somerset in August 1549, also contributed to England's woe: while the French king is powerful, Paget warns the Lord Protector and the council, "how we are exhausted and worn to the bones with these eight years wars both of men and money all other things for the wars your grace and my lords know better than I."[27] In short, England was in deep economic trouble, and **Somerset**, who sympathized with the poor to an astonishing degree, tried to legislate England back to economic health by attacking enclosures and aristocratic greed.

On June 1, 1548, **Somerset** announced in a royal proclamation the formation of commission to investigate infractions of the various statutes against enclosures; the language is extraordinarily hostile toward landowners, and the proclamation contrasts an idealized past, in which farming produced a cornucopia of food and supported a community, with a monoculture that serves only a tiny minority:

> All that land which heretofore was tilled and occupied with so many men, and did bring forth not only divers families in work and labor, but also capons, hens, chickens, pigs, and other such furniture of the markets, is now gotten, by insatiable greediness of mind, into one or two men's hands and scarcely dwelled upon with one poor shepherd, so that the realm thereby is brought to a marvelous desolation, houses decayed, parishes diminished, the force of the realm weakened, and Christian people, by the greedy covetousness of some men, eaten up and devoured of brute beasts and driven from their houses by sheep and bullocks.[28]

The committee reported that "all this groweth through the great dropsy and the insatiable desire of riches of some men, that be so much given to their private profit that they pass nothing on to the commonwealth."[29] Parliament thus passed a tax on sheep and cloth in order to discourage enclosures and encourage labor-intensive farming. Next, **Somerset** created two commissions to travel the country and examine the problems caused by enclosures. **Sir John Hales** (1516–72), a member of the enclosure commissions, condemned the rich in no uncertain terms. In a paper on the causes of dearth, he blamed hoarding, "when the most part of victuals be gathered into a few men's hands who may defer to sell but when they see their most profit."[30] In a letter to **Somerset** defending himself, **Hales** vociferously denounced the rich as responsible for England's decline. His accusers, the landowners, "will have no alterations, and they themselves make great innovations. They destroy towns, they pull down houses, they enclose poor men's commons and take away all their livings ...."[31] As one might expect, landowners did not rush to amend their ways, and on April 11, 1549, Somerset issued another proclamation, announcing that "it is come to his majesty's and his said councilor's knowledge that through the greediness of some persons, blind and ignorant in brotherly love and charity, that ought to be between Christian man and Christian man, and the natural love and amity of one Englishman to another ... the said laws and statutes ... have not been observed ..."[32]

Somerset's views on enclosure may have made him very popular among the poor, but they alienated the aristocracy, especially since the poor reacted to **Somerset's** policies by rioting and armed uprisings. In fact, while the participants of the **Western Rebellion** thought of themselves as opposing the government, the participants in the somewhat misnamed **Kett's Rebellion** and the surrounding lesser uprisings did not at all see themselves as rebelling against their king. While the demands of the Western rebels' all begin "We will have ...," Kett and his followers used a very different formulation: "We pray that ...." Far from taking arms against their government, they thought that **Somerset's** commissions gave them *permission* to act against enclosure and other economic ills. On May 8, 1549, for example, rioters in Frome (in Somerset) claimed that it "was meet and lawful" for them to tear down enclosure hedges.[33] Furthermore, while the bills of grievance from Robert Kett may be the only surviving document, the evidence shows that the government received a blizzard of such bills pouring into Westminster from the countryside, and the government responded in kind with multiple communications.[34] However, Kett and his followers were not trying to replace the government with one more to their liking, and the amount of paper flowing back and forth between the Lord Protector and the supposed rebels strongly suggests that Kett and his followers did not at all believe that **Somerset's** government had lost all legitimacy. Rather than a "rebellion," the uprising in Norfolk seems more an armed demand for good government.

Somerset's empathy for the anti-enclosure rioters – the Imperial ambassador reported that Somerset "had declared to the Council the peasants' demands were fair and just"[35] – and his repugnance at religious persecution (e.g., the repeal of the act allowing the burning of heretics) helps explain his extraordinarily patient response to the disorders. The usual Tudor way with rebels, exemplified by **Henry VIII's** response to the **Pilgrimage of Grace,** was to offer amnesty, disarm the mob, and then execute as many as possible. Somerset, however, approached the Western uprising with a confused mixture of carrots and sticks. On May 23, 1549, he issued a proclamation ordering the punishment of enclosure rioters, whom he called "seditious and lewd persons" who have "most arrogantly and disloyally" pulled down enclosures, "by the sword and with all force and extremity."[36] But at the proclamation's end, he says that if they have any complaints, then "his majesty will command such order to be given for redress thereof ...."[37] And three weeks later (June 14, 1549), he issued another proclamation "Pardoning Enclosure Rioters" while also "Ordering Martial Law against Future Rioters."[38] His letters exhibit the same inconsistencies. On one hand, he would condemn the rioters as "lewd, seditious and evil disposed persons" and "vile wretches,"[39] but then, in the same document, offer them pardons while admitting that their grievances were "for the most part founded upon great and just causes."[40] In a letter to Sir Thomas Hoby, ambassador to the Holy Roman Emperor, Somerset calls Kett an "archtraitor," but says that "the thing we most desire [is] to spare as much as may be the effusion of blood, and namely, that of our own nation."[41] These vacillations drove even **Somerset's** closest allies to distraction. In the same letter in which he reminded the Lord Protector of the promises made before "the breath was out of the body of the King that dead is," **William Paget** complained that **Somerset's** allegiance to the poor only made a bad situation worse: "What seeth your Grace over the King's subjects out of all discipline, out of obedience, caring neither for Protector nor King, and much less for any other mean officer. And what is the cause? Your own lenity, your softness, your opinion to be good to the poor."[42]

Somerset's "lenity" extended only so far, however, and eventually even his patience ran out. Despite his sympathy with their demands, he called the uprising's participants "lewd, seditious, and ill-disposed persons,"[43] and his descriptions of the uprising reveals only frustration and disgust at their confused demands and class warfare:

> The causes and pretences of their uproars and risings are divers and uncertain, and so full of variety almost in every camp, as they call them, that it is hard to write what it is, as ye know is like to be of people without head and rule, and would have that they wot [know] not what. Some cry, Pluck down enclosures and parks; some for their commons; others pretend religion; a number would rule and direct things, as gentleman have done, and indeed all have conceived a wonderful hate against gentlemen, and them all as their enemies.[44]

At the Lord Protector's behest (and nominally, also **King Edward's**), **John Dudley, Earl of Warwick,** later **Duke of Northumberland** (1504–53, the son of **Henry VII's** servant, **Edmund Dudley,** whom **Henry VIII** executed upon his accession), commanded the royal forces which crushed the Norfolk uprising while a second army took care of the Western rebels.[45] Calm once more reigned, but at a horrible cost: over 200,000 lives were lost over the course of the uprisings. Furthermore, **Somerset's** enemies on the council blamed him for the realm's descent into chaos. According to a document prepared by the Privy Council in

October 1549, the fundamental problem was that **Somerset** refused to listen to anybody other than himself:

> these and sundry other great disorders had proceeded of [from] the ill government of the Lord Protector, who being heretofore many times spoken unto both in open council and otherwise privately, hath not only refused to give ear to their advises [advice], but also minding to follow his own fantasies (wherefrom all the said disorders and mischiefs had before grown and arisen), did after persist in the same.[46]

In a more personal vein, **William Paget** begged **Somerset** to stop yelling "In great choleric fashion" at people who disagreed with him because "no man shall dare speak to you what he thinks, though it were never so necessary."[47] Paget reminded Somerset of "Poor Sir Richard Alte [who] this afternoon, after your Grace had very sore, and too much more than needed, rebuked him, came to my chamber weeping, and there complaining, as far as became him, of your handling of him, seemed almost out of his wits and out of heart."[48] Stubbornness and a refusal to consult with others, not greed, not lust for power, brought about the Lord Protector's downfall. In 1550, **John Dudley, Earl of Warwick** finally engineered **Somerset's** removal from office, but while **King Edward** elevated Dudley to **Duke of Northumberland**, he did not become the Lord Protector. As for **Somerset**, rather than accept his lesser position as another councilor or retire gracefully, he started plotting against his rival, and was duly executed in January, 1552.

By 1550, **Edward VI** was thirteen years old, and while he was not yet ready to rule by himself, he was more than capable of making his preferences known. The young king was a precocious intellectual, and he received the best humanist education possible at the hands of such tutors as **Sir John Cheke** (1514–57), who in 1544 was appointed to teach Edward "of tongues, of the scripture, of philosophy and all liberal sciences."[49] Cheke and Edward's other tutors, such as **Roger Ascham** (1514–68; Ascham also taught Princess Elizabeth and would write, among other works, a masterpiece of

Elizabethan pedagogy, *The Schoolmaster* [posthumously published in 1570]), were all committed to evangelical reform, and under their influence **Edward** leaned heavily toward reform. While **Northumberland** enlisted the religious conservatives as allies when he pushed out **Somerset**, he had to please **Edward** if he were to stay in power, and so **Northumberland** dropped his erstwhile allies and committed himself to religious reform with a vengeance. In 1552, he and **Archbishop Cranmer** issued a second **Book of Common Prayer** that was even more Protestant than the first (no more prayers for the dead; the bread and wine of the Eucharist were now purely symbolic), and Parliament passed a new **Act of Uniformity**, one that made failure to attend Sunday services a crime punishable by imprisonment (the third offense meant life imprisonment). **Northumberland** also issued his own formulary, the **Forty Two Articles** (1553), which reduced the sacraments to two (baptism and the Eucharist); embraced predestination as "the everlasting purpose of God"; affirmed that "Bishops, priests and deacons are not commanded to vow the state of single life without marriage, neither by God's law are they compelled to abstain from matrimony"; condemned purgatory and the worship of saints' relics as "a fond thing vainly feigned, and grounded upon no warrant of Scripture, but rather repugnant to the word of God"; declared that the king of England is "Supreme head in earth, next under Christ, of the Church of England and Ireland"; affirmed that "The Bishop of Rome hath no jurisdiction in this realm of England"; and finally, struck at the ideological center of the Norfolk uprising by affirming that "Christian men's goods are not common," meaning, the right to private property.[50]

By 1553, the illness that would eventually kill **Edward VI** had started to manifest itself, and **Northumberland**, both to preserve himself and the Protestant reformation, knew that he needed to direct the accession away from **Princess Mary**, who remained devoutly Roman Catholic. **Northumberland** understood that if Edward died and Mary became queen, he would shortly follow the late king. Consequently, he persuaded **Edward** to follow his father's example and will the kingdom to someone other than his closest blood relative, **Mary**. Northumberland's choice was **Lady Jane Grey** (1537–54), granddaughter of Henry VIII's sister, Mary, and therefore not an entirely implausible candidate. With the examples of Thomas More, Cardinal Wolsey, and Thomas Cromwell in mind (who were all servants of the crown who reached great heights and then ended either disgraced or on the block), **Northumberland** married **Lady Jane** to his son, Guilford, to ensure his future safety. The plan did not work.

The Reigns of Jane Grey and Mary Tudor

Edward VI died of tuberculosis on July 6, 1553, and **Lady Jane Grey** was immediately proclaimed queen. When she heard that the king's demise was imminent, **Mary Tudor** fled to Norfolk, home to the Catholic Howard family, and announced her claim to the throne on July 9. Two armies then marched toward each other, but Mary's forces reached London before Queen Jane's reached her enemy's. Once there, **Henry Fitzalan, the Earl of Arundel** (1511–80), the army's general, convinced the Privy Council to reverse itself. Arundel's success did not arise from his diplomatic skills, but from the massive upsurge of popular sentiment for Mary ("the only successful popular rising of the century," notes one historian[51]), due to her being Henry VIII's daughter combined with **Jane's** complete lack of support. On July 19, the Council proclaimed **Mary Tudor** queen. In one of the great reversals of history, the woman who had known little other than disgrace, imprisonment, rejection by her royal father and brother, and constant pressure to abandon her religion, now ruled England.

Jane's army deserted her, and despite an attempt by **Northumberland** to do the same, he, his son, and **Queen Jane** were all committed to the Tower and tried for treason. As everyone understood that **Jane** was a pawn, albeit a brilliant, highly educated one who corresponded with some of the leading continental reformers, such as Heinrich Bullinger in Zurich, **Mary** inclined toward sparing her life, "telling a disapproving imperial ambassador that her conscience would not allow her to have Jane put to death, although she promised to take every precaution before setting her free."[52] Unfortunately, events intervened.

Like her father, **Mary** realized that the success of her reign depended on producing a Catholic heir, and so the question became whom would she marry? On the advice of her longtime ally and confidante, the Holy Roman Emperor, **Charles V**, she decided to marry his son, **Philip II** (1527–98; King of Naples from 1554, king of Spain from 1556), an arrangement sure to cause alarm because the match would potentially subjugate England to the Holy Roman Empire; "This would be Habsburg conquest of England by marriage."[53] The thought of a foreign, papist king of England was immediately opposed by both her council and parliament, and her choice sparked an attempted coup in 1554 led by **Thomas Wyatt** (son of the famous poet). Jane's father, **Henry Grey, the Duke of Suffolk** (1517–54), participated, thus sealing both his fate and his daughter's. According to an eyewitness account, **Lady Jane Grey** was entirely composed at her execution. She asked the executioner to "dispatch me quickly"; after tying on a blindfold, "then feeling for the block, said 'What shall I do? Where is it?'"[54]

As for **Elizabeth**, Mary had her imprisoned first in the Tower, and then under house arrest at Woodstock, where, according to several reports, she inscribed this short poem "with her diamond in a glass window":

> Much suspected by me,
> Nothing proved can be
> *Quod* [said] Elizabeth the prisoner[55]

While Mary clearly did not trust her sister, neither could anyone demonstrate that Elizabeth behaved in anything other than an exemplary fashion. As the poem says, nothing could be "proved" against her. What she thought inwardly, however, remains anyone's guess. Even so, proof was not always necessary, and **Queen Jane's** judicial murder (she had no knowledge of or involvement in Wyatt's uprising) was an ominous sign of what was to come.

Mary's primary mission upon becoming queen was the restoration of Roman Catholicism. The Protestant Reformation, as we have seen, required acts of Parliament, and therefore its repeal required parliamentary co-operation as well. On the one hand, parliament obliged their new monarch by rolling back the Act of Uniformity, retracting the Book of Common Prayer, and re-instating the heresy laws (of which Mary would make ample use). But the return of monastic lands presented a major sticking point; changing the nature of the service, the official theology, and the details of the mass are one thing, giving up a major revenue source is quite another. These lands, sold and resold, were too valuable for their present owners to give them up, and the Pope conceded the point, thus allowing the reconciliation between England and Rome to proceed. The alteration in religion also meant a revolving door of clergy. Catholic bishops who were excluded by the previous regime, such as **Stephen Gardiner** (c. 1495–1555) and **Cuthbert Tunstall** (1474– 1579), returned.[56]

On the other hand, clergy who espoused Protestantism were ejected, and approximately 2000 priests found themselves out of a job for their beliefs or for marrying. Many opted for exile in the Protestant centers of Frankfurt and Geneva, including **John Foxe** (1516–87), whose massive work, the *Acts and Monuments* (first ed. 1563) would become, next to the Bible, the most widely read work in early modern England, and two prime architects of Protestant resistance theory, **Christopher Goodman** (c. 1521–1603) and **John Ponet** (c. 1514–56), who argued that it is one's religious duty to violently resist tyranny, and tyranny is synonymous with Catholicism.

In 1557, the enterprising publisher, **Richard Tottel** (c. 1528–93) brought out *Songs and Sonnets written by the Right Honorable Lord Henry Howard, Late Earl of Surrey, and Others*, usually referred to as *Tottel's Miscellany* and reprinted at least eight times before 1600. This book made available to the buying public Surrey's and Sir Thomas Wyatt's poems, which previously circulated only in manuscript.

However, many faced considerably worse fates than either imprisonment in the Tower or exile. **Queen Mary** and her religious adviser, **Cardinal Reginald Pole** (1500–58), the papal legate, did not share the Edwardian regime's distaste for religious persecution. While Pole initially assured Parliament that his aim was "not to pull down, but to build; to reconcile, not to censure; to invite, but without compulsion," that is not what happened.[57] John Rogers, a translator of the Bible, has the dubious honor of being the first to go to the stake, and shortly afterward, three of the most prominent Protestant voices were silenced. In 1555, **Hugh Latimer**, Bishop of Worcester and **Nicholas Ridley**, Bishop of London, went to the stake. According to Foxe, as the fires started, Latimer called out to his companion: "be of good comfort, Master Ridley, and play the man. We shall this day light such a candle, by God's grace, in England, as I trust shall never be put out."[58] (Latimer was right, but whether this happened because of God's grace or the extraordinary popularity of Foxe's *Acts and Monuments* remains an open question.) The next year, **Archbishop of Canterbury, Thomas Cranmer**, had his turn at the stake. All told, **Queen Mary** burned 237 men and 52 women as heretics.[59] Most, it is important to note, came from society's lower orders, and the hunt for heretics at times reeked of hypocrisy. When a linen draper from a small Essex town appeared before a Justice of the Peace to answer heresy charges, the judge demanded to know who taught him these Protestant ideas, and the man responded, "forsooth, even of you sir. You taught it to me, and none more than you. For in King Edward's days in open session you spoke against this religion now used; no preacher more."[60] Sickening as these numbers may be, the move toward killing heretics reflects a generalized raising of the stakes in this period. **Thomas Wyatt's** 1554 revolt attempted tyrannicide in the name of religion,[61] and the Protestant "monar-chomachs," such as **Goodman** and **Ponet**, gave religious cover to violent resistance. The numbers also pale before such later acts as the 1572 **St. Bartholomew's Day Massacre** in Paris in which Catholics murdered untold thousands of Protestants (nobody is quite sure of the number).

However, **Queen Mary's** attempt to restore the old religion could not succeed. While the physical accoutrements of Catholicism, the images, the crucifixes, the stained glass windows, could be restored along with the traditional forms of Catholic worship, the beliefs that underscored them had disappeared. Simple demographics tell the story: in 1553, approximately half the population was under twenty, and so had never known papal authority, received the Mass, or prayed for the dead in purgatory.[62] They knew no other religion than Edwardian Protestantism. They had not fallen away from Catholicism, because they never knew it. And yet, they could now be burnt alive for practicing the religion they were taught from birth.

Queen Mary's political and personal lives failed along with her religious program. By all accounts, Mary genuinely loved her husband, **Philip**, and she was overjoyed at her possible pregnancy. But **Mary** experienced a hysterical pregnancy, not a real one, and her husband regarded **Mary** as a diplomatic convenience, not a "help meet." Considerable friction developed between **Philip**, who spoke no English, and Mary's courtiers. He left England in 1555, and would not return until 1557, when events on the continent, not love, spurred his return. In 1555, Pope Julius III died, and the new Bishop of Rome, Paul IV, hated Spain. He started negotiating a peace treaty with France, and in response, **Philip** decided to try to seize the Papal States in present-day Italy. Philip came back to England to enlist **Mary** in his efforts, and so, despite England's fragile economy and inner turmoil, she declared war on France. The only result of this venture was the loss of the sole remaining English outpost in France: the port city of Calais, militarily insignificant, but psychologically, a devastating blow, sadly symbolic of Mary's failures. She seemed to have understood this: "when I am dead and opened," she reportedly said, "you will find Calais lying in my heart."[63] That, however, would not be long. In the summer of 1558, Mary thought she was pregnant again, but a tumor rather than a child grew inside her. To avoid the problems of 1553, the Privy Council finally persuaded Mary to recognize **Elizabeth** as her successor, and **Mary Tudor** died on November 17, 1558. The Elizabethan era was about to begin.

Notes

1 Quoted in Chris Skidmore, *Edward VI: The Lost King of England* (New York: St. Martin's Press, 2007), 45.

2 Sir William Paget to the Lord Protector, letter dated July 7, 1549, in John Strype, *Ecclesiastical Memorials relating chiefly to Religion* (Oxford: Clarendon Press, 1822), vol. 2, part 2, 429. See also Skidmore, *Edward VI*, 49.

3 Skidmore, *Edward VI*, 71.

4 Skidmore, *Edward VI*, 63.

5 *Hall's Chronicle*, 828.

6 Skidmore, *Edward VI*, 82.

7 François's early death in 1560 would lead to Mary's return to Scotland, her disastrous reign, and her flight to England, where she would eventually be executed for plotting against her cousin, Queen Elizabeth I.

8 See Chapter 3, p. 86.

9 Skidmore, *Edward VI*, 72.

10 Quoted in G. W. Bernard, "Seymour, Thomas, Baron Seymour of Sudeley (*b.* in or before 1509, *d.* 1549)," *The Oxford Dictionary of National Biography*, Oxford University Press, September 2004; online edn., January 2008. http://www.oxforddnb.com/view/article/25181, accessed December 28, 2009.

11 Skidmore, *Edward VI*, 76.

12 Quoted in Bernard, *Seymour*.

13 Quoted in Bernard, *Seymour*. See also Skidmore, *Edward VI*, 103–11.

14 Quoted in Skidmore, *Edward VI*, 107.

15 John N. King, *English Reformation Literature: The Tudor Origins of the Protestant Tradition* (Princeton: Princeton University Press, 1982).

16 *Injunctions given by the Most Excellent Prince, Edward the Sixte* (London, 1547). Sig. a4v.

17 *Injunctions*, sigs. Biv-r.

18 Quoted in Skidmore, *Edward VI*, 109.

19 Skidmore, *Edward VI*, 81.

20 Robert Bucholz and Newton Key, *Early Modern England 1485–1714: A Narrative History* (Oxford: Blackwell, 2004), 99.

21 Skidmore, *Edward VI*, 80.

22 Barrett L. Beer, *Rebellion and Riot: Popular Disorder in England during the Reign of Edward VI*, rev. ed. (Kent, OH: Kent State University Press, 2005), 66, 224n58.

23 "The Demands of the Western Rebels, 1549," in *Tudor Rebellions*, ed. Anthony Fletcher and Diarmaid MacCulloch, 5th ed. (Harlow: Pearson, 2008), 151–2. The list of demands is also reprinted in Beer, *Rebellion and Riot*, 64–5.

24 "The Demands of the Western Rebels," in *Tudor Rebellions*, 151.

25 Beer, *Rebellion and Riot*, 54.

26 Quoted in Skidmore, *Edward VI*, 114.

27 *The Letters of William, Lord Paget of Beaudesert, 1547–63*, ed. Barrett L. Beer and Sybil M. Jack, *Camden Miscellany* 4th ser., vol. 13 (1977), 77.

28 *Tudor Royal Proclamations*, ed. Paul L. Hughes and James L. Larkin (New Haven: Yale University Press, 1964), vol. 1, 428.

29 Quoted in Bucholz and Key, *Early Modern England*, 100.

30 Sir John Hales, "Causes of Dearth," in *A Discourse of the Common Weal of this Realm of England*, ed. Elizabeth Lamond (Cambridge: Cambridge University Press, 1893; rpt. New York: Lenox Hill, 1971), xlii.

31 "The Defence of John Hales," in *A Discourse*, liii.

32 *Tudor Royal Proclamations*, 451–2.

33 Quoted in Skidmore, *Edward VI*, 113.

34 Ethan H. Shagan, "Protector Somerset and the 1549 Rebellions: New Sources and New Perspectives," *English Historical Review* 114, n. 455 (1999), 39–40.

35 Skidmore, *Edward VI*, 113–14; Shagan, "Protector Somerset," 35.

36 *Tudor Royal Proclamations*, 461, 462.

37 *Tudor Royal Proclamations*, 462.

38 *Tudor Royal Proclamations*, 462.

39 Quoted in Shagan, "Protector Somerset," 35.

40 Skidmore, *Edward VI*, 117.

41 Strype, *Ecclesiastical Memorials*, vol. 2, part 2, 424.

42 Skidmore, *Edward VI*, 118. In a letter to Somerset dated July 7, 1549, Paget repeated this charge: his eagerness to appease had "give evil men a boldness to enterprise as they do and cause them to think you dare not meddle with them but are glad to please them" (Quoted in Shagan, "Protector Somerset," 34).

43 Strype, *Eccelsiastical Memorials*, vol. 2, part 2, 426.

44 Strype, *Eccelsiastical Memorials*, vol. 2, part 2, 425.

45 After the royal army ousted Kett's forces from the city of Norwich, they retreated to Mousehold Heath, where the woods offered them protection. According to *Holinshed's Chronicles*, one of the "wizards" came up with this prophecy:

The country gnoffs [a low-class person, a lout], Hob, Dick
and Hick
With clubs and clouted shoon [shoes],
Shall fill up Dussindale [with blood
Of slaughtered bodies soone.

"Dussindale" was the name of a nearby, open field, and on the basis of this prophecy, Kett moved his forces to this much more exposed area. Warwick took advantage of their vulnerability, and a massacre ensued. Warwick's forces captured Robert Kett the day after the battle. He and his brother were tried for treason in London, but to discourage others, they were returned to Norwich for execution. On 7 December, 1549, Robert Kett was hung in chains from the castle wall, and his body was left to rot (*Holinshed's Chronicles*, 981–4; Skidmore, *Edward VI*, 129–30. See also John Walter, "Kett, Robert (*c.* 1492–1549)," *Oxford Dictionary of National Biography*, Oxford University Press, 2004. http://www. oxforddnb.com/view/article/15485, accessed December 27, 2009.

46 *Acts of the Privy Council of England: 1547–1550*, ed. John R. Dasent (London: HMSO, 1890), new series, vol. 2, 330.

47 Strype, *Ecclesiastical Memorials*, vol. 2, part 2, 429, 428.

48 Strype, *Ecclesiastical Memorials*, vol. 2, part 2, 428.

49 Quoted in Alan Bryson, "Cheke, Sir John (1514–1557)," *Oxford Dictionary of National Biography*, Oxford University Press, Sept 2004; online ed., October 2008 [http://www.oxforddnb.com/view/article/5211, accessed December 27, 2009].

50 *Articles Agreed on by the Bishops and Other Learned Men in the Synod at London in the Year of Our Lord, 1552* (London, 1553), sigs. B2v, C2r, B4v, C3r, and C4r.

51 Susan Brigden, *New Worlds, Lost Worlds: The Rule of the Tudors 1485–1603* (New York: Viking, 2000), 198.

52 Alison Plowden, "Grey, Lady Jane (1537–1554)," *Oxford Dictionary of National Biography*, Oxford University Press, September 2004; online ed., October 2008. http://www.oxforddnb.com/view/article/8154, accessed 27 December 2009.

53 Brigden, *New Worlds, Lost Worlds*, 201.

54 *The chronicle of Queen Jane, and of two years of Queen Mary, and especially of the rebellion of Sir Thomas Wyat : written by a Resident in the Tower of London*, ed. John Gough (Camden Society, old series, 48 [1850]; rpt. New York: AMS, 1968), 59.

55 *Elizabeth I: Collected Works*, eds. Leah S. Marcus, Janel Mueller, and Mary Beth Rose (Chicago: University of Chicago Press, 2000), 46. Leah Marcus perfectly captures this couplet's ambivalence: "This deceptively simple poem can be taken in at least two senses: much was suspected *of* Elizabeth by Mary Tudor's ministers as they interrogated her in hopes of linking her to one or another plot against Mary's crown; much was suspected *by* Elizabeth herself of others' nefarious plans for her destruction" ("Elizabeth I as Public and Private Poet: Notes toward a New Edition," *Reading Monarchs Writing: The Poetry of Henry VIII, Mary Stuart, Elizabeth I, and James VI/I*, ed. Peter C. Herman [Tempe, AZ: MRTS, 2002], 139). On Elizabeth's poetry generally, see Peter C. Herman, *Royal Poetrie: Monarchic Verse and the Political Imaginary of Early Modern England* (Ithaca: Cornell University Press, 2010), 99–156.

56 While Stephen Gardiner, Bishop of Westminster, served Henry VIII as a diplomat and theological adviser, he opposed Somerset's and Cranmer's religious innovations (as he saw them). After a sermon in which he upheld clerical celibacy, he was imprisoned in the Tower, where he continued to write religious polemics. Cuthbert Tunstall, bishop of London, also served as a diplomat for Henry VIII, and he maintained his position until Somerset's fall, when Northumberland committed him to the Tower, where, like Gardiner, he remained, writing religious polemics, until Mary's accession.

57 Quoted in Jeremy Collier, *An Ecclesiastical History of Great Britain* (London: William Straker, 1852), vol. 6, 90.

58 Quoted in Bucholz and Key, *Early Modern England*, 107.

59 Bucholz and Key, *Early Modern England*, 107.

60 Quoted in Roger Lockyer, *Tudor and Stuart Britain: 1471–1714* (Harlow, Essex: Longman, 1985), 103.

61 Brigden, *New Worlds, Lost Worlds*, 202.

62 Brigden, *New Worlds, Lost Worlds*, 207.

63 Quoted in Bucholz and Key, *Early Modern England*, 110.

5

The Elizabethan Era (1558–1603)

I. 1558–88

When **Elizabeth Tudor** became queen of England in 1558, she inherited a depressed, dispirited nation. In a document entitled "The Distresses of the Commonwealth," the clerk to the Privy Council, Armigail Waad, despaired at sufficiently describing England's troubles "as they are so infinite there is such a throne of them, as no one man is able to rehearse or comprehend them."[1] Even so, one must try, and the clerk gave this summary of England's state in 1558:

> The Queen poor. The realm exhausted. The nobility poor and decayed. Want of good captains and soldiers. The people out of order. Justice not executed. All things dear. Excess in meat, drink, and apparel. Division among ourselves. Wars with France and Scotland. The French King bestriding the realm., having one foot in Calais and the other in Scotland. Steadfast enmity but no steadfast friendship abroad.[2]

A Short History of Early Modern England: British Literature in Context, First Edition.
Peter C. Herman.
© 2011 Peter C. Herman. Published 2011 by Blackwell Publishing Ltd.

Figure 5.1 Queen Elizabeth I ('The Ditchley portrait') by Marcus Gheeraerts the Younger, c. 1592. © National Portrait Gallery, London.

While Waad clearly likes engaging in the early modern penchant for exaggeration (after beginning to enumerate the "many and most grievous diseases" of the commonweal, he laments the term's inappropriateness: "alas! What say I 'weal,' when in manner we have none at all"[3]), his assessment accurately describes England's condition in 1558. England remained embroiled in a disastrous war with France – the late Queen Mary had lost England's remaining outpost, Calais, and the heir to the French throne, the *dauphin* François, married Mary Stuart, creating the possibility of a French invasion from England's northern border. The economy lay in ruins thanks to war coupled with the dilution of the currency, the crown was deeply in debt, and the populace both exhausted and traumatized by the violent gyrations over religion since Henry VIII separated from Rome.

Certainly, the new queen had her virtues. She was young (25 years old), very attractive (no small advantage on the marriage market), exceedingly smart, and exceedingly well educated. Fluent in Latin, French, Italian, and Spanish, **Elizabeth Tudor** (like her father) played the virginal (an early keyboard instrument) and composed verse. She also wrote prayers in a variety of languages, and translated Boethius. Most importantly, however, Elizabeth possessed extremely good political skills. She knew whom to trust, and she brought into her council such eminently capable men as **William Cecil**, later **Baron Burghley** (1520–98) and **Sir Francis Walsingham** (c. 1532–1590), who would serve her well. Elizabeth also possessed two other qualities, seemingly opposed, that would prove essential to her success. First, she had, as Shakespeare's Kent says of King Lear, *authority*, something the Spanish ambassador noted two weeks after her accession: "she seems to me incomparably more feared than her sister was, and she gives her order and has her way as absolutely as her father did."[4] Second, Elizabeth knew how to make people love her. But nobody knew at the time how this untested queen would work out, and the recent past did not give much cause for optimism.

However, it is important to note at the outset that Elizabeth's gender did not pose as great an obstacle as one might imagine. True, a prejudice against women rulers certainly existed, as demonstrated by John Knox's attack on female rule, *The First Trumpet Blast against the Monstrous Regiment of Women*, which begins by declaring how female rule is fundamentally blasphemous:

> To promote a woman to bear rule, superiority, dominion or empire above any realm, nation or city is repugnant to nature, contumely to God, a thing most contrarious to his received will and approved ordinance, and finally, it is the subversion of good order, of all equity and justice.[5]

While Knox's primary targets were the Catholic queens, **Mary Tudor** and **Mary of Guise**, Elizabeth took Knox's book very personally, and she did not have to commission a rebuttal. John Aylmer, Bishop of London, took it upon himself to publish *An Harbor for Faithful Subjects*, which rejected Knox's argument in no uncertain terms. He intends, Aylmer writes, to "lay before men's eyes the untruth of the argument, the weakness of the proofs, and the absurdity of the whole."[6] Elizabeth never forgave Knox for writing *The First Trumpet Blast*. While the fiery preacher wrote several letters to the queen and to **Cecil** trying to explain himself, neither responded. Instead, Knox was repeatedly denied permission to enter England.[7] Elizabeth's gender clearly shaped how she ruled, but Elizabeth knew how to turn a possible debility into an advantage. From the start of her reign, for example, Elizabeth associated herself with the prophetess, Deborah, also the fourth judge of Israel (Judges 4:4–5:31), which simultaneously promoted Elizabeth as divinely elected while deferring to the ultimate male authority figure, God.[8]

Elizabeth and her government had enough problems to make their lives difficult, and they faced two major challenges at the outset of her reign: religion and marriage, and for both, as we will see, domestic concerns and foreign policy overlapped to the point where they are nearly indistinguishable.

To review, from **Henry VIII's** split from Rome in 1533 (the **Act in Restraint of Appeals**) onward, England's population endured a constant stream of shifting pronouncements as to what constituted the true religion. Starting with the document issued in 1536, there were at least five different sets of injunctions, including acts of parliament, attempting to fix the content of English Protestantism and to stop the arguments about religion. Then in 1553, with the accession of **Mary Tudor**, the Protestant tide reversed and England officially reverted to Catholicism; making things worse, Mary also reverted to burning "heretics" (meaning, Protestants) alive, which may have given **John Foxe** material for *The Book of Martyrs*, but did nothing to ease the trauma of radical shifts in officially sanctioned beliefs. The question on people's minds as **Elizabeth** became queen was what she would do with religion? Would she embrace Protestantism, and if so, which brand of Protestantism? The issue had foreign policy implications, as her treatment of Catholics might antagonize Spain and France, which also had an alliance with Scotland. Ireland, primarily Catholic and deeply resentful of attempts to impose Protestantism, also represented a possible invasion route for Catholic powers. The great fear in 1558 and beyond was that a Catholic league would invade a militarily weak, economically crippled England. Whatever moves Elizabeth would make in settling the question of religion had to take this threat into consideration.

Therefore, Elizabeth came up with a compromise that her government hoped would thread the needle between placating the more radical Protestants, including those returning from the Marian exile, and not antagonizing the remaining Catholics to the point that their foreign allies would take up arms on their behalf. Essentially, Elizabeth and her councilors devised a Church that "thinks Protestant, but looks Catholic."[9] In the spring of 1559, parliament passed a new **Act of Supremacy** (although to do so, the Catholic bishops in the House of Lords had to be locked up in the Tower), which undid Mary's restoration of papal jurisdiction over England and confirmed Elizabeth's position as "Supreme Governor" of the Church (not, in deference to her gender, "Supreme Head," the title Henry VIII claimed). That same year, parliament also passed another **Act of Uniformity**, mandating that everyone attend church on Sundays, and that services would follow the second **Book of Common Prayer**, the more radically Protestant prayer book introduced by **John Dudley, Duke of Northumberland** in 1552. In 1563, parliament passed a new **Treason Act**, which made it a capital crime to support papal jurisdiction and to refuse twice to take the Oath of Allegiance. Also in 1563, Elizabeth's government issued the **Thirty-Nine Articles of Faith**, which in their rejection of purgatory and embrace of predestination and justification by faith were strongly Protestant, even Calvinist. But Elizabeth also allowed the wearing of colorful vestments by the clergy, a move that might seem indifferent today but sparked a huge controversy at the time because allowing the use of elaborate vestments blurred the distinction between the rival versions of Christianity. Most significantly, Elizabeth retained the hierarchical, or **episcopal**, structure of the old religion (see Table 5.1).

Table 5.1 Varieties of Early Modern Christianity

Catholicism	Elizabethan Settlement	"Godly" or Radical Protestant
Pope	Monarch as Governor or Head of Anglican Church	No Pope, Governor, or Head
Bishops	Bishops (**Episcopacy**)	No Bishops (**Presbyterian**)
Colorful vestments	Colorful vestments	Plain vestments
Purgatory	No purgatory	No purgatory
Tradition as authoritative as Bible	Bible alone	Bible alone
No predestination	Predestination	Predestination
Eucharist/Holy Supper: Belief in transubstantiation (actual substance of bread and wine mystically transformed to body and blood of Christ)	Eucharist/Holy Supper: no transubstantiation, but spiritual consumption of body and blood of Christ	Eucharist/Holy Supper: strictly in memory of Last Supper
Latin service	English	English

At the same time that Elizabeth had to take conservative opinion into account, she also needed to accommodate the more uncompromising Protestants, insultingly referred to at the time as **puritans**, many of who suffered for their faith or went into exile under Mary, and who resisted any compromises with Catholicism.

In its original usage and throughout the early modern period, "puritan" was a term of abuse lobbed against those who "think themselves to be ... more pure than others ... and separate themselves from all other Churches and congregations as spotted and defiled."[10] A participant in King James's 1603 Hampton Court conference offered this definition: "a Puritan is a Protestant strayed out of his wits."[11] Since then, "puritan" has attracted other connotations (primarily anti-sex and anti-joy) that do not fit with sixteenth and seventeenth-century usage. Consequently, referring to early modern Protestants who sought further reform to the English Church as "puritans" – as many contemporary literary critics and historians do – is both anachronistic and misleading. Christopher Hill once called the term "an admirable refuge from clarity of thought."[12] I agree, and therefore, in this chapter and others, I do not use this term.

They demanded that the hierarchical structure exemplified by bishops (**episcopacy**) be replaced by a "flat" structure (**Presbyterian**) in which a "presbyter" leads the congregation. According to the early English Protestant, **William Tyndale**, a "presbyter" is "an elder and is nothing but an officer to teach and not to be a mediator between God and us."[13] The threatening implications for secular authority and the monarch's authority over church affairs should be evident. If each congregation could make up its mind about religion, then why should they not decide on their own which secular laws to follow? If one does not need a bishop, why do we need a monarch? These questions would shape English politics through the Restoration and beyond.

In terms of church doctrine and government, **Elizabeth** and her government situated themselves squarely in the middle, embracing neither the "hot" reformers nor Catholicism. Indeed, if anything, Elizabeth detested radical Protestants even more than Catholics, asserting that they are "greater enemies to her than the papists."[14] Which is not to say that Elizabeth's council was entirely united in its approach to religion. To simplify, on one side, **William Cecil, Lord Burghley** represented moderation and caution, both at home and abroad, although he could be entirely fierce when he believed Elizabeth's interests were threatened, as in the case of Mary, Queen of Scots. On the other side, **Robert Dudley**, made **Earl of Leicester** in 1563 (1532–88), sympathized more with the "hot" Protestants and advocated aggressively intervening abroad against Catholic powers. Elizabeth, who generally preferred to delay tough decisions (much to the impatience of her courtiers), would tilt one way, then another, over the course of her reign.

Yet moderation makes one vulnerable to attacks by the extremes, which is exactly what happened. Throughout her reign, **Elizabeth** endured the destabilizing efforts by both Catholics and radical Protestants, and they endured her government's persecution. For example, in 1576, Elizabeth ordered **Edmund Grindal** (1519?–1583), Archbishop of Canterbury, to suppress "prophesyings," or unofficial group discussions on religious matters. Grindal, who went into exile during Queen Mary's reign, not only refused, but in a letter to the Queen defending the "prophesyings," asserted that her authority in religious matters was limited, that she could not "pronounce so resolutely and peremptorily" as she could on secular matters, and concluded, "Remember, Madam, that you are a mortal creature."[15] Elizabeth did not take kindly to this attack on her authority, and she suspended him from performing his office. When Grindal died in 1583, Elizabeth replaced him with her ally, **John Whitgift** (1531?–1604), once the Bishop of Worcester, who used his new position as Archbishop of Canterbury to eject radical Protestant clerics from their posts.

The second major problem that **Elizabeth** and her government had to confront, and like religion, this would shape Elizabethan politics, both domestic and foreign, for her entire reign, was the issue of the Queen's marriage and the related issue of the succession. I will deal with this topic in more detail later in the chapter, but for the moment, it is important to know that while Elizabeth would never marry, that does not mean that she never intended to marry. As we will see, **Elizabeth** seriously explored this option twice, first at the start of her reign, and second, in late 1570s, with a foreign, Catholic prince.

The question of marriage was inseparable from foreign policy concerns, and those concerns in turn overlapped with the war between Catholicism and Protestantism. There are five moving parts, as it were, to this situation: France, Scotland, Spain, the

Netherlands, and Ireland. Further complicating matters, France and Scotland were at war among themselves over religion, and the Netherlands was in open revolt against a monarchy, albeit a Catholic one. Before moving further, I will review each in turn.

France and Scotland (including Mary, Queen of Scots)

When Elizabeth came to the throne in 1558, she had to deal with the aftermath of England's humiliating loss of its last outpost on French soil, the port city of Calais. (The late **Queen Mary** had declared war on France at the behest of her husband, **Philip II of Spain**.) None of the warring parties could afford to continue hostilities; France and Spain were bankrupt, England nearly so. But everyone needed to salvage something from this humiliating wreckage, and for **Elizabeth**, the face-saving concession was that France would after eight years return Calais to England or pay a substantial amount of money. The **Treaty of Câteau-Cambrésis**, signed in April 1559, may have brought Mary and Philip's French adventure to its ignominious end, but it also opened the door to further troubles, as the Catholic powers, France and Spain, could now train their sights on Protestant England. In particular, the French monarchy could now focus on intervening more forcefully in Scotland,[16] and in an ominous sign, **Pope Paul IV** refused to endorse the treaty, as that would mean recognizing **Elizabeth's** legitimacy as queen.

To understand why the French would be interested in Scotland in the first place, and why Elizabeth and her government would be so concerned, we need to understand something of their collective history. Two facts are of prime importance. First, when the king of Scotland at the turn of the sixteenth century, **James IV** (1473–1513) married in 1503 **Henry VII's** daughter, **Margaret Tudor** (1489–1541), their children joined the line of succession to the English throne, being the descendants of a blood relative to an English monarch. Next, James IV and Margaret Tudor's son, **King James V** (1512–42) tied together French and Scottish interests when he married **Mary of Guise** (1515–60), a scion of the very powerful and virulently Catholic **house of Guise**. Their daughter, **Mary Stuart** ("Stuart" is the last name of the Scots kings), eventually known as **Mary, Queen of Scots** (1542–87; much more on her below), was sent to France after Henry VIII invaded Scotland in the hopes of forcing a marriage between Mary and his son, Edward ("the Rough Wooing"). In France, the young Mary was raised to consider herself as the future queen of France.[17] When James V died in 1542, he left an increasingly Protestant Scotland in the hands of a determinedly Catholic, French regent, **Mary of Guise**.

Protestantism was very much ascendant in Scotland; the regent, **Mary of Guise**, responded with persecution, which in turn led to a rebellion in 1557 by a group known as the **Lords of the Congregation** (led by the truculent **John Knox**). Then, in 1559, **Henri II** of France died, leaving the throne to the young **François II**, who that year married **Mary Stuart**. This meant that France could press its dominance in Scotland as well as **Mary Stuart's** claims to the English throne (Elizabeth's Protestantism made her an illegitimate monarch in Catholic eyes). By the end of 1559, French troops had landed in Scotland, raising the very real possibility of a Scots–French (read "Catholic") invasion from England's north. To counter this danger, Elizabeth ultimately decided to align her government with the Protestant **Lords of the Congregation** (although it took Cecil's threatened resignation to convince Elizabeth to go along), sending them both money and military support. While the land battles ended badly for the English, the appearance of a fleet, which blocked the French supply lines, combined with the death of **Mary of Guise**, ended hostilities, resulting in the **Treaty of Edinburgh**, signed on July 6, 1560, which enshrined Protestantism and formally abandoned Mary Stuart's claim to the English throne. But then, mortality intervened once again to completely change the situation: the young and sickly **François II** died,[18] and **Mary Stuart** was sent back to Scotland, becoming **Mary, Queen of Scots**. Significantly for the future, **Mary** did not ratify the treaty.

Given her sex and her devout Catholicism, the odds were clearly stacked against **Mary** when she returned to Scotland in 1562 as that country's ruler. Yet **Mary** successfully negotiated these difficulties in the first years of her reign. While she continued to worship as a

Catholic, she did not insist that anyone else follow suit, and while she maintained her independence, refusing to sign the Treaty of Edinburgh and insisting on her right to choose her husband, she understood just how far she could push fundamental beliefs without reaching the breaking point. **Mary** in fact established a reputation for being "modest, intelligent and anxious to do her best as a rule by taking wise advice."[19] She also tried to establish her own relations with Elizabeth, based on their family connections, but also on their common gender. In 1562, for example, **Mary** sent **Elizabeth** a diamond accompanied by a poem in which the jewel hopes that it will "bind the hearts of these [queens] / with adamantine bonds."[20]

What eventually happened to Mary resulted from a politically fatal combination of bad luck and even worse judgment. The unraveling of Mary's reign began with her marriage to **Henry Stewart, Lord Darnley** (1545–67) in July 1565. Despite Mary's infatuation with Darnley before their marriage, it became evident very quickly that she had made a serious mistake. **Darnley** was "was arrogant, vain, and unreliable, preferring pleasure to the affairs of state,"[21] and the royal couple argued bitterly over Mary's refusal to grant him the "crown matrimonial" (meaning, the spouse's right to co-rule with equal power and authority as the original monarch). **Thomas Randolph** (1525–90), the English ambassador to the Scots court, reported: "'He claims the crown matrimonial, and will have it immediately. The Queen tells him that that must be delayed till he be of age, and done by consent of Parliament, which does not satisfy him."[22] Despite the birth of the future **James VI** (eventually **James I** of England) in 1566, **Darnley's** behavior deteriorated to the point where everybody knew that something had to be done. That "something" was Darnley's murder, but what exactly happened on the night of February 9, 1567 remains unclear: the house Darnley was staying at in Kirk o'Field blew up, but Darnley and a servant were found dead underneath a tree, probably having been strangled. **Darnley's** violent end came as a relief to everybody, and **Mary's** rule could have survived even this crisis, had she at least pretended to find and prosecute those responsible. Instead, Mary made the inexplicable, politically disastrous decision to marry **James Hepburn,**

Lord Bothwell (1534–78). Bothwell's sudden elevation upset Scotland's delicate political balance, and consequently, Mary was deposed (actually, she was told to either sign her deposition papers or be killed). Rather than returning to France, **Mary, Queen of Scots** fled to England, arriving, unexpected and uninvited, on May 16, 1568, where she would remain, despite increasingly restrictive captivity, as a magnet for Catholic plots against Queen Elizabeth until her execution on February 8, 1587.

In 1586, Mary's former servant, **Thomas Babington**, organized a plot to invite a Spanish invasion of England that would place Mary on the throne. What made this conspiracy different is that Babington planned to assassinate Elizabeth, and Mary approved in writing. With that evidence, Walsingham quickly had Mary arrested, tried, and condemned. But then, Elizabeth hesitated, signing the death warrant but not giving permission for its use. The Secretary of State, **William Davison** (c. 1542–1608), with the Privy Council's permission, took matters into his own hands and had Mary beheaded. **Elizabeth** was furious, gave Mary a state funeral, sacked Davison, imposed a huge fine, and sent him to the Tower. But within a short time, Davison was released, the fine remitted, and his salary restored. To this day, it is not clear if Elizabeth's contradictory behavior demonstrated Machiavellian statecraft, tortured indecision, or some combination of the two.

Mary's deposition and arrival in England meant that by 1568, Scotland no longer loomed as the gateway for a foreign invasion of England, and the French threat was more or less neutralized by a series of weak, boy-kings controlled by their mother, **Catherine de Medici** (1519–89). Furthermore, the country was increasingly embroiled in religious tensions between Catholics and the Calvinist–Protestant minority known as the **Huguenots. Elizabeth** was convinced by **Dudley** to intervene militarily on the Huguenot side in 1563, but unlike the aid she sent to Scotland to help the Lords of the Congregation, this venture ended in disaster. Not only were her troops decimated by the plague, but when the regent, **Catherine de Medici**, and the Huguenots agreed to a truce, they turned on Elizabeth, thus confirming for the rest of her reign Elizabeth's distrust of foreign ventures.[23]

The marriage of Catherine's daughter, Margaret, to **Henri of Navarre** (later **Henri IV of France**) in August 1572, would lead to the **St. Bartholomew's Day Massacre**. Catherine, worried that her future son-in-law was far too much under the influence of the Huguenot leader, **Admiral Gaspard de Coligny**, tried to have him assassinated. The attempt failed, but Catherine then ordered the massacre of thousands of Protestants gathered in Paris for the wedding. The title of the French lawyer, humanist, and "monarchomach" (opponent of absolutism and proponent of "resistance theory") François Hotman's report of the massacre (which he wrote to counter Catherine de Medici's own propagandists, who had "shamefully set forth things feigned or falsely imagined"[sig. A3r]), gives a sense of the horror this event inspired among Protestants: *A True and Plain Report of the Furious Outrages in France and the Horrible and Shameful Slaughter of Chastillon … And of the Wicked and Strange Murder of Godly Persons Committed in Many Cities of France without any Respect of Sort, Kind Age or Degree* (London, 1573; also published in Latin and French). This atrocity may have had the salutary effect of eliminating the French threat to England for over a generation, but it intensified the French **Wars of Religion** and only confirmed English Protestant suspicions of Catholic perfidy. But as the decade progressed, relations between England and France would warm, as Elizabeth needed an ally to balance Spain's increasingly hostility.

Spain and the Netherlands

In 1558, England and Spain were allies, not enemies, but as the decades progressed, that relationship would deteriorate to the point where Spain would attempt to invade England in 1588 (the infamous

Spanish Armada). In one sense, it was very much in England's interest to keep Spain as an ally: not only would maintaining a friendship balance France's power and possibly disrupt an alliance between the two Catholic powers, but also Spain's empire was immensely vast, stretching into southern Italy and including the Netherlands as well as all of South and Central America, and immensely wealthy, thanks in good part to the silver (mined by slaves) imported from the New World.

Spain, in short, was much more powerful than England, and so it would make strategic sense to keep on its good side. But that was not what happened, at least partly because of the entirely reasonable fear that **Philip II of Spain** would leverage his vast wealth into supporting a Catholic rebellion in England that would replace Elizabeth with a monarch (such as **Mary, Queen of Scots**) more to his religious liking. **Elizabeth** therefore moved on two fronts. First, she secretly supported piracy against Spanish shipping and raids on the treasure fleets that left South America twice a year.

Some of the most storied names in English navigation and exploration, such as **Sir Francis Drake** (1540–96; the first Englishman to circumnavigate the globe) and **Sir Martin Frobisher** (1535?–1594; who explored Canada's north in his search for the fabled Northwest Passage) were also pirates allowed to conduct their own private war against Spain. **Sir John Hawkins** (1532–95), who played a key role in designing the ships that would defeat the Spanish Armada, also has the dubious honor of being among the first Englishmen to participate in the slave trade. **Queen Elizabeth** participated in the syndicate bankrolling these ventures (as well as the pirating voyages by Drake and Frobisher), and neither she nor anyone "expressed reservations then or later about involving themselves in such a loathsome business."[24] Indeed, Hawkins included a bound slave in his coat of arms.

While these attacks cost Spain a good deal of money, **Philip II** decided that the losses could be absorbed. The problems in the **Netherlands**, however, posed a threat that could not be ignored. Once more, we need to go back in time a bit to understand the issues faced by Elizabeth and her government. In 1554, the Holy Roman Emperor, **Charles V**, gave the Netherlands to his son, **Philip**, and in 1566, the Dutch, Calvinist leader, **William of Orange** (1533–84), started a rebellion against Spanish rule spurred as much by antipathy toward Catholicism as by nationalism. **Philip** responded by importing the **Inquisition** and 20,000 troops, led by the vicious Fernando Alvarez de Toledo, Duke of Alva (1508–83), described by a contemporary as a malign, unstoppable force: nothing "could pluck him from his purpose .... And going on a determined course (neither revocable nor to be controlled) ... used his force and extremities to subdue by violence that which some governors by sweet persuasions would have performed."[25] Despite Alva's ferocity, the revolt lasted for decades. The question Elizabeth faced was how much should she support the rebels? On the one hand, Elizabeth looked at any insurgency against a royal power, regardless of religion, with the greatest suspicion. On the other hand, many in her government believed that they needed to support a Protestant rebellion against a Catholic power hostile to England and bent on extirpating heresy. Much to everyone's frustration, Elizabeth chose a middle path, not necessarily abandoning the Dutch to their fate, but only half-heartedly giving military and economic support to the anti-Spanish, Protestant insurgency.

The tensions between England and Spain were further exacerbated by the undiplomatic behavior of their ambassadors. First, the English representative to Spain, a Protestant cleric named John Mann, made his contempt for Catholicism so obvious that **Philip** made him *persona non grata* at the Spanish court. The Spanish representative to England, Guzman de Silva, smoothed things over and Elizabeth agreed to recall Mann. But then, de Silva was himself replaced by Guerau DeSpes, a man "ready to stir up controversy and who saw the Protestants as the enemy."[26] Relations between the two countries started to deteriorate rapidly. In 1568, when bad weather forced a ship carrying £80,000 (a lot of money) intended to pay Alva's troops into Plymouth, Elizabeth seized the cash; in return, Alva seized English goods and ships in the Netherlands; Elizabeth responded by seizing all Spanish property in England and placing DeSpes under house arrest. While nobody in either country wanted a war, and while this incident was eventually resolved, the downward spiral continued. Elizabeth secretly supplied the Dutch rebels with money while publicly denouncing the rebellion, and Philip closed Antwerp, the main entry point for English cloth merchants, for five years.

Philip II also started secretly supporting plots against Elizabeth that centered on **Mary, Queen of Scots**. In 1568, **Thomas Howard, fourth Duke of Norfolk** (1536–72), devised a plot to wed Mary, displace Cecil, and thus control Elizabeth. It didn't work, and led to the **Northern Rebellion** of 1569–70 (which resulted in the publication of the Homily against Willful Rebellion). In an attempt to drum up support for the rebels, **Pope Pius V** issued a bull excommunicating Elizabeth and absolving her subjects of allegiance. Strategically, the attempt was a serious blunder, as it forced English Catholics to choose between their religion and their country, with most opting for the latter. In the fall of 1571, **Robert Ridolfi** plotted to put **Mary Stuart** and **Thomas Howard** on the throne. While the attempt failed (**Sir Francis Walsingham's** spies had infiltrated the conspiracy), the plot served to intensify anti-Catholic sentiment in England and led to further strictures on Catholics by parliament. In 1585, for example, being a Catholic priest was in itself made a treasonous offence. It was not a plot, however, that led England to war against the most powerful nation in Europe, but the near-collapse of the Dutch revolt after the assassination in 1584 of **William of Orange**. Elizabeth had to decide if she was going to support the Dutch or not. Half measures and duplicitous condemnations no longer sufficed, and she sided with her co-religionists. In December, 1585, **Dudley** landed in the Netherlands, and in response **Philip II** planned the invasion of England: **the Spanish Armada.**

In 1586, Elizabeth finally allowed **Sir Philip Sidney**, (b. 1554) author of *The Apology for Poetry*, the sonnet sequence *Astrophil and Stella*, and the unfinished prose romance, *The Countess of Pembroke's Arcadia*, and a "hot" Protestant, to join his uncle, **Robert Dudley**, **Earl of Leicester**, then the Governor-General of the Netherlands (he had accepted this position without Elizabeth's position, and she was furious). But on September 23, 1586, **Sidney** and his uncle participated in an ambush of Spanish troops near Zutphen, where **Sidney** was wounded in the leg, dying of gangrene on October 17.

Ireland

Elizabeth inherited a complex, difficult situation. Nominally under the authority of the English monarchy, the crown's authority did not extend beyond **the Pale** (the area around Dublin); further complicating matters, the English habitants of the Pale, known as the "Old English," developed their own identity and loyalties, and they resented increasing taxation from London as well the attempt to impose Protestantism upon them. Over the course of Elizabeth's reign, Ireland witnessed a series of insurrections against colonial rule (which the English interpreted as rebellions against legitimate authority) that were met with increasingly bloody repression. The English desire to control Ireland, however, stemmed from more than a desire for empire. In a very real sense, Ireland was to England what the Netherlands was to Spain: the focus of religious resistance that also served as an entry point for threatening foreign powers. So, in 1580, wrote **Sir Christopher Hatton** (c. 1540–91), a member of Elizabeth's Privy Council and eventual Lord Chancellor, to **Burghley**:

> this rule I hold in all certainty, that in Ireland and Scotland the entries and ways to our destruction most aptly to be found. If there we safely

shut up the postern-gate, we are sure to repulse the peril; but if our enemy make himself the porter, it will be then too late to wish we had the keys.[27]

Irish resistance to English colonization had to be crushed in order to prevent Spain, France, and the other Catholic powers from using Ireland as a staging ground to invade England, and these fears were not unfounded. In 1566, the Irish chieftain, **Shane O'Neill** (c. 1530–67) negotiated with **Charles IX of France** and **Mary Stuart** for military help against England. In response, Elizabeth told her deputy in Ireland, **Sir Henry Sidney** (1529–86; father of the Protestant hero and poet, **Sir Philip Sidney**) to take all necessary steps to bring **O'Neill** down. In 1569, the leader of another rebellion, James Fitzmaurice Fitzgerald, turned to **Philip II** for help.[28]

Sidney was among the first to attempt the pacification of Ireland through the establishment of **plantations**, or colonies of "New English" loyal to Protestantism and the British crown. As one might expect, both the "Old English" and the native Irish bitterly resisted being supplanted by these colonists, and the English responded ferociously, committing numerous atrocities. The ease with which English forces slaughtered men, women, and children is explained by the fact that the English scarcely considered their adversaries (whose land they were taking) human. "How godly a deed it is," one man declared, "to overthrow so wicked a race the world may judge; for my part I think there cannot be a greater sacrifice to God"; Elizabeth told Sir Henry Sidney that he was entering a world "replenished with ravening beasts," and she complimented **Walter Devereux, Earl of Essex** (1539–1576; father to her ill-fated favorite, **Robert Devereux, second Earl of Essex** [1565–1601]) on his savagery in bringing that "rude and barbarous nation to civility … and to oppose yourself and your forces to them whom reason and duty cannot bridle."[29] Ireland, as the anonymous saying goes, is the graveyard of English reputations.

In 1580, **Edmund Spenser** (b. 1552?) became private secretary to **Arthur Grey, Baron Grey of Wilton** (1536–93), **Sir Henry Sidney's** successor as Lord Deputy of Ireland, and while he would occasionally return to London, he lived there for nearly the rest of his life. Grey, like his predecessors, treated the Irish rebels brutally, most notably at Smerwick, when on November 9, 1580 Grey massacred approximately 600 Spanish and Italian troops who had surrendered, an event that Spenser may have witnessed. Spenser wrote his most famous work, the unfinished yet magnificent Protestant epic, *The Faerie Queene*, in Ireland, and in about 1596, Spenser wrote *A View of the Present State of Ireland*, a defense of English policy and his employer, Grey. In 1598, his estate was overrun and burnt by Irish rebels, and he fled to London, where he died in 1599.

Marital Negotiations

Elizabeth did not lack for suitors once she became queen in 1558. During the early years of her reign, she received no fewer than ten offers, ranging from her late sister **Mary's** husband and eventual antagonist, **Philip II** of Spain, to King Eric IV of Sweden, various archdukes, and the Earls of Arran and Arundel. Nor did Elizabeth lack encouragement from her government, as both her Privy Council and parliament repeatedly importuned her to marry and provide England with an heir, as did various preachers, diplomats, courtiers, and other well-wishers.[30] All of England, it seemed, urged Elizabeth to choose a husband. But the task, as indicated earlier, was much more complicated than it might seem, as marriage posed three overlapping sets of problems. The difficulties with **Philip II** and **Mary** demonstrated the pitfalls of marrying a foreign prince. Since the husband was expected to be the dominant figure in the marriage, how does one prevent England from being ruled, to use the early modern term for someone not English, by a "stranger"? Yet **Henry VIII's**, and further back in history, **Edward IV's** marital experiences amply demonstrated that wedding an English subject also created tremendous problems, because that would mean Elizabeth, by definition, would marry someone beneath her station, and then there would be the question of how one dealt with the various relatives. Finally, there was the question of what would happen if Elizabeth never married? Who would be her heir? What would happen to Protestantism? Would there be a civil war, or even a foreign invasion?

While we know that **Elizabeth** would choose the third option and that the crown would descend to **James VI**, son of **Mary, Queen of Scots**, without challenge, the future was not clear at the time, and during the latter part of her reign, the succession question caused genuine and deep anxiety. It would be a mistake, however, to assume that Elizabeth intended a single life from the moment she became queen. Elizabeth's celibacy resulted more from political circumstances than a deliberate strategy on her part. In fact, she seriously contemplated marriage twice, first in the beginning of her reign with her favorite, **Lord Robert Dudley**, and then, in the 1570s, with **François**, Duke of Anjou and Alençon, brother to **King Henri III** of France.

It was apparent to everyone that Elizabeth's disinterest in foreign suitors at the start of her reign did not stem from the problem of religion, but from her infatuation with **Dudley**. While the two may have met while children, their intimacy started when Dudley was appointed Master of the Horse, a position that not only included minding the royal stables but also accompanying the Queen when she went hunting or riding. By the spring of 1559, scurrilous gossip started swirling among the court and diplomatic circles. The problem was twofold: Elizabeth did not hide her affections, and Dudley was married. Furthermore, Dudley's prominence made him the object of considerable jealousy among the more established nobility. Then, on September 8, 1560, Dudley's wife, **Amy Robsart**, was found dead at the foot of a staircase.

What precisely happened is not clear, and her ostensibly convenient demise caused suspicions of murder, and even though Dudley was cleared (he was not even home at the time), those suspicions never entirely went away. But perhaps even more importantly,

Robsart's death deeply embarrassed the Queen politically both at home and abroad. **Nicholas Throckmorton**, the English ambassador to France, complained to a friend about how the Dudley affair had sullied both Elizabeth's and Protestantism's reputation:

> One laugheth at us, another threateneth, another revileth the Queen. Some let not to say [do not stop themselves from saying], "What religion is this that a subject shall kill has wife, and the Prince not only bear withal but marry with him?"[31]

It became increasingly clear that Elizabeth could not marry Dudley, as much as she may have wanted to. The damage to her reputation, and consequently her effectiveness as a monarch, would have been too great, and so she backed away. In response, **Dudley** did something extraordinary: he turned to the Spanish ambassador to ask for support in his suit to marry Elizabeth, offering, apparently, to help with the restoration of Catholicism. This move put the Dudley marriage into an entirely different category, and it brought in **Cecil**, always alive to the threat Catholicism posed to the queen. Spanish duplicity in this matter quickly brought an end to negotiations, but with two lasting results. The first was that Dudley's aborted alliance with Spain drove home to Elizabeth that she could not marry her favorite, and while he retained his position at court, all talk of a more personal union ended. Second, Dudley's experience with Spain at least partly led him to champion an aggressive, hawkish foreign policy against Catholicism (Cecil focused more on the domestic front) and in favor of supporting continental Protestants with both cash and arms.

Religion also scuttled Elizabeth's plans to marry **François, Duke of Alençon and Anjou**. Elizabeth had carried on a desultory negotiation for some years before he arrived in England in January, 1579, when the amazing happened: the two fell in love with each other. But the prospect of Elizabeth marrying a Catholic prince was too much for many of her subjects and her closest advisors to bear, and the match was called off late that year, but not before one John Stubbe was publicly mutilated for publishing a book condemning the match, and **Sir Philip Sidney** probably banished from the court for his writing a private pamphlet on the same topic. Everybody, including Elizabeth, realized that marriage would no longer be an option.

II.   1588–1603

Foreign Affairs

The execution of **Mary, Queen of Scots** in 1586 gave **Philip II** of Spain the final impetus to invade England and replace Elizabeth, a Protestant thorn in his side, with a Catholic monarch more to his liking. The invasion was far from a surprise. In 1587, the Queen sent Sir Francis Drake on a mission to disrupt and delay Spain's military preparations, and so Drake invaded Cadiz harbor, sinking between two and three dozen ships, thus forcing Philip to wait until his fleet could be replenished. In May 1588, a huge fleet of ships and soldiers finally set sail, their object being the conquest of England and the restoration of Catholicism. The plan was for the fleet to sail not directly to England but to the Dutch port of Flushing, where they would pick up yet more troops, and that proved to be a fatal mistake. While the English ships were smaller and much more agile than the huge, lumbering Spanish galleons, they could only harry their enemies while at sea, not defeat them. The Dutch Protestant forces had also retaken Flushing, and so the Spanish fleet was forced to pull into Calais. On the night of the 28th, the English sent fireships (old vessels filled with combustibles which were then ignited) into the anchored Spanish fleet, and while the fireships destroyed only a few of the Spanish ships, they accomplished their purpose by creating panic. Out of formation, the English picked off the enemy ships one by one. Since the English navy now had control of the English channel, the remnants of the Armada could not retreat south, and so they were forced to sail north, around Scotland, where they ran into fierce gales – the "Protestant wind" – sinking yet more ships. Fewer than half of the 130 vessels limped back to Spain.

On the one hand, both the preparations for the Armada and its eventual defeat look like an unqualified success for England. Elizabeth was never so popular, and her famous speech at Tilbury on August 9, 1588 ("I know I have the body but of a weak and feeble woman, but I have the heart and stomach of a king and of a king of England too"[32]) enshrined her mystique. The Armada's defeat signaled not just a national success but validated England's sense that God was on their side and that England was indeed God's chosen nation. To commemorate the victory, Elizabeth's government issued a commemorative medal with the inscription "*Afflavit Deus et dissipati sunt*" (God blew, and they were sunk), and Elizabeth composed a hymn that was performed for her that again interprets the Armada's defeat in providential terms: "This Josephs Lord and Israel's God, / The fiery Pillar and day's Cloud, / That saved his saints from wicked men / And drenched the honor of the proud."[33]

Yet the sinking of the 1588 Armada did not end the Spanish threat or usher in a Protestant Golden Age. Nearly every year afterward brought fears of another Spanish invasion, and the war with Spain would continue. In 1596, for example, **Robert Devereux, Earl of Essex** (more on him later in this chapter) and Charles, Lord Howard of Effingham would lead a massive, pre-emptive assault on the port of Cadiz to destroy the fleet Philip was preparing for another attempted invasion of England. Furthermore, the situations in France, the Netherlands and Ireland also caused England to expend both treasure and lives. In France, a crazed monk assassinated **Henri III** in 1589, leaving the throne to his Protestant brother, Henri of Bourbon, who became **Henri IV**. The prospect of a Protestant monarch prompted Spain's **Philip II** to renew the Wars of Religion. The new French king appealed to Elizabeth for help, and Elizabeth immediately responded by sending a major military force (4000 men) and two more contingents arrived in 1591. All suffered heavy losses, mainly from disease. **Henri IV**, however, understood that military strength alone would never defeat the Catholic League. Therefore, Henri decided to convert to Catholicism, apparently saying, "Paris is worth a mass," thus giving the Catholic side what it wanted (a co-religionist as monarch) while insisting on toleration for the Protestants. Henri signed peace treaties with the Catholic League in 1596, then with Spain in 1598, and made Protestantism secure with the **Edict of Nantes** that same year.

England also continued to pour money and men into the Netherlands. Unfortunately, **Robert Dudley, Earl of Leicester**, was not a very effective general and a poor diplomat to boot. Elizabeth was furious at his decision to accept the position of Governor-General, as that would imply a degree of commitment that the Queen would not tolerate. To make matters worse (or more embarrassing), when **Leicester** returned to England in 1586 to report on the situation, he left Sir William Stanley, a Catholic, in charge, who then betrayed his trust by promptly surrendering two towns to the Spanish general, **Alexander Farnese, Prince of Parma** (1545–92). Leicester came back for good in 1588, a broken man, dying that fall. His absence, however, coupled with more competent English and Dutch leadership along with the worsening situation (for the Catholic League) in France, which drew Parma's attention away from the Dutch and towards Paris, allowed the Dutch forces to continue the rebellion on their own, and by the end of the decade, they even started repaying their debt.

Adding to the complexity and troubles, in 1594, **Hugh O'Neill, Earl of Tyrone** (c. 1550–1616) started a rebellion in the northern province of Ulster that would eventually be known as the **Nine Years War**. By 1595, he started negotiating with the Pope and Philip II for support, "and posed a greater threat to the English control of Ireland than any Irish lord previously that century."[34] By the fall of 1598, England had lost control of all but a small portion of the country. In 1599, Elizabeth sent an army of over 16,000 men to Ireland, under Essex's command. After suffering a humiliating defeat, **Essex** rushed back to the court, even though **Elizabeth** expressly ordered him not to abandon his post. He was replaced by a much abler soldier, **Charles Blount, Lord Mountjoy** (1563–1606), who crushed the rebellion in 1603 using the same scorched earth tactics employed by Spenser's employer, **Lord Grey**, earlier. According to one account of the campaign, "we have killed, burnt and spoiled all along the lough .... We spare none of what quality or sex soever, and it hath bred much terror in the people."[35] Tyrone surrendered a few days after Elizabeth died.

While in one sense, the story of England's foreign involvements over the last years of her reign ends more or less successfully – the Spanish kept at bay, Protestantism defended in the Netherlands and France, Ireland subdued – these results came at a tremendous financial and social cost. "Between 1558 and 1603 over 105,000 men served in the army,"[36] and people did not volunteer but were "pressed" into service, meaning, they were conscripted whether they wanted to fight or not, which led to all sorts of corruption and abuses. When Shakespeare's Falstaff admits that he used the opportunity for greater profit – "I have misus'd the King's press damnably. I have got, in exchange of a hundred and fifty soldiers, three hundred and odd pounds" by allowing able-bodied men to buy their way out, and so his whole company consists of "slaves as ragged as Lazarus in the painted cloth" (*I Henry IV*, 4.2.12–14, 25) – the audience would have likely recognized the reality behind the fiction. In 1600, the Privy Council agreed in language that seems to echo Shakespeare's: the recruits "seem they were picked so as to disburden the counties of so many idle, vagrant and loose persons rather than for their ability and aptness to do service."[37] Nor did those lucky enough to return enjoy any social services. Those injured in England's service were left, as Falstaff says, "for the town's end, to beg during life" (*1 Henry IV*, 5.3.38). England's foreign entanglements left the country exhausted, demoralized, and nearly broke.

Domestic Affairs

Elizabeth's Tilbury speech and the defeat of the Armada in 1588 mark the high point of her reign. England had not only triumphed over its greatest enemy but confirmed its sense of divine mission, and Elizabeth ruled over the chosen nation as the Virgin Queen. The sense of triumph, however, very quickly started to fade. Paintings of Elizabeth from this period, such as Nicholas Hilliard's miniatures consistently depicted her as a beautiful, young woman, idealized as Astraea, goddess of justice, or, as in the Ditchley Portrait (see page

116), as the imperial, virgin empress of the world. Edmund Spenser would cast Elizabeth as "the faerie queene" in his epic of the same name. The sense of triumph, however, very quickly started to fade, just as the distance between Elizabeth's iconography and her actual appearance, became increasingly undeniable.

Elizabeth had kept in her Privy Council many of her original advisers, and mortality started taking its toll. **Leicester** died in 1588, **Walsingham** in 1590, and **Sir Christopher Hatton** in 1591, and these are only the most notable departures. The sense of an era ending permeates the chronicles of the period. William Camden's *History of the Life and Reign of the Most Renowned and Victorious Princess, Elizabeth*, for example, ends each chapter after 1588 with a long litany of notable deaths. An increasingly dour and infirm **Burghley** survived until 1598 – "Old Saturnus," he was called, "a melancholy and wayward planet."[38] As each great man functioned as a gateway for offices and patronage, their clients needed to find new avenues of support in a cut-throat, highly competitive atmosphere. "There was never in court," wrote one observer in 1589, "such emulation, such envy, such back-biting, as is now at this time."[39]

The earlier polarity in Elizabeth's court between **Leicester** and **Burleigh**, a tension qualified by mutual respect and friendship, was replaced by the competition between the Queen's new favorites, **Sir Walter Ralegh** (who would unsuccessfully try to colonize Virginia) and **Essex**. But **Ralegh**, perhaps because of his common ancestry, never became part of Elizabeth's ruling circle, the Privy Council. The more telling and consequential competition was between **Essex** and Burleigh's son, **Robert Cecil** (1563–1612), who may have been physically unimpressive, but carried on his father's administrative dedication and brilliance: "Sir Robert goes and cometh very often between London and the court," writes one of **Essex's** men with a combination of contempt and grudging admiration, "so that he comes out with his hands full of papers, and head full of matter, and so occupied [that he] passeth through the presence like a blind man, not looking upon any."[40]

Essex, however, was a highly unstable man who had a highly inflated sense of his importance that was not matched by a record of achievement. He botched the Cadiz expedition by not occupying the town, which could have been used as an English base, and he infuriated **Elizabeth** by having the temerity to knight 33 men without her knowledge or permission. His behavior soon veered from the impolitic to the seriously unbalanced. In 1599, after the collapse of his campaign in Ireland, **Essex** – against Elizabeth's express orders – ran back to the court, ostensibly to retrieve his reputation, and he burst in upon Elizabeth in her bed chamber, "where he found the Queen newly up, the hair about her face," a huge breach of protocol, especially for a person as vain as the Queen. **Elizabeth** was initially gracious, but as one person reports, "'tis much wondered at here that he went so boldly to her Majesty's presence, she not being ready, and he so full of dirt and mire, that his very face was full of it."[41] After Elizabeth had time to dress and to collect herself, however, her aspect darkened considerably: "She began to call him to question for his return, and was not satisfied in the manner of his coming away, and leaving all things at so great hazard."[42] Despite his great opinion of himself, **Essex** had relatively little influence over the Queen and the machinery of patronage. Despite strenuous efforts, for example, he could not get Elizabeth to appoint his client, **Sir Francis Bacon** (1561–1626) as Solicitor-General (Bacon's time would come during the reign of King James). Instead, **Cecil's** man, the great constitutional lawyer, **Sir Edward Coke** (1552–1634), got the job. After a few months of deadlock (he refused to submit, she refused to reconcile), Elizabeth charged Essex with "great and high contempts and points of misgovernance" in Ireland along with "divers notorious error and neglects of duty."[43]

The final straw, however, came when **Essex** lost his lease on the customs revenues from imported sweet wines, his main source of income. **Sir John Harington** (Elizabeth's godson and translator of Ludovico Ariosto's epic poem, *Orlando Furioso*) recorded that from that moment on, Essex started behaving extremely erratically. He

> shifteth from sorrow and repentance to rage and rebellion so suddenly, as well proveth him devoid of good reason as of right mind. In my last discourse he uttered strange words, bordering on such strange designs

that made me hasten forth and leave his presence …. His speeches of the Queen become no man who hath *mens sana in corpore sano*.[44]

Essex then had the completely daft idea that he would lead a rebellion against his enemies at court (mainly **Cecil**). Fascinatingly, the day before the planned insurrection, some of Essex's followers commissioned a performance of Shakespeare's *Richard II*, including the deposition scene (left out of the quarto edition), which prompted Elizabeth later to make her celebrated remark, "I am Richard II, know ye not that?"[45] Elizabethans may have been seriously disillusioned by 1601, yet there was no chance they would join a revolt against Elizabeth, and so **Essex's** attempt collapsed. He was executed on February 25, 1601.

The uproars and factionalism at court led to a widespread sense that the government was no longer entirely in control. One writer complained about the factionalism, suspicion, and outright paranoia gripping Elizabeth's government:

> They [the Privy Counselors] suffer very few to be acquainted with matters of state for fear of divulging it, whereby their practices are subject to be revealed, and therefore they will suffer few to rise to places of reputation that are skillful or studious in matters of policy, but hold them low and far off so that the greatest politicians that rule most will not have about them other then base pen clerks that can do nothing but write as they are bidden, or some mechanical dunce that cannot conceive his Master's drifts and polices, for if they have lynx's eyes, they must look into their actions.[46]

Even Elizabeth admitted the decline. "Now the wit of the fox is everywhere on foot," she complained to William Lambarde, "so as hardly a faithful or virtuous man may be found."[47] Adding to the dismay was the pervasive uncertainty over the succession. While in hindsight, the accession of **James VI of Scotland** (the son of Mary, Queen of Scots) may seem like a foregone conclusion, the murky legal situation (was Henry VIII's final will valid because it was signed with a stamp, not his hand?) plus the lack of direction from the top caused tremendous uncertainty. As one person in 1600 remarked, "this crown is not like to fall to the ground for want of heads that claim to wear it, but upon whose head it will fall is by many doubted."[48]

Incertitude about the succession and the generalized disillusionment certainly contributed to the "crisis of authority" characterizing Elizabeth's final years. Radical Protestants, such as the author (or authors) of the **Marprelate Tracts**, declared that Elizabeth's authority in ecclesiastical affairs was misplaced, even illegitimate, and in response, the government tightened the laws against religious dissidents, both Catholic and Protestant. Partly as a result of government pressure, a small group led by **Robert Browne** (c. 1550–1633), known as either **Brownists** or **Separatists**, decided that the Elizabethan Church could not be salvaged, and therefore they decided to establish their own congregations. Officially, the punishment for leaving the Anglican Church was banishment, but many did not wait for the government to catch them before decamping voluntarily to the Netherlands (which was not only the focus of Protestant resistance against Spain and Catholicism, but had a tradition of religious toleration), and then, under the reign of King James, to America.

The political and ideological quarrels, however, likely concerned only a small portion of England's population. The four disastrous harvests of 1594–97 (memorialized in Titania's lines from *A Midsummer Night's Dream*: "The ox hath therefore stretch'd his yoke in vain, / The ploughman lost his sweat, and the green corn / Hath rotted ere his youth attain'd a beard" [2.1.93–5]) had a profound impact on just about everybody. "Every man complains against the dearth of this time," wrote one observer, and for good reason.[49] The lack of food caused riots, starvation, and a severe spike in mortality.[50] The crop failures strained the social fabric to the breaking point, as the poor believed that the authorities had either abandoned them or were helpless. *The Homily on Obedience* assured listeners that while God created a hierarchy, "every one have need of other."[51] But that assurance started to ring hollow in the face of dearth and starvation.

A libel delivered in Norfolk in 1595 reveals the profound anger against the avarice of the rich and the government, which despite issuing numerous proclamations against hoarding, is revealed to be impotent:

> For seven years the rich have fed on our flesh. Bribes make you jus-
> tices blind and you are content to see us famished. What are these
> edicts and proclamations, which are here and there scattered in the
> country concerning kidders, corn-mongers and those devilish cormo-
> rants, but a scabbard without the sword, for neither are those mur-
> dering malsters nor the bloody corn-buyers stayed? We thought to
> have pressed higher to our L[ord] Admiral, to entreat him to shut up
> the gate of his gain awhile and content himself with that he hath got.
> Sir William Paston, who might have been called Passion for his former
> pity, but now is Paston [Pass-stone] because he is become as hard as a
> stone …. There are 60,000 craftsmen in London and elsewhere, besides
> the poor country clown that can no longer bear, therefore their
> draught is in the cup of the Lord which they shall drink to the dregs,
> and some barbarous and unmerciful soldier shall lay open your
> hedges, reap your fields, rifle your coffers, and level your houses to
> the ground. Meantime give license to the rich to set open shop to sell
> poor men's skins. Necessity hath no law.[52]

One of the more serious disorders – called either the Oxfordshire Rebellion or the Enslow Hill Rising – was led by Bartholomew Steere, who claimed, according to a deposition taken afterward, that "there were 100 in Whitney who would go with them to throw down enclosures, and [that] it would never be well until the gentry were knocked down."[53]

While Steere did not get his revolution (any more than Essex got his), that does not mean that Elizabethans were not deeply unhappy with their situation, as evidenced by the extraordinary pressure on those in authority in late Elizabethan literature. This critical sensibility is especially evident (despite the presence of licensing and censorship) on the public stage. In 1599, for example, Shakespeare creates a scene in *Henry V* in which two common soldiers express the utmost skepticism over the disguised king's assertion that the war is justified: "That's more than we know," replies Michael Williams (4.1.129), who then states "if the cause be not good, the King himself hath a very heavy reckoning to make" (4.1.134). In a lighter vein, Thomas Dekker's *The Shoemaker's Holiday*, also staged in 1599, fundamentally challenges the social structure exemplified by the Homily on Obedience with Simon Eyre's redefinition of nobility: "Prince am I none, yet am I nobly born, as being the sole son of a shoemaker" (sc. 7, 48–9). In this play, the rich London merchant, Oatley, does not want his daughter to marry an aristocratic courtier because such people are wastrels "who will in silks and gay apparel spend / More in one year than I am worth by far" (sc. 1, 13–14). While today we can focus on the glories of Elizabeth's reign, especially since "she was perhaps the only really popular monarch between Henry V and Queen Victoria,"[54] we should not lose sight of the fact that most of the canonical literature of this era was written during a period of tremendous social unrest and genuine misery.

Elizabeth's final years were lonely. She keenly felt the loss of her servants; **Burleigh's** passing in 1598 especially pained her. In a letter written in 1600 to Sir John Harington, **Sir Robert Sidney** (Philip Sidney's brother) describes her decline: "she doth wax weaker since the late troubles, and Burghley's death often draws tears from her goodly cheeks; she walketh out but little, meditates much alone."[55] In 1601, she told the French ambassador "she was tired of life, for nothing now contented her spirit, or gave her any enjoyment."[56] She did not have to wait long for the end. In February 1603, she fell ill, yet she refused medicine, preferring to remain on cushions rather than take to her bed, because, according to a contemporary report, "she had a persuasion that if she once lay down she should never rise."[57] **Elizabeth I** died on March 24, 1603, amid conflicting reports as to whether in her last moments she finally designated an heir. It didn't matter, as **Robert Cecil**, had long since arranged for the crown to pass to **King James VI** of Scotland, son of the Scots queen whom Elizabeth executed for plotting to assassinate her. The Tudor age done, the reign of the Stuarts was about to begin.

Notes

1 "The Distresses of the Commonwealth, with the Means to Remedy Them," in Henry Gee, *The Elizabethan Prayer-book and Ornaments* (London: Macmillan, 1902), 207. See also Penry Williams, *The Later Tudors: England 1547–1603* (Oxford: Clarendon Press, 1995), 229.

2 Gee, *The Elizabethan Prayer-book*, 211.

3 Gee, *The Elizabethan Prayer-book*, 207.

4 Quoted in Roger Lockyer, *Tudor and Stuart Britain: 1471–1714* (Harlow, Essex: Longman, 1985), 147.

5 Knox, *The First Trumpet Blast against the Monstrous Regiment of Women* (Geneva, 1558), sig. B1r.

6 John Aylmer, *An Harbor for Faithful Subjects* (London, 1559), sig. B2v.

7 Robert M. Healey, "Waiting for Deborah: John Knox and Four Ruling Queens," *The Sixteenth Century Journal* 25 (1994), 379.

8 See Alexandra Walsham, 'A Very Debora?' The Myth of Elizabeth I as a Providential Monarch," *The Myth of Elizabeth*, ed. Susan Doran and Thomas S. Freeman (New York: Palgrave Macmillan, 2003), 143–70. The literature on Elizabeth and the various uses of royal imagery is extensive, to say the least. See, for example, Roy Strong, *The Cult of Elizabeth* (Berkeley: University of California Press, 1977); Winfried Schleiner, "*Divina virago*: Queen Elizabeth as an Amazon," *Studies in Philology* 75 (1978): 163–80; and Louis A. Montrose, *The Subject of Elizabeth* (Chicago: University of Chicago Press, 2006).

9 Robert Bucholz and Newton Key, *Early Modern England 1485–1714: A Narrative History* (Oxford: Blackwell, 2004), 119.

10 Archbishop John Whitgift, *An Answer to a Certain libel entitled "An admonition to the Parliament"* (London, 1572), sig. D2v.

11 William Barlow, *The Sum and Substance of the Conference … at Hampton Court* (London, 1604), sig. F3.

12 Christopher Hill, *Society and Puritanism in Pre-Revolutionary England*, 2nd ed. (New York: Schocken, 1967), 13.

13 William Tyndale, *Obedience of a Christian Man* (London, 1548), sig. K8r.

14 Quoted in Lockyer, *Tudor and Stuart Britain*, 155.

15 Quoted in Patrick Collinson, "Grindal, Edmund (1516×20–1583)," *Oxford Dictionary of National Biography*, Oxford University Press, September 2004; online edn., January 2008. http://www.oxforddnb.com/view/article/11644, accessed March 1, 2010.

16 Williams, *The Later Tudors*, 238.

17 The most recent and, in many ways, the best biography of Mary, Queen of Scots, is John Guy, *Queen of Scots: The True Life of Mary Stuart* (New York: Houghton Mifflin, 2004).

18 François II was succeeded by Charles IV, whose reign was dominated the Wars of Religion.

19 Antonia Fraser, *Mary, Queen of Scots* (New York: Delacorte Press, 1970), 113.

20 "Adamas Loquitur" (The Diamond Speaks), quoted in Peter C. Herman, *Royal Poetrie: Monarchic Verse and the Political Imaginary of Early Modern England* (Ithaca: Cornell University Press, 2010), 69.

21 Elaine Finnie Greig, "Stewart, Henry, duke of Albany [Lord Darnley] (1545/6–1567)," *Oxford Dictionary of National Biography*, Oxford University Press, September 2004; online edn., January 2008. http://www.oxforddnb.com/view/article/26473, accessed March 17, 2010.

22 Quoted in Greig, "Stewart, Henry."

23 Carole Levin, *The Reign of Elizabeth I* (New York: Palgrave, 2002), 43.

24 Harry Kelsey, *Sir John Hawkins: Queen Elizabeth's Slave Trader* (New Haven: Yale University Press, 2003), 69.

25 Thomas Churchyard, *A Lamentable and Pitiable Description of the Woeful Wars in Flanders* (London, 1578), sig. E2r.

26 Levin, *The Reign of Elizabeth I*, 48.

27 Nicholas Harris Nicolas, *Memoirs of the Life and Times of Sir Christopher Hatton* (London: Richard Bentley, 1847), 159–60.

28 Levin, *The Reign of Elizabeth I*, 52–3.

29 Quoted in Bridgden, 227, and Levin, *The Reign of Elizabeth I*, 55.

30 The best survey of Elizabeth's various courtships is Susan Doran, *Monarchy and Matrimony: The Courtships of Elizabeth I* (London: Routledge, 1996). This section relies heavily on Doran's book.

31 *Calendar of State Papers, Foreign Series, of the Reign of Elizabeth*, ed. Joseph Stevenson (London: HMSO, 1865), vol. 3, 348. See also Doran, 42.

32 *Elizabeth I: Collected Works*, ed. Leah S. Marcus, Janel Mueller, and Mary Beth Rose (Chicago: University of Chicago Press, 2000), 326.

33 *Elizabeth I: Collected Works*, 411. See my analysis of this poem in *Royal Poetrie*, 149–56.

34 Levin, *The Reign of Elizabeth I*, 77.

35 Quoted in Williams, *The Later Tudors*, 380.

36 Levin, *The Reign of Elizabeth I*, 79.

37 Quoted in Bucholz and Key, *Early Modern England*, 140.

38 Quoted in Williams, *The Later Tudors*, 342.

39   Letter from Francis Allen to Anthony Bacon, quoted in Thomas Birch, *Memoirs of the Reign of Queen Elizabeth* (London, 1754), vol. 1, 57.

40   Letter from Sir Anthony Standen to Anthony Bacon, quoted in Birch, *Memoirs*, vol. 1, 155.

41   Letter from Rowland White to Sir Robert Sidney, in Arthur Collins, *Letters and Memorials of State* (London, 1746), vol. 2, 127.

42   Letter from Rowland White, 128.

43   Quoted in Williams, *The Later Tudors*, 372.

44   John Harington, *Nugae Antiquae* (London: Vernon and Hood *et al.*, 1804), vol. 1, 179.

45   Quoted in Louis A. Montrose, *The Purpose of Playing: Shakespeare and the Cultural Politics of the Elizabethan Theatre* (Chicago: University of Chicago Press, 1996), 79.

46   Thomas Wilson, *The State of England, Anno Dom. 1600*, ed. F. J. Fisher, *Camden Miscellany* 16 (1934), 42.

47   Quoted in J. E. Neale, "The Elizabethan Political Scene," *Essays in Elizabethan History* (New York: Cape, 1958), 78.

48   Quoted in Williams, *The Later Tudors*, 383.

49   Quoted in Peter Clark, "A Crisis Contained? The Condition of English Towns in the 1590s," *The European Crisis of the 1590s: Essays in Comparative History*, ed. Peter Clark (London: George Allen, 1985), 45.

50   In 1595, there were food riots in both the southeast and the southwest of England, and in 1597, riots broke out in the West Country, East Anglia and on the Kent–Sussex border (John Walter "'A Rising of the People?': The Oxfordshire Rising of 1596," *Past and Present* No. 107 [1985], 92).

51   "The Exhortation concerning Good Order and Obedience to Rulers and Magistrates," in *Certain Sermons or Homilies* (London, 1547), sigs. Riir–Riiiv.

52   *Historical Manuscripts Commission: Calendar of the Manuscripts of the Marquis of Salisbury*, ed. E. Salisbury (London: HMSO, 1915), ser. 9; vol. 13, 168–9.

53   *Calendar of State Papers, Domestic series, of the Reign of Elizabeth, 1595–97* (London: Longman, Brown, Green, Longmans, & Roberts, 1867), 344.

54   Williams, *The Later Tudors*, 388.

55   Quoted in J. R. Black, *The Reign of Elizabeth 1558–1603* (Oxford: Clarendon Press, 959), 493.

56   Black, *The Reign of Elizabeth*, 494.

57   John Nichols, *The Progresses and Public Processions of Queen Elizabeth* (London, 1823), vol. 3, 604.

6

The Reign of King James VI/I (1603–25)

The accession of King **James Stuart** (1566–1625), the sixth of that name to rule Scotland, the first to rule England (hence the two numbers), seemed to come as a great relief (for how a Scots king came to rule England, see the earlier discussion in Chapter 5). In 1603, James appeared as the opposite of Elizabeth in 1558. As a man, he did not come burdened with the controversies surrounding female rule; and as a family man – married in 1589 to **Anna of Denmark** (1574–1619), they had three children: **Henry** (1594–1612), **Elizabeth** (1596–1662), and **Charles** (1600–49) – another succession crisis seemed unlikely. Adding further cause for optimism, James came to England's throne as an experienced monarch, having successfully ruled the fractious kingdom of Scotland for over a decade, and as a pacifist, he would bring England's wars to an end, thus saving treasure and lives. Their similarities also gave cause for hope. Both Elizabeth and James were exceedingly intelligent and highly educated. James also enjoyed engaging in theological controversies, and very unusually for a monarch, he was

A Short History of Early Modern England: British Literature in Context, First Edition.
Peter C. Herman.
© 2011 Peter C. Herman. Published 2011 by Blackwell Publishing Ltd.

Figure 6.1 King James I of England and VI of Scotland by Daniel Mytens, 1621. © National Portrait Gallery, London.

also an author who had published both poetry and prose.[1] *The True Law of Free Monarchies* (1598; reprinted in England, 1603) would become a classic of absolutist theory, and his book of practical advice for Prince Henry, the *Basilicon Doron* (The Gift of a King), first published in 1599, would become an international best-seller, translated into Latin, French, Dutch, German, and Swedish, among other languages. Initial impressions were highly favorable. One person who met James recorded that "The King is of sharpest wit and invention, ready and pithy speech, an exceeding good memory; of the sweetest, pleasantest and best nature that ever I knew ...."[2] Another contemporary, Thomas Wilson, wrote to a friend in Paris: "our virtuous king makes our hopes to swell."[3]

150

Yet there were other differences that in time would cause very significant problems. First, **James** was a Scot, and while nobody doubted the legitimacy of his claim to the throne, overall the English did not like the Scots or Scotland very much. A popular "description" of James's home (first circulated c. 1617) begins by confessing that the country "is too good for them that possess it and too bad for others to be at charge to conquer it. The air might be wholesome but for the stinking people that inhabit it; the ground might be more fruitful had they the wit to manure it; the beasts are generally small (women only excepted), of which sort there are none greater in the world."[4] Next, James was a very different kind of politician than Elizabeth. For one, he hated crowds, whereas **Elizabeth** understood their utility, a fact immediately noted to James's disadvantage. In the same letter quoted above, Wilson writes, "the people according to the honest English nature approve all their prince's actions and words, saving that they desire some more of that gracious affability which their good old queen did afford them."[5] **James** could also be crude, as exemplified by an incident at the start of his reign. Told of a crowd who had come to express their love and loyalty, he is reported to have said (in Scots): "God's wounds! I will pull down my breeches and they shall also see my arse."[6] Needless to say, Elizabeth never reacted to offered adulation like that.

James's personal hygiene left a great deal to be desired, even by early modern standards. According to one report, "his skin was soft as taffeta sarsnet [very fine, soft silk cloth], which felt so because he never washed his hands, only rubbed his finger ends slightly with the wet end of a napkin."[7] James, in short, never washed. Unlike the Tudors, **James** did not cut an impressive or attractive figure. Oddly proportioned, his spindly legs (blamed "on some foul play in his youth, or before he was born, that he was not able to stand at seven years of age"[8]) supported a large frame and a rather bulbous head. Also, James spoke with a thick accent exacerbated by a lisp caused by his tongue being

> too large for his mouth, which ever made him speak full in the mouth, and made him drunk very uncomely, as if eating his drink, which came out into the cup of each side of his mouth.[9]

151

Whereas Elizabeth's court had its problems and its rivalries, it maintained a fundamental dignity, but James presided over a court infamous for its rampant corruption, sexual scandals, and generally tawdry behavior. While some still some resist admitting this fact, there is little doubt that James's attraction to young, handsome men whom he then showered with favors, wealth, and public displays of affection was physical in nature. In other words, **James** was, to use contemporary terms, bisexual, if not homosexual. In a time when such behavior could get one executed, his sexual preferences did not endear James to his subjects.[10]

More ominously, **James** firmly believed in absolute monarchy (meaning, the monarch is above the law and accountable only to God), which led to a series of gradually escalating confrontations with parliament, the House of Commons in particular. An event that occurred while James made his way from Scotland to be crowned in London illustrates James's different approach to the rule of law.[11] A thief was discovered among the crowds surrounding the new king. But rather than letting justice take its course, James ordered the man immediately hanged, "which was accordingly executed."[12] The problem is that James had the thief executed without the benefit of a trial. At least one courtier, **Sir John Harington**, understood full well the implications of this rash act: "I hear our new king hath hanged one man before he was tried; 'tis strangely done; now if the wind bloweth thus, why not a man be tried before he hath offended?"[13] While worrisome, nobody at the time thought this event merited deposition, civil war, and the execution of a king. But in hindsight, one can see the first hints of what was to come almost as soon as James entered England.

Historical interpretations of the Stuart era and the causes of the English Revolution era veer between two poles. On one side, one has the **Whig** interpretation of history, named after the political group (the Whigs, very broadly, were anti-Catholic and pro-parliament) who in 1689 removed **James II** from the throne and brought in William of Orange. The term itself derives from "whiggamore," like "puritan," originally a derisive term for an extreme Protestant. Whig history, especially popular during the nineteenth century, sees the English past as a progressive march toward greater and greater liberty. It takes a **teleological** approach to history, seeing events moving toward a pre-determined goal. In the 1970s, however, a group known as the **Revisionists** challenged this view, rejecting the teleological basis of **Whig** history, arguing that events are not produced by long-term causes, but by short-term contingencies.[14]

First Acts: Spain, the Hampton Court Conference, and the Gunpowder Plot

James saw himself as a "rex pacificus," a peaceful king, and in his first speech to parliament in 1604, he declared that:

> outward peace … is no small blessing to a Christian commonwealth, for by peace abroad with their neighbors the towns flourish, the merchants become rich, the trade doth increase, and the people of all sorts of the land enjoy free liberty to exercise themselves in their several vocations without peril or disturbance.[15]

By this time, the war between England and Spain had nearly bankrupted both countries, plus, the 1601 collapse of the Spanish intervention in Ireland, made continuing the war seem pointless to Spain's rulers. Despite the virulent hatred of Catholicism on the part of the English and the equally virulent desire to restore the "old religion" on the part of Spain, both sides were willing to strike a deal. James showed his good faith by almost immediately upon his accession issuing a "Proclamation to Repress All Piracies and Depredations upon the Seas" (1603), and the two countries signed the **Treaty of London** in August 1604, ending hostilities until 1625 (more on the resumption of war later in this chapter). In many ways, this treaty was a brilliant diplomatic success for England, since the English negotiators, led by the able **Robert Cecil**, James's Chief Minister (who James referred to as his "little beagle"), conceded almost nothing to the Spanish delegation, who had hoped for freedom of religion for English Catholics, breaking the alliance between England and the Protestant Dutch rebels, and banning English trade in the New World.[16]

James also had to deal immediately with the tensions among the more radical reformers, Catholics, and the more moderate Protestants. His accession raised the hopes of both Protestants and Catholics. On the one hand, Catholics looked to the new king to ease their lot, and James gave them some encouragement. In his first speech to parliament, he declared his willingness to consider re-examining the recusancy laws "in case they have been at times part further or more rigorously extended by judges than the meaning of the law was, or might tend to the hurt as well of the innocent as of guilty persons," and he distinguished between "quiet and well-minded men, peaceable subjects" and those who have become "factious stirrers of sedition and perturbers of the commonwealth."[17] To be sure, there were limits to what James will tolerate. Any cleric who maintains papal supremacy or justifies the assassination of kings will not be tolerated. But otherwise, **James** suggested that so long as Catholics remained quiet and loyal to the commonwealth (as most were), he would tolerate them. On the other hand, James also had to contend with the more radical wings of Protestantism, which, we should remember, **Elizabeth's** government severely repressed in her last years. They too looked to enlist James as an ally, and on his procession from Scotland to London in 1603, the new king was handed the **Millenary Petition** (allegedly signed by 1000 ministers). While the petition asked for moderate reforms, such as urging stricter Sabbath observance, granting these requests would have landed James solidly in the camp of the "godly."

Therefore, James decided that the best approach to the problem was to convene the **Hampton Court Conference** in January 1604. The conference itself did not resolve much in terms of doctrine, but it did have two lasting effects. First, James not only made clear his distaste for "puritans," which a participant defined as "a Protestant strayed out of his wits," but grounded his support for **episcopacy** on the integral connection between church and civil government. Getting rid of one meant getting rid of the other. As James succinctly put it, "No bishop, no king."[18] Second, James agreed with a request for "a new translation of the Bible, because those which were allowed in the reigns of Henry VIII and Edward VI were corrupt and not answerable to the truth of the original."[19] James, who thought the Geneva translation "the worst of all," agreed, and ordered that the new translation

> should be done by the best learned in both the universities, after them to be reviewed by the bishops and the chief learned of the Church; from them to be presented to the Privy Council; and lastly to be rati-fied by his royal authority, and so this whole church to be bound unto it, and none other.[20]

The result of course would be the **King James Bible**, published in 1611.[21]

If the more radical Protestants were disappointed at James's refusal to tilt entirely in their direction, the Catholic minority felt entirely devastated. Many expected that the peace treaty with Spain would contain a provision for easing the laws against Catholicism in England, or that James would have some sympathy for Catholics, given his mother's religion. But these hopes were shattered. Not only did the **Treaty of London** not allow Catholics freedom to worship as they pleased, but in February 1605, James increased pressure by conducting a purge of secret recusants, and approximately 5000 people were caught up in the net. As a consequence, a group of disaffected Catholics plotted to blow up both Houses of Parliament along with the king on November 5, 1605 – **the Gunpowder Plot**. The Plot was motivated, according to a contemporary narrative by a Catholic priest, by an overwhelming sense of despair: "How great was the grief and bitter the anguish of those poor folk who had suffered for so many years under the harsh yoke of Elizabeth when they began to see hope vanish once more from before their eyes."[22] Believing they had no other options, a small group turned to political violence. They rented a house next to the parliament building, and broke down the cellar wall separating the two structures. **Robert Catesby**, and his fellow-conspirators, including **Guy Fawkes**, then rolled some 20 barrels of gunpowder into the cellar, and they hoped to blow up the building during the opening ceremonies, thus destroying in one blow both Houses and the royal family.

Aiming, as the Attorney-General, **Sir Edward Coke**, put it in his opening statement at the conspirators' trial, at "the destruction and dissolution of the frame and fabric of this ancient, famous and ever-flourishing monarchy, even the deletion of our whole name and nation,"[23] the **Gunpowder Plot** went beyond all precedent. **James** himself recognized that while monarchs had been murdered before, "the ruin of a whole kingdom along with the King and his offspring, that truly was without parallel."[24] While today we might call this deed an act of "terrorism," early modern culture had no such term, and they grappled with the problem of what to call the **Gunpowder Plot**. **Coke** himself admitted that "this treason doth want an apt name,"[25] and subsequent accounts tried to capture the plot's horror by piling up superlatives. William Barlow (the same man who wrote the summary of the Hampton Court conference) called it "an inhumane cruelty, a brutish immanity [inhumanity] a devilish brutishness, and an hyperbolical, yea, an hyperdiabolical devilishness."[26]

Perhaps because of its radically unprecedented nature, the **Gunpowder Plot** did not have an obvious effect on the period's literature. Shakespeare's *Macbeth* (1606) and Ben Jonson's *Catiline* (1611) have been linked to the plot, but only indirectly. When the Porter in Shakespeare's play welcomes his imaginary visitors to Hell, he exclaims: "'Faith, here's an equivocator that could swear in both the scales against either scale, who committed treason enough for God's sake, yet could not equivocate to heaven' (2.3. 7–11). It's likely that these lines allude to the Jesuit leader, **Henry Garnett** (1555–1606), who knew about the Gunpowder Plot through the confession of one of the participants but failed to inform the government, and who defended equivocation at his trial. The young **John Milton** wrote several poems about the plot, including "In Quintum Novembris" (written 1626, published in the 1645 *Poems*).[27]

Fortunately for the government, the plot was discovered in time (**Fawkes** was caught in the basement with the gunpowder, and he gave up the names of the other conspirators after torture). Immediately afterward, there was much thanking of God for providentially saving England, and certainly, the **Gunpowder Plot** deeply unsettled James (the Venetian ambassador reported that "the King is in terror. He does not appear nor does he take his meals in public as usual. He lives in the innermost rooms with only Scotsmen about him"[28]), yet the **Gunpowder Plot** did not have much of a long-term effect beyond forcing Catholics to sign the Oath of Allegiance and the establishment of November 5 as a national day of thanksgiving (and now Guy Fawkes Day). Furthermore, **James** acted to limit the fallout. He did not embark on an inquisition against Catholics, and in fact, he tried to divert attention away from the divisive issue of Catholicism. The king announced in parliament that while "it appeared that religion was the cause of the conspiracy, yet in reality it had another object" (all of the participants, James said, were "of broken estate, which they hoped to better under the cloak of conscience"), and the peace with Spain remained in place.[29]

Indeed, throughout his reign, **King James** pursued the via media ("the middle way") in religious matters. One of his favorite theologians was **Richard Hooker** (b. 1554) whose work, *Of the Laws of Ecclesiastical Polity* (1593, 1597) masterfully defends the compromises of the Elizabethan Settlement, and he asked to meet him when he arrived in London in 1603, only to be informed that Hooker had died in 1600. Throughout his reign, **James** consistently resisted calls for more vigorous persecution of the Catholic minority. For example, in 1620, he denied a petition from the viciously anti-Spanish, anti-Catholic House of Commons banning recusants from London when parliament is in session on the grounds that "he would not be an example of such severity to other princes," arguing that such an act would only set a precedent for the persecution of their fellow religionists abroad: "the French king might also take the same course, to banish all the Protestant from Paris, etc." When a member complained at the same session that he hears "never a word spoken against the puritans, or so much as a mousetrap proposed for them," he was literally thrown out of the chamber.[30]

While King James preferred to spend his time hunting, **Queen Anna's** household became a something of a counter-court, especially as a center for literary men and artists. She patronized such poets, playwrights, artists, and musicians as **Samuel Daniel**, **John Donne**, **Ben Jonson**, **Inigo Jones**, and **John Dowland**.[31]

Royal Finances, the Union, and the Ancient Constitution

James's problems with money and the subsequent constitutional problems had a more lasting consequence. When **James** became king of England in 1603, he was faced with the perennial problem of royal supply. The monarch, we should remember, had no independent source of income, and could not (yet) impose taxes without the explicit approval of parliament. James's money problems, however, were greatly exacerbated by two factors. Unlike Elizabeth, **James** came with a wife and three children, all of whom had their own courts, and that cost money. Also unlike Elizabeth, **James** had no sense at all when it came to generosity, and he spent wildly without regard to his actual means. Consequently, **Cecil** (made **Earl of Salisbury** in 1605) sought various means to improve royal finances. In 1608, he decided to increase revenues by "farming out" its collection, meaning, the right to collect customs revenues was sold to the highest bidder, who then gave the government a lump sum and pocketed the rest as profit. In 1611, **Salisbury** started selling honors and titles, which may have been economically prudent, but diluted the cultural capital inherent in elevation to the peerage. Selling titles turned a matter of honor into a financial transaction.

The most portentous idea, however, was to add new items to the customs rolls. This seemingly innocuous move caused a firestorm because it meant that the king created a new tax without parliamentary approval. Merchants balked at these new measures, and one of the most substantial, **John Bate**, nearly caused a riot when he refused to allow the impounding of his merchandise to pay the tax.[32] The Lord High Treasurer at the time, **Thomas Sackville, Earl of Dorset** (c. 1536–1608) was also the head of the Court of Exchequer, and **Dorset** not only arranged for his court to hear **Bate's Case** (1606), he consulted with the judges on the verdict, which articulated a new and expansive view of royal prerogative, stating that levying impositions belonged to the king's absolute, or unfettered, prerogative. While the crown won **Bate's Case**, it did so at the cost of deep and lasting resentment, and it would serve as a touchstone for absolutism's threat to England's fundamental liberties well into the 1640s.

It is ironic that **Sackville** would become such an enthusiastic supporter of royal prerogative because in his earlier years, when he had a literary bent, his works were much more skeptical of unfettered monarchic power. He contributed with Thomas Norton on *Gorboduc* (1561), a tragedy written and performed by the lawyers-in-training at the Inns of Court as well as the "Induction" and "The Tragedy of Buckingham" for *The Mirror for Magistrates* (1559).

In 1610, **Salisbury** proposed a **"Great Contract"** to put the king's finances on a more stable footing (James would give up certain feudal dues in return for a permanent revenue), but the deal fell apart because of the wrangling over impositions and James's insistence, as he told parliament in his infamous Whitehall speech, that "The state of monarchy is the supremest thing upon earth," and "Kings are justly called gods."[33] James warned his listeners that it is "sedition in subjects to dispute what a king may do in the height of his power,"[34] but they kept on disputing. One member proposed that the judgment in **Bate's Case** contradicted "the Decalogue [the Ten Commandments], which is that subjects as well as kings should enjoy their own."[35] Another warned the House that if the Commons allowed the king to tax in this manner, "the ancient frame of the commonwealth [would be] much altered," because this decision challenged the key elements of the Ancient Constitution:

> One is that we are masters of our own and can have nothing taken from us without consents; another that laws cannot be made without our consents, and the edict of a prince is not a law; the third is that the parliament is the storehouse of our liberties. All these are in danger to be lost by this power …. We know not how this may stretch.[36]

Bate's Case was the first of several court cases over the course of the Stuart era affirming an expansive view of royal prerogative, but with every legal victory came a nearly equal increase in anger and alienation. The question of royal finances had been transformed into a battle over the relative powers of the monarch and parliament, which was really a battle over the nature of England itself.

For his part, James was intensely frustrated by the resistance to his first great project, **the union of England and Scotland into one nation.** While he regularly described the great advantages of combining the two nations, the House of Commons refused to embrace the proposals, fearing, they said, that changing the nation's name from "England" to "Great Britain" would mean erasing all the laws. Rather than spending their time enacting his will, the 1604 parliament occupied itself with an election dispute that James made worse by telling the Commons that he would resolve the dispute on his own, without their participation. The king's proposal did not go over well, and the Commons responded with a document (never delivered) called *The Form of Apology and Satisfaction*, in which they told James that he had been misinformed, that "our privileges and liberties are our right and due inheritance, no less than our very lands and goods."[37] This would not be the only time James received instruction. After attempting to usurp judicial authority by deciding a case by himself, rather than "in some court of justice," **Edward Coke** told **James** (according to his report) that "no man shall be put to answer without presentment before the justices, matter of record, or by due process ..., according to the ancient law of the land," and what is more, "his Majesty was not learned in the laws of his realm of England."[38] The King, **Coke** continues, "was greatly offended, and said, that then he should be under the law, which was treason to affirm. To which [Coke] said, that Bracton saith, [The king ought not be under any man, but under God and the law]."[39] This fundamental conflict led to a series of failed parliaments (1604, 1610, 1614 [called **"the Addled Parliament"** because it enacted nothing], and 1621), in which the monarchy's attempt to raise money foundered on the question of royal prerogative versus the Ancient Constitution.

Disillusionment, Court Favorites, and the Death of Prince Henry

This slow-motion constitutional crisis should not be considered an abstruse event, of concern only to lawyers and members of the House of Commons. The government's victory in **Bate's Case** cost merchants a lot of money, but that was not enough to feed the king's extravagant spending habits. By 1618, the royal debt rose to approximately one million pounds, "the largest peacetime debt in English history up to that point,"[40] and many both inside and outside parliament resisted further grants, loans or "benevolences" because they thought the money would go to lining the pockets of one or another of the king's favorites rather than to a good purpose. **Thomas Wentworth**, a member of the House of Commons who furiously protested the increase in royal prerogative signaled by **Bate's Case**, asked "to what purpose is it for us to draw a silver stream out of the country into the royal cistern, if it shall daily run out thence by private [taps]."[41]

The debates over royal prerogative, James's alienation from parliament, and parliament's alienation from their monarch contributed to the general unhappiness with **James**, which set in very quickly after his accession.

On the one hand, the onset of the Stuart era seems to have ushered in a cultural efflorescence. **Shakespeare** completed many of his greatest plays, such as *King Lear* (1605) and *The Tempest* (1611), the public theater continued to thrive, **John Donne** wrote most of his verse, and translations of the Homeric epics as well as the essays of **Michel de Montaigne** and Seneca appear. Yet there is also a significant darkening of tone, as evidenced by Shakespeare's "problem plays," such as *Measure for Measure*, and the increasingly grotesque violence of such Jacobean tragedies as *The Revenger's Tragedy* (1607; published anonymously but thought to be written by Thomas Middleton) and Webster's *The White Devil* (1612), in which the court is figured as a fountain of corruption.

Indeed, **James** gave people many reasons for losing patience with him. He was, for one, obsessed with hunting, spending most of his time at his various lodges in the countryside, to the point where it severely impacted the nation's governance. "He seems to have forgotten that he is a king," reported the Venetian ambassador, "except in his kingly pursuit of stags, to which he is quite foolishly devoted."[42] James's active dislike of courting the people also created significant tensions. In 1607, the Venetian ambassador repeated Thomas Wilson's observation that the king "does not caress the people nor make them that good cheer the late Queen did, whereby she won their loves," but unlike in 1603, mutual dislike had started to set in:

"[the English] like their King to show pleasure at their devotion, as the late Queen knew well how to do, but this King manifests no taste for them, but rather contempt and dislike. The result is he is despised and almost hated."[43] The behavior of James's court inspired disgust rather than awe. For example, **Sir John Harington** reported on a masque performed before the King of Denmark (Anna's brother) that degenerated into a sodden fiasco:

The **"masque"** is an early modern art form combining spectacle, learned iconography, elaborate scenery, music, poetry, and dance that quite literally centered on the monarch. Ostensibly, masques were used to project "the triumph of an aristocratic community" (the anecdote below suggests that the performances might not have always succeeded) through allegorical representations.[45] While the two would quarrel over the primacy of words or images, the partnership of **Ben Jonson** (1572–1637) and **Inigo Jones** (1573–1652), also a prominent architect, produced the most famous masques of the period.

[The woman playing the Queen of Sheba fell,] spilling wine, cream, jelly, beverage, cakes, spices and other good matters [all over the king of Denmark]. The entertainment and show went forward, and most of the presenters went backward, or fell down, wine did so occupy their upper chambers. Now did appear, in rich dress, Hope, Faith, and Charity. Hope did assay [try] to speak but wine rendered her endeavors so feeble that she withdrew, and hoped the King would excuse her brevity. Faith was then all alone, for I am certain she was not joined with good works, and left the court in a staggering condition. Charity came to the King's feet, and seemed to cover the multitude of sins of her sisters had committed. In some sort she made obeisance and brought gifts, but said she would return home again, as there was no gift which heaven had not already given his Majesty. She then returned to Hope and Faith, who were both sick and spewing in the lower hall. ... I ne'er did see such lack of good order, discretion, and sobriety as I have now done.... I wish I was at home.[44]

The King's notorious privileging of favorites also detracted from the court's reputation. James had a record of lavishing attention on young men, but he had not allowed them to become politically important. **Robert Carr** (c. 1585–1645) would be different. A young Scot, **Carr** came to James's attention in 1607 after he broke his leg at a tilt celebrating the king's accession, and the king's infatuation was quickly noted: "The Prince leaneth on his arm, pinches his cheek, smoothes his ruffled garment," a court observer informed **Sir John Harington**.[46] (Carr's fashion sense apparently determined who would have access to James: "The King is nicely heedful of such points, and dwelleth on good looks and handsome accoutrements. Eighteen servants were lately discharged and many more will be discarded who are not to his liking in these [sartorial] matters…. [Carr] hath changed his tailors and tiremen [attire men, or tailors] many times, and all to please the Prince, who laugheth at the long grown fashion of our young courtiers, and wisheth for change every day."[47]) James quickly elevated Carr to the peerage, adding him the Privy Council in 1612 and making him **Earl of Somerset** in 1613. Carr's ambitions led him to get involved in one of the seamier sex scandals of the age: the **Overbury** affair.

Somerset decided to marry his mistress, **Lady Frances Howard**, who inconveniently was already married to **Robert Devereaux, Earl of Essex** (son of Elizabeth's favorite who was later executed for treason; **Essex** would later lead the Parliamentary army against Charles I). The two were granted a divorce after a trial in which **Essex** admitted that despite her obvious charms, he could not perform with her: "he hath found an ability of body to know any other woman, and hath oftentimes felt motions and provocations of the flesh … but that he hath lain by the lady Frances two or three years last past, and hath no motion to know her, and he believes never shall."[48] Making matters even more complicated, **Somerset's** friend, **Sir Thomas Overbury**, objected to the match, and he threatened to reveal damaging information. **Overbury** found himself locked up in the Tower, where he promptly died, freeing **Somerset** and **Howard** to marry in 1613. However, it came out that **Howard** had **Overbury** murdered by a poisoned enema, and the couple were tried (Essex returned to London to observe the trial) and found guilty in 1616. Despite their death sentences, they would remain in the Tower until 1622, when James pardoned them.

> **Somerset** also developed a significant art collection that demonstrated almost avant-garde tastes, and he patronized such literary figures as **George Chapman** and **William Davenant**. After his pardon, **Somerset** was forbidden to attend court or parliament. His experiences seems to have chastened him, and possibly altered his politics: Somerset "initially refused to pay the controversial forced loan of 1626 [see the next chapter], and in 1630 he was among a group of Robert Cotton's friends arrested for circulating a treatise on arbitrary rule that was taken to be a critique of **Charles I's** political ambitions …. [While there] is little evidence of Somerset's response to the political crisis of the late 1630s and early 1640, [he did not] side with the king during the civil war, and appears to have remained instead in the parliamentarian stronghold of London.[49] **Somerset's** final portrait depicts him dressed soberly in a black shirt with a white ruff, the opposite of the gay courtier he once was. He seems to wear the forced smile of someone who has little to smile about.

By the time of his fall, **Somerset** had already been eclipsed by **George Villiers, Duke of Buckingham** (1592–1628). **Somerset's** enemies, who wanted to distract the king with a new face, put Villiers forward and the ploy succeeded brilliantly. In short order, **Villiers** rose to gentleman of the Bedchamber in 1615, master of the Horse and knight of the Garter in 1616, Earl of Buckingham in 1617, Marquess of the same in 1618, Admiral of England in 1622, and finally, **Duke of Buckingham** in 1623. **Buckingham** made himself fabulously wealthy in the process, and he ensured his political longevity (until an assassin's blade put an end to him) by befriending the heir apparent, **Charles**, who reciprocated even though the man was also his father's lover. Yet **Buckingham**, like **Cardinal Thomas Wolsey** a century earlier, combined rapaciousness with a genuine desire to improve the commonwealth. He used his position as master of the Horse to import superior Continental horses to crossbreed with domestic stock, and as Lord Admiral he "encouraged the appointment of an investigative commission into the state of the navy."[50] He brought in **Sir Francis Bacon** (1561–1626) to tutor him on politics, and the very wealthy London merchant, **Lionel Cranfield** (1575–1645; made Earl of Middlesex in 1622), to teach him economics. Yet like **Wolsey**, the good **Buckingham** did was eclipsed by his reputation as the center of all corruption and vice, a reputation both created and shaped by "the escalating numbers of verse libels that, by the mid- and later-1620s, increasingly came to focus on the favourite's sins as an explanation for the troubles of the age."[51]

The event, however, that crystallized the sense of decline and cast a pall for years afterward was **Prince Henry's** death, probably of typhoid fever, in 1612. From the start, **Henry** seemed to be the opposite of his father. Inclined to martial affairs whereas **James** thought of himself as a peacemaker and showed no skill in military arts, **Henry** did not much like studying, whereas **James** was intellectual to the point of pedantry. Furthermore, **Henry** overtly disapproved of his father's policies, and his dislike was not kept private. In 1607, when Henry was 13, the Venetian ambassador reported that James chastised his son for his indifference to his lessons, and he warned that if Henry did not buckle down to his books, James might leave the throne to his younger brother, Charles. Henry, out of respect for his father, kept quiet, but when his tutor continued in the same vein, he replied, "I know what becomes a Prince. It is not necessary for me to be a professor, but a soldier and a man of the world. If my brother is as learned as they say, we'll make him Archbishop of Canterbury."[52] In 1610, **Henry** was installed as Prince of Wales, but more than that, Henry set up his own court that was designed as a barely disguised rebuke of his father's. **Henry** commissioned the team of **Jonson** and **Jones** to create an Arthurian masque for his political coming of age which depicted **Henry** as reviving the lapsed spirit of English chivalry: "bring forth thy knight," says the Lady of the Lake, "Preservèd for his times, that by the might / And magic of his arm he may restore/ These ruined seats of virtue, and build more."[53] Early in 1612, however, Henry started to fall ill, and he died on November 6, 1612. While the death of any teenager is sad, many thought that Henry's premature demise symbolized England's decline. The late prince "came to stand for a glory that England had lost," and after Henry's death, far more elegies and lamentations were written for him than for Elizabeth.[54] A letter written by the Earl of Dorset sums up the widespread sense of national eclipse: indifferent to the good health of both **James** and Henry's siblings, **Charles** and **Elizabeth**, Dorset writes that "our rising sun is set ere scarce he had shone, and ... all our glory lies buried."[55]

Foreign Policy, 1603–23: Ireland and the Continent

In his first speech to parliament in 1604, **James** announced the first of the blessings he has brought is "out peace, that is, peace abroad with all foreign neighbors."[56] When he first arrived, he found England "embarked in a great and tedious war," and now, "only by mine arrival here, and by the peace in my person, is now amity kept."[57] **James** understood something that the more ideologically driven hawks in England did not – that war is bad for business: "for by peace abroad with their neighbors the towns flourish, the merchants become rich, the trade doth increase, and the people of all sorts of the land enjoy free liberty to exercise themselves in their several vocations without peril or disturbance."[58] And this principle guided James's foreign policy throughout nearly the entirety of his English reign, much to the frustration of those who wanted war against Spain and Catholicism. Even so, resisting the siren call for war on the Continent and acting as both moderator and chief negotiator was central to James's self-conception. As the Spanish ambassador, Count Gondomar, Diego Sarmiento de Acuña (1567–1626) observed (not altogether positively) in 1618, "The vanity of the present King of England is so great that he will always think it of great importance that peace should be made by his means, so that his authority will be increased."[59]

Ireland

As noted above, the first fruit of James's irenic approach to foreign policy was the **Treaty of London**, which halted the war between Spain and England. The cessation of hostilities also had a major effect on the situation between **Ireland** and England. While the Irish rebels surrendered to Elizabeth in 1603, their leader, **Hugh O'Neill, Earl of Tyrone**, had not completely given up. He realized in 1607 that with the end of Spanish military support, his cause had no hope, and so he left for poverty and exile on the Continent (he ended his days in Rome), thus ending Irish resistance to English colonialism for the time being. **James**, however, had further plans for Ireland. Even though the king showed little interest in the New World (more on this below), he actively promoted the plantation of Ulster (in the north of Ireland). With very little to no resistance, native Irish inhabitants were ejected, and Scots and English immigrants settled in their place. While this scheme would eventually come back to haunt England with the rebellion of 1641, "until then the plantation went on apace peacefully, and was one of the most successful colonization schemes of the reign of James I."[60]

The Continent

Unlike **Henry VIII** and **Elizabeth I**, who with greater and lesser degrees of enthusiasm, involved themselves and England in military conflicts on the European continent, James did his best to keep England out of it, preferring to act as Europe's peacemaker. This proved to be an exceptionally wise strategy, as the conflict known as the **Thirty Years War**, an especially vicious war fought mainly in central Europe between the various Protestant and Catholic powers, would start in 1618. In addition to trying to act as a mediator, James's favored approach for creating and maintaining peace was the diplomatic marriage. First, against both public opinion and the Prince's own inclinations, James pushed for a match between **Henry** and a Spanish princess. Obviously, Henry's premature death put an end to that project. Next, James arranged for his daughter, **Elizabeth**, to marry the Protestant **Frederick V**, Count Palatine of the Rhine and an Elector of the Holy

Roman Empire (1596–1632), a match that would have far-reaching consequences. In 1618, Protestant rebels in Bohemia deposed the Catholic Holy Roman Emperor as their king, and then offered the Protestant Frederick their crown. Much to everyone's surprise, he accepted. James was furious because his son-in-law had just endorsed rebellion against a monarch, an act that according to James, was not ever, under any circumstances, justified: "What hath religion to do to decrown a king? [...] For may subjects rebel against their prince in quarrel of religion? Christ came into the world to teach subjects obedience to the king, and not rebellion!"[61] The Spanish and the Holy Roman Emperor were furious because this act upset the delicate balance in Europe. Rather than waiting for negotiations, Ferdinand fought back, not only regaining the Bohemian throne, but also throwing Frederick out of the Rhine. Elizabeth and Frederick spent the rest of their lives as exiles.

Elizabeth and **Frederick**, despite their dire circumstances, enjoyed a happy, fruitful marriage (13 children) until Frederick's death in 1632. **Elizabeth** lived until 1662, and so witnessed her brother's execution and the restoration of **Charles II**, her nephew. After living in great poverty in the Netherlands, she returned to England in 1661. Her youngest daughter, Sophia, would marry Ernst August, who would become the first elector of **Hanover**. In 1714, their eldest son would become **King George I**, who would finally bring about the union of England and Scotland in 1701.

James came under tremendous pressure to join the Protestant powers against the Catholic League, which he continued to resist. His refusal to commit England stemmed partly from good sense (fielding an army to fight a battle so far away would have been hideously expensive and difficult), and partly from his own growing lack of interest in foreign policy. The Venetian ambassador noted in 1620 that James "seemed utterly weary of the affairs that are taking place all over the world at this time," and when reminded that the Spanish army was marching toward the Palatinate, he snapped,

"What do you know? You are ignorant. I know quite well what I am about. All these troubles will settle themselves. You will see that very soon. I know what I am talking about."[62]

Even so, **James** called a parliament in 1621 to deal with the European crisis, and at first, everything went well. Far from averse to voting money to subsidize a military venture supporting Protestantism, the Commons approved two subsidies even though England was suffering from a severe economic depression. **James** and **Buckingham** actually had to restrain the desire for a full-scale war against Spain (partly because James still wanted to purse a marriage between **Charles** and Philip IV's daughter, the Spanish infanta; see pg. 171). The Commons, however, added conditions for their support. First, many wanted to abolish monopolies, which they believed restricted trade because James awarded them to unscrupulous people who used them to reward themselves. **Sir Edward Coke** asserted that there were two thousand monopolies, that their yearly income amounted to £400,000, but the government netted only £400, and that many monopolies "were in the hands of base fellows, and the rest of them bestowed upon such as had never deserved anything, either of the king or kingdom."[63] James conceded some of their demands, including the impeachment and removal of **Sir Francis Bacon**, ostensibly for judicial corruption. But then, the Commons added further conditions that led to a breakdown. First, a member added a stipulation to the motion urging war that **Charles** should marry a Protestant. That was too much for **James** (and **Charles**), who responded that the Commons had no right to debate foreign policy or the Prince's marriage; the Commons responded with a protestation declaring that "the liberties franchises, privileges, and jurisdictions of Parliament are the ancient and undoubted birthright and inheritance of the subjects of England," and as for trying to restrict the scope of allowed topics, that every member of the Houses of Parliament has "freedom of speech to propound, treat, reason, and bring to conclusion" anything concerning "the arduous and urgent affairs concerning the King, State, and defence of the realm and of the Church of England …."[64] **James**, furious, dissolved parliament (thus losing the subsidies already approved), and he personally ripped the protest out of the Commons Journal.

The years 1622–23 witnessed one of the stranger events in English history. Frustrated with the snail's pace of negotiations with Spain, **Charles** and **Buckingham** decided to take matters into their own hands, and they travelled (in disguise, complete with false beards that had a habit of falling off inopportunely) to the Spanish court in Madrid to pursue the courtship in person. After a year of temporizing, the two returned empty-handed, but to great celebrations precisely *because* the negotiations had failed. (Indeed, it was possibly the only time crowds cheered **Charles** and **Buckingham**.)

> Thomas Middleton's drama, *A Game at Chess* (1624) depicts how the White Duke (Buckingham) and the White Knight (Charles) outwit the Black Knight, or Gondomar, the former Spanish ambassador and representative of the "gins, traps and alluring snares" (4.4.5) of Spain.

Their amorous failure turned their thoughts from love to war. Whatever reservations they may have harbored against open hostilities against Spain disappeared, and the increasingly fragile **King James** no longer had the power to restrain them. James called his last parliament in 1624 specifically to deal with funding the war, and it would prove much more successful than the debacle of 1621 (although **Buckingham** and **Charles** orchestrated **Cranfield's** impeachment because of his opposition to resuming war against Spain on the grounds that England could not afford it).[65] Yet the constitutional tensions remained and would only get worse in years to come.

> The letters **James** wrote to his son and **Buckingham** during their Spanish sojourn reveal a very different, much more sympathetic side to the king's personality. He constantly refers to both as his "babies" and prays for "a comfortable and happy return to their sweet and dear dad."[66]

James did not have much longer on this earth. He fell ill in March 1625, and in short order suffered a stroke, which loosened his face muscles. His tongue "was swollen so big in his mouth that either he could not speak at all, or not be understood," and adding to his woes, he contracted dysentery, suffering "in filth and misery."[67] Perhaps mercifully, **King James VI/I** died on March 28, 1625.

New Thinking, New Worlds, New Continents

The world changed during the reign of King James. First, the foundations for what we call today "science" were laid during this period. To be sure, not everything occurred in the seventeenth century. **Nicolaeus Copernicus** proved that the earth revolved around the sun, not the other way around, in the mid-sixteenth century (he published *On the Revolution of the Heavenly Spheres* in 1543), and **Andreaus Vesalius** published his textbook on human anatomy that same year. But the invention of the telescope and **Galileo's** subsequent descriptions of sunspots and mountains on the moon pretty much shattered the old conception of a universe made up of immutable spheres. For some, this shifting paradigm of the universe itself did not much matter. **John Milton**, for example, refuses to choose between the Copernican and the Ptolemaic universes in *Paradise Lost* (4.592–7), but for others, the shifts represented by Copernicus and Galileo's telescope and his description of the moon had a jarring effect, such as **John Donne**, who famously wrote: "And new philosophy calls all in doubt, / The element of fire is quite put out, / The sun is lost, and th'earth, / And no man's wit / Can well direct him where to look for it."[68] The major figure for this development in England is **Sir Francis Bacon**, whom we have already met as a politician and lawyer. **Bacon's** great project, as elaborated in *The Advancement of Learning* (1605) and the *Novum Organum* (The New Organon; 1620), aimed at re-organizing all of human knowledge away from reliance on book authorities and toward direct observation of nature and experimentation.

While **King James** is reported to have said that **Bacon's** "last book" (probably *The Great Instauration*) resembles "the peace of God, which passeth all understanding,"[69] the king wrote a letter to the author suggesting a much more appreciative and insightful response: "I can, with comfort, assure you that ye could not have made choice of a subject more befitting your place and your universal methodic knowledge."[70]

Second, England's physical horizons expanded along with its intellectual and cultural ones, laying the foundations for both the English empire and the United States of America. While religion motivated some of those who moved from England to the New World, the primary impetus was economic expansion and the necessity of finding new markets. The wool trade, long England's staple export commodity, went into a severe decline exacerbated by the closings of the port in Antwerp due to various wars. In addition, English merchants had certainly noted the stream of goods and profits emanating from Asia, Africa, and the New World. To make up for lost revenues and to take advantage of these opportunities, the crown started granting charters to find new markets. The first successful attempt to found a colony occurred in 1607, when Sir Thomas Smith established **Jamestown** in present-day Virginia. Over the next forty years, the English expansion focused on three areas:

Virginia, with the Bermuda islands from 1615 and Maryland from 1633, became the centre of the tobacco colonies of mainland America; Barbados, St. Christopher, Nevis, and Antigua in the Lesser Antilles in the Caribbean from the late 1620s, after a false start as tobacco islands, developed sugar-based economies; and thirdly, the colonies of New England (Plymouth 1621, Massachusetts 1629, and its offshoots) emerged as farming, fishing, and trading communities.[71]

Famously, the American colonies offered a refuge from religious persecution by the Church of England. The group who embarked from Leiden on the *Mayflower* in 1620 consisted of radical Protestants, and as a balance, Maryland became a refuge for Roman Catholics.

> Usually, but mistakenly, the Mayflower's passengers are called "Puritans." More accurately, they are **separatists**, or **Brownists**, followers of the radical firebrand, **Robert Browne** (1550?–1633), people who wanted to separate from the Church of England because they believed it did not go far enough in purging Roman Catholic doctrine and practices.

The overall context, however, for English emigration to the colonies was trade, and the goal of the colonies, whatever their religious affiliation, was to fill England's coffers.[72] Indeed, by 1620, the situation had become so desperate that at the start of the 1620 parliament, an observer noted that while the Commons wanted to supply "the king's wants …, the difficulty will be how and where these supplies should be raised, for it is most certain that England was never generally so poor since I was born as it is at this present."[73]

Notes

1   See *Royal Subjects: Essays on the Writings of James VI and I*, ed. Daniel Fischlin and Mark Fortier (Detroit: Wayne State University Press, 2002).

2   Quoted in Alan Stewart, *The Cradle King: The Life of James VI & I, The First Monarch of a United Great Britain* (New York: St. Martin's Press, 2003), 171.

3   "Thomas Wilson to Sir Thomas Parry, at Paris," *Original Letters Illustrative of English History*, ed. Henry Ellis (London: Harding and Leopard, 1827), vol. 3, 201.

4   [Sir Anthony Weldon], *A Description of Scotland*, 4th ed. (London, 1626), sig. A2.

5   "Thomas Wilson to Sir Thomas Parry," 201.

6   Quoted in David Harris Willson, *King James VI and I* (London: Jonathan Cape, 1956), 165.

7   Anthony Weldon, *The Court and Character of King James* (London, 1650), sig. N2v.

8   Weldon, *The Court and Character of King James*, sig. N2v-r.

9   Weldon, *The Court and Character of King James*, sig. N2v.

10 Homosexuality meant something very different in the early modern period than today. The best introduction to the subject remains Alan Bray, *Homosexuality in Renaissance England* (London: Gay Men's Press, 1982; rpt. New York: Columbia University Press, 1995).

11 *The Progresses, Processions, and Magnificent Festivities of King James the First*, ed. John Nichols (rpt. New York: Burt Franklin, 1966). See also Adam Nicolson, *God's Secretaries: The Making of the King James Bible* (New York: HarperCollins, 2003), 14–15. I am grateful to Adam Nicolson for directing me to the source of this anecdote.

12 *Progresses*, vol. 1, 89.

13 *Progresses*, vol. 1, 48.

14 For two excellent surveys, see Glenn Burgess, "On Revisionism: An Analysis of Early Stuart Historiography in the 1970s and 1970s," *The Historical Journal* 33.3 (1990): 609–27, and Kevin Sharpe, "Remapping Early Modern England: From Revisionism to the Culture of Politics," *Remapping Early Modern England: The Culture of Seventeenth-Century Politics* (Cambridge: Cambridge University Press, 2000), 3–37.

15 *Constitutional Documents of the Reign of James I*, ed. J. R. Tanner (Cambridge: Cambridge University Press, 1930), 25.

16 Pauline Croft, *King James* (New York: Palgrave, 2003), 52–3.

17 *Constitutional Documents*, 28, 29.

18 William Barlow, *The Sum and Substance of the Conference ... at Hampton Court, January 14, 1603* (London, 1604), sig. F3r, F3v.

19 Barlow, *The Sum and Substance*, sig. G3r.

20 Barlow, *The Sum and Substance*, G4v. On the creation of the King James Bible, see Adam Nicolson's excellent *God's Secretaries: The Making of the King James Bible* (New York: HarperCollins, 2003).

21 See Chapter 3, pp. 73 for a brief history of translating the Bible into English.

22 *The Gunpowder Plot: The Narrative of Oswald Tesimond alias Greenway*, ed. and trans. Francis Edwards (London: Folio Society, 1973), 25.

23 *A True and Perfect Relation of the whole Proceedings against the Last Most Barbarous traitors, Garnet a Jesuit, and His Confederates* (London, 1606), sig. D4v.

24 *Calendar of State Papers and Manuscripts, relating to English Affairs, Existing in the Archives and Collections of Venice*, ed. Horatio F. Brown (London: HMSO, 1900), vol. 10, 513 (hereafter referred to as *CSPV*).

25 *CSPV*, sig. D4v.

26 William Barlow, *The Sermon Preached at Paul's Cross, the Tenth Day of November, Being the Next Sunday After the Discovery of this Horrible Treason* (London, 1606), sig. C3v.

27 The best treatment of this topic is Robert Appelbaum, "Milton, the Gunpowder Plot, and the Mythography of Terror," *Modern Language Quarterly* 68.4 (2007): 461–91. See also Gary Wills, *Witches and Jesuits: Shakespeare's "Macbeth"* (New York: Oxford University Press, 1995). "In Quintum Novembris" (On the fifth of November) can be found in *The Complete Poetry and Essential Prose of John Milton*, ed. William Kerrigan, John Rumrich and Stephen M. Fallon (New York: Modern Library, 2007), 205–13.

28 *CSPV*, vol. 10, 293; see also Stewart, *The Cradle King*, 223.

29 *CSPV*, vol. 10, 294.

30 Reverend Joseph Meade to Sir Martin Stuteville, February 25, 1620, *Court and Times of James the First*, ed. Thomas Birch (London: Colburn, 1849), vol. 2, 230.

31 See Leeds Barroll, *Anna of Denmark, Queen of England: A Cultural Biography* (Philadelphia: University of Pennsylvania Press, 2001).

32 For a full explication of the complexities surround this event, see Pauline Croft, "Fresh Light on Bate's Case," *The Historical Journal* 30.3 (1987): 523–39.

33 "A Speech to the Lords and Commons of the Parliament at Whitehall on Wednesday the 21 of March, anno 1609," *King James VI and I: Political Writings*, ed. Johann P. Sommerville (Cambridge: Cambridge University Press, 1994), 181.

34 "A Speech," 184.

35 *Parliamentary Debates in 1610*, ed. Samuel R. Gardiner (London: Camden Society, 1862), 61.

36 *Proceedings in Parliament 1610*, ed. Elizabeth Read Foster (New Haven: Yale University Press, 1966), vol. 2, 109.

37 *Constitutional Documents*, 221.

38 *The Selected Writings of Sir Edward Coke*, ed. Steve Sheppard (Indianapolis: Liberty Fund, 2003), vol. 1, 481.
39 *Selected Writings*, 481. The Bracton quote is in Latin, and I have substituted the editor's translation.
40 Robert Bucholz and Newton Key, *Early Modern England 1485–1714: A Narrative History* (Oxford: Blackwell, 2004), 212.
41 Quoted in D. L. Smith, *The Stuart Parliaments 1603–1689* (London: Arnold, 1989), 108.
42 Quoted in Willson, *King James VI and I*, 179–80.
43 *CSPV*, vol. 10, 513.
44 Sir John Harington, *Nugae Antiquae*, vol. 1, 351–52, 353.
45 Stephen Orgel, *The Illusion of Power: Political Theater in the English Renaissance* (Berkeley: University of California Press, 1975), 40.
46 *Nugae Antiquae*, vol. 1, 392.
47 *Nugae Antiquae*, vol. 1, 392.
48 Quoted in John Morrill, 'Devereux, Robert, third earl of Essex (1591–1646)', *Oxford Dictionary of National Biography*, Oxford University Press, September 2004; online edn., January 2008. http://www.oxforddnb.com/view/article/7566, accessed June 2, 2010.
49 Alastair Bellany, "Carr, Robert, earl of Somerset (1585/6?–1645)," *Oxford Dictionary of National Biography*, Oxford University Press, September 2004; online edn., January 2008. http://www.oxforddnb.com/view/article/4754, accessed June 1, 2010. See also A. R. Braunmuller, "Robert Carr, earl of Somerset, as Collector and Patron," *The Mental World of the Jacobean Court*, ed. Linda Levy Peck (Cambridge: Cambridge University Press, 1991), 230–50.
50 Mark Kishlansky, *A Monarchy Transformed: Britain 1603–1714* (London: Penguin Books, 1996), 96.
51 Alastair Bellany and Andrew McRae, "King and Favorite: James, Buckingham, and the Villiers Clan", *Early Stuart Libels: An Edition of Poetry from Manuscript Sources*, ed. Bellany and McRae. *Early Modern Literary Studies* Text Series I (2005). http://www.purl.oclc.org/emls/texts/libels/.
52 *CSPV*, vol. 10, 513. See also Stewart, *The Cradle King*, 217.
53 Ben Jonson, "Prince Henry's Barriers," *The Complete Masques*, ed. Stephen Orgel (New Haven: Yale University Press, 1969), lines 83–6.
54 Roy Strong, *Henry, Prince of Wales and England's Lost Renaissance* (London: Thames and Hudson, 1986), 221.

55 Strong, *Henry, Prince of Wales*, 221.
56 *King James VI and I: Political Writings*, 133.
57 *King James VI and I: Political Writings*, 133.
58 *King James VI and I: Political Writings*, 134.
59 Quoted in Stewart, *The Cradle King*, 298.
60 Barry Coward, *The Stuart Age: England 1603–1714*, 3rd ed. (London: Pearson, 2003), 127.
61 Quoted in Stewart, *The Cradle King*, 302.
62 Stewart, *The Cradle King*, 306.
63 Reverend Joseph Meade to Sir Martin Stuteville, March 3, 1620, *Court and Times*, vol. 2, 234.
64 *Constitutional Documents*, 288–9.
65 David L. Smith, *The Stuart Parliaments: 1603–1689* (Oxford: Oxford University Press, 1999), 111.
66 Letter of 10 April 1623, *Letters of King James VI&I*, ed. G. P. V. Akrigg (Berkeley: University of California Press, 1984), 407.
67 Quoted in Stewart, *The Cradle King*, 345.
68 John Donne, *The First Anniversarie: An Anatomie of the World* (London, 1621), sig. B8v.
69 John Chamberlain to Sir Dudley Carleton, February 3, 1620, *Court and Times*, vol. 2, 219.
70 Letter of 16 October 1620, *Letters of King James VI/I*, 375.
71 Coward, *The Stuart Age*, 25.
72 For an excellent, accessible exploration of who sailed on the *Mayflower* and why, see Nick Bunker, *Making Haste from Babylon: The "Mayflower" Pilgrims and Their World* (New York: Alfred A. Knopf, 2010).
73 John Chamberlain to Sir Dudley Carleton, February 10, 1620, *Court and Times*, vol. 2, 221.

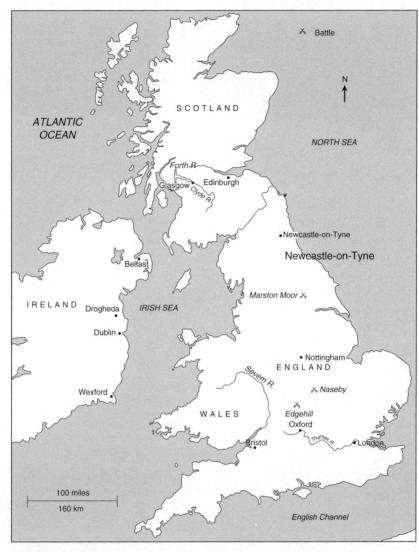

Map 7.1 Major Places and Battles of the Civil Wars.

7

Charles I (1625–42): From Accession to the Beginning of the Civil Wars

On the one hand, the shift from **King James** to his son, **King Charles I**, appears seamless, without any of the anxieties or sudden alterations in religion accompanying the previous monarchic transitions. Unlike his father, **Charles** was a known quantity in England, as he had started attending parliamentary sessions and participating in government in the early 1620s. Legally, **Charles I** became ruler of England, Scotland and Ireland the moment **James** died on March 28, 1625, but by that point, he was king in all but name. Indeed, the coronation ceremony in 1626 may have seemed a mere formality. The transition, however, brought about a number of important alterations. First, **Charles**, a fastidious man who loved order and hierarchy, had a very different personality than his father, and the style and culture of the court changed accordingly. Deeply impressed by the formality of the Spanish court, even before his father's funeral he sought to import that sort of conduct into England. According to the Venetian ambassador:

A Short History of Early Modern England: British Literature in Context, First Edition.
Peter C. Herman.
© 2011 Peter C. Herman. Published 2011 by Blackwell Publishing Ltd.

Figure 7.1 King Charles I after Sir Anthony Van Dyck, c. 1635–36. © National Portrait Gallery, London.

> [Th]e king observes a rule of great decorum. The nobles do not enter his apartments in confusion as heretofore, but each rank has its appointed place … The king has also drawn up rules for himself, dividing the day from his very early rising, for prayers, exercises, audiences, business, eating and sleeping. It is said that he will set apart a day for public audience and he does not wish anyone to be introduced to him unless sent for.[1]

Charles also got rid of the louche atmosphere and sleazy behavior characterizing the Jacobean court. "The face of the court," Lucy Hutchinson recalled, "was much changed in the king, for King Charles was temperate and chaste and serious, so that the fools and bawds, mimics and catamites of the former court grew out of fashion."[2] However, the political situation Charles faced in 1625 was not so easily repaired.

Charles faced the same complex mélange of money, foreign policy, and domestic pressures that his father had to negotiate. Like **Elizabeth, James** had managed to successfully balance the contrary pressures of the radical Protestants, whose anti-hierarchical views on religion spilled over into secular politics, and the Catholic minority, who may have been small and in the main but whose persecution rankled the Catholic powers on the Continent, Spain especially. Furthermore, any moves toward toleration caused howls of protest from the pulpits and the "hot" Protestants in the House of Commons, horrified that "papistry" would rear its head again in England. As we will see, Charles would be much less successful in threading this needle. Next, **Charles** had to deal with the perennial problem of royal finances. Lacking an independent source of income, the Crown relied on a variety of means to fund itself and its foreign ventures, but by the end of his father's reign, those options were no longer available. Thanks to James's wildly improvident spending and various economic depressions, both Parliament and England's merchants were unwilling to grant or lend the Stuarts any more money. Charles dealt with this problem by continuing and intensifying his father's belief in absolutism, which in his view allowed him to impose taxes without parliamentary approval, leading to a series of increasingly fractious confrontations with Parliament.

Elizabeth carefully balanced her own sense of the monarchy's privileges with accommodating **the Ancient Constitution**, which limits the power of the crown by forbidding taxation without representation, imprisonment without cause, and unjustified seizure of property, among other provisions. **James** upset that balance though speeches and books arguing that the monarchy is the "supremest thing upon earth,"[3] imposing a tax without parliamentary approval, and then engineering a judicial confirmation of the legitimacy of this procedure, with the result that many both inside and outside parliament grew alarmed by what they perceived as a growing threat to the liberties of the English subject. Yet James tempered his absolutism with a sense of political reality. He qualified his assertion that kings remain above the law by granting that kings are

183

"glad to bound themselves with the limits of their laws."[4] **Charles**, on the other hand, lacked that flexibility, and very much unlike his loquacious father, he did not jump at the chance to explain himself to Parliament or his people. At the opening of his first parliament, he said that it did not "stand with my nature to spend much time in words."[5] While the king and his Privy Council tried to shape public opinion through proclamations and sermons, **Charles** interpreted dissent as disloyalty, and disagreement as a threat to his monarchy. **Charles** was not an easy man to advise, especially since he considered advice that countered his own views as originating in a moral defect.

The foreign and domestic situations that Charles inherited in 1625, which, given his involvement since the early 1620s, he had a hand in creating, were by no means hopeless. Nobody in 1625 dreamed that his reign would end with a trial and an execution. But the problems required diplomacy, tact, and a willingness to compromise, all qualities Charles lacked. Consequently, within a few short years, he and his policies provoked many of his subjects, including some of the highest peers in the land, into seriously thinking about the limits of monarchy and what one could, or should, do if a monarch went over the line.

Marriage to a Catholic Princess

James, as we noted in Chapter 6, had little taste for involving England in a war against Spain, even though it would mean recovering the Palatine for his Protestant son-in-law, Frederick. But rather than refusing to engage at all, he temporized: taking money to support a war he never fought, perhaps never intending to fight. The failure of **Buckingham's** and **Charles's** mad venture to woo the Spanish infanta (**Philip IV's** daughter) changed the equation. Fed up with Spanish deceitfulness, they returned determined to declare war on Spain, and for a royal bride, England's diplomats turned to France, arranging a marriage with Henry IV's youngest daughter, the fifteen-year-old **Henrietta Maria** (1609–69).

> Henrietta Maria inherited her father's wit and a winning resistance to intimidation. When she first met her husband, the King of England, Charles glanced at her feet because she was "higher than report she was," apparently wondering if his bride was wearing high heels. Noticing this, Henrietta Maria quipped: "Sire, I stand upon mine own feet. I have no help by art. This high am I, and neither higher nor lower."[6]

The marriage of a Catholic princess and a Protestant king in 1625 was fraught with difficulty, and the French drove a hard bargain: the marriage treaty guaranteed that **Henrietta Maria** could continue to practice her religion, have her own chapel, and bring up their children as Catholics (a stipulation that would have immense consequences for the future of the Stuart dynasty in England). A secret annex promised to relax restrictions against English recusants, but that condition was never fulfilled (and perhaps never intended to be fulfilled). While royal marriages are always political, this match seemed especially calculated. The couple married "by proxy. There were no dashing escapades, only the cold realities of diplomacy."[7] **Charles** and **Buckingham** decided to risk the unpopularity of a Catholic–Protestant match because they needed France as an ally in their fight against Spain, and they needed the huge dowry to resupply the crown's dwindling cash reserves.

War, Supply, and the Constitution

Wars, however, cost money, and they require competence, both of which were sorely lacking on the English side. After using up all of Henrietta Maria's dowry to supply the fleet, it finally set out in October 1625 with the intent, as **Buckingham**, now the Lord Admiral, told the fleet's commander, of achieving "some notable effects to move those that have dispossessed His Majesty's dear sister [Elizabeth] of her inheritance to lose that prize."[8] The result was a debacle. The English ships missed the Spanish treasure fleet, "and the attempt to take the port of Cadiz – to relive the glories of Sir Walter Ralegh – failed."[9] Indeed, everything about this attempt failed. The troops were unprepared and poorly provisioned, the commanders inexperienced, and the planning wholly inadequate. Adding to the fiasco, the English ships lent to the French as part of the marriage treaty were used against the Protestant rebels in the port city of La Rochelle.

Bad as the results of these disasters may have been for English foreign policy (not to forget that half the sailors died, mainly due to disease), the domestic fallout was, if anything, even worse. **Buckingham** already had many enemies in the Commons. In the 1625 session (adjourned before the Cadiz expedition), one member complained that the duke's "nearness to his Majesty was too much; his greatness and exorbitance offensive; his power and practice were both doubted and disliked. In his person was contracted the cause of all [England's] miseries."[10] Due to worsening finances, **Charles** had to convene a parliament at the beginning of February 1626, but to forestall what he knew was coming, **Charles** tried to remove Buckingham's enemies by selecting some of them as sheriffs (sheriffs had to remain in their district and so could not sit in parliament). While clever, the tactic did not work, and in fact left the House of Commons less conciliatory and angrier than before because of the royal interference. Significantly, **Charles** also alienated the House of Lords by attempting to exclude two members for the same reason. The king's actions "represented a practical authoritarianism that went far beyond anything his father had done, and they reflected a much more high-handed attitude towards parliamentary privilege than James had ever displayed."[11]

Following a time-honored tradition, members of both houses blamed the king's objectionable actions on bad counsel, **Buckingham** in particular, and so, when parliament reconvened, the duke's enemies started impeachment proceedings against him. The issue of the royal favorite, however, had become a constitutional crisis. The Commons, according to one report, told the king that:

the kingdom was overburdened with grievances, all spring from one root, which named [Buckingham]; and therefore desired his majesty might inquire into and question any subject without exception. Otherwise, they had nothing to say to the subsidies or supply which his majesty demanded; for they would not give their posterity a cause to curse them for losing their privileges by restraint, which their fore-fathers left them.[12]

"Remember," the king said in response, "that parliaments are altogether in my power for the calling, sitting and continuance of them. Therefore as I find the fruits either good or evil they are for to continue or not to be."[13] Indeed, there were good reasons to fear that the king wanted to do without parliaments altogether even though he was a prince "bred up in parliaments," as a contemporary put it.[14] On May 12, 1626, Sir Dudley Carleton, a member of the Privy Council, warned the Commons their continual resistance to meeting the king's demands put at risk their existence:

I beseech you, gentlemen, move not his Majesty with trenching upon his prerogatives, lest you bring him out of love with Parliaments. In his message he hath told you that if there were not correspondency between him and you, he should be enforced to use new counsels. Now I pray you to consider what these new counsels are, and may be. I fear to declare those that I conceive. In all Christian kingdoms you that Parliaments were in use anciently, until the monarchs began to know their own strength; and, seeing the turbulent spirit of their Parliaments, at length they, by little and little, began to stand upon their prerogatives, and at last overthrew the Parliaments throughout Christendom, except here only with us.[15]

Apparently, this history lesson was also on the mind of the king: the Venetian ambassador reported home that **Charles** asked the French bishop who had previously run his queen's household about "the means used by the Kings of France to rid themselves of parliament."[16] (The ambassador also reported that he didn't think Charles could do it since one needed "plenty of money and they could not take such steps in time of need," circumstances that obviously did not apply to Charles.[17]) The Commons didn't listen, and they voted to supply the king with money only if **Buckingham** was sacked. **Charles** refused the offer and dissolved parliament in June 1626. The House of Lords sent a delegation to the King "to let him know how dangerous this abruption would be to the State, and to beseech him the parliament might sit but two days longer. [Charles] answered, *"Not a minute."*[18] Three months later, when someone mentioned parliament in the Privy Council, "the King who was present said he did abominate that name."[19] While some of the Privy Councilors thought "that the old and usual way was best; that in Kingdoms harmony was sweetest where the Prince and people tuned well together," **Charles** yearned for a new way of ruling, one that did not include parliament.[20]

> The phrase "new counsels" would resonate throughout this period and is often cited by historians. **Milton** possibly alludes to it when Satan criticizes God's sudden (and to him, inexplicable) elevation of the Son: "new laws thou seest imposed; / New laws from him who reigns, new minds may raise/ In us who serve, new counsels" (5.679–81).

The Forced Loan and the Five Knights' Case

Charles still needed money, especially since in 1626, despite marriage to a French princess, he also declared war on France for a variety of reasons, including a major trade dispute (both sides had seized merchant ships belonging to the other), and France's reneging on their promise to help England's war against Spain (in fact, Spain and France signed their own peace treaty). England was now in the highly perilous position of being at war with both major European powers. To pay for the fleet against France, Charles turned to the expedient of the **Forced Loan,** really an unauthorized tax, as Charles had no intention of paying back the money. This expedient may have temporarily resolved the monarchy's financial woes, but at a terrible cost to the trust between ruler and ruled. For example, in July 1626, "the judges sat in Westminster Hall to persuade the people to pay subsidies; but there arose a great tumultuous shout amongst them, 'A parliament! A parliament! Or else no subsidies.'"[21] Resistance to **the Forced Loan** extended well beyond London. "In Kent, the whole country denied, saying, that subsidies were matters of too high a nature for them to meddle withal."[22]

In the face of such widespread resistance, **Charles** tried a public relations blitz of his own. In early 1627, three divines, Robert Sibthorpe, Roger Manwaring, and Isaac Bargrave, gave sermons arguing that the subject's property belonged to the king, resisting the loan equaled rebellion, and that the mark of a true subject was absolute obedience. Indeed, the king took the unusual step of personally ordering the sermons by Sibthorpe and Manwaring be licensed for print (the title page of Manwaring's *Religion and Allegiance* proclaims that the sermon was printed "By his Majesty's Special Command," a key phrase, as we will see later in the chapter).[23] The attempt did not work, and there was widespread opposition to **the Forced Loan**. Theophilus Clinton, the Earl of Lincoln, (c. 1600–67) circulated a pamphlet accusing the monarchy of seeking "the overthrow of Parliament and the freedom that we now enjoy …. If it [the Forced Loan] goes forward, we make ourselves and our posterity subject to perpetual slavery."[24] The Yorkshire commissioners outright refused to collect a "loan" they considered fundamentally illegal: "having no legal power to levy the same upon the subject, we dare not presume to do it."[25]

> The most fervent opposition to the Loan in London centered on Bread Street, where **John Milton, Sr.**, father of the poet, lived (although the records indicate that he paid up).

Because **Charles** turned **the Forced Loan** into a loyalty test, he took an exceptionally hard line against those who refused to pay, including Lincoln, who spent two years in the Tower (unsurprisingly, he joined the Parliamentary army in 1642), leading to another constitutional–legal crisis: the **Five Knights' Case**. As the name implies, the case concerned five peers who were imprisoned for refusing to pay the Loan and then sued for a writ of *habeas corpus*, meaning, they demanded their right to have a judge on the King's Bench (England's Supreme Court) examine the reason for their incarceration, like the sanctity of private property, one of the pillars of the English legal system since Magna Carta. In response, Attorney-General Sir Robert Heath argued that the defendants were imprisoned "by his majesty's special commandment" (the same phrase that appears on the title page of Manwaring's sermon), meaning, they were held by **Charles's** royal prerogative of discretionary imprisonment, and therefore not subject to judicial review.[26] The judges in the case remanded the prisoners, but did not make any decision about the larger issues. As Judge Dodderidge explained to the Commons, "In this case a *remitittur* [the prisoners were returned to prison, not freed as they asked] was granted … that we might take better advisement upon the case."[27]

What happened next is almost unbelievable. Because the judges did not make a substantive ruling, only a procedural one, the decision did not confirm the king's expansive view of royal prerogative. Attorney-General Heath then tried to *change the record* so that the court's ruling would become a binding precedent, thus "settling the substantive issue of discretionary imprisonment for unknown causes permanently in favour of the Crown."[28] Needless to say, the lawyers in both Houses of Parliament were outraged, and the **Five Knights' Case** would ultimately lead to the **Petition of Right** in the 1628 parliament, but we are getting ahead of the story.

In June 1627, **Buckingham** himself led a fleet to relieve the siege at La Rochelle by taking the Isle of Rhè, an island just out La Rochelle's harbor. Hoping to erase the memory of the Cadiz fiasco, the Lord Admiral this time tried to do everything right. "He ensured that the ships were serviceable, the provisions fresh, and the soldiers stout-hearted. He spent generously from his own coffers, and omitted nothing necessary for his success."[29] **Buckingham's** efforts and personal attention didn't work, however, and the invasion

190

ended in another debacle. **Charles** had no choice now but to call another parliament, since another forced loan was out of the question, and the Crown had run out of options. Even so, before the 1628 parliament met the chances for success seemed vanishingly small. The Commons included elected members who openly worried about the dangers the Crown's view of royal prerogative posed to the subject's liberties, and some were among those imprisoned for refusing to pay the Forced Loan. **Charles** and his supporters thought that that parliament wanted to alter the fundamental rights of the monarchy. The 1628 parliament thus gathered in a confrontational mood.

At first, moderates on both sides prevailed. **Charles** was persuaded not to speak in person to the Commons, as he always aggravated the situation when he did. In his opening address to the 1628 parliament, for example, after warning both Houses of what may happen if they (in his view) neglected their duties, Charles needlessly added: "I would not have you take this as a threatening, for I scorn to threaten any but my equals ... ."[30] Instead, "his views were relayed through messages, usually drafted and delivered by Secretary [John] Coke who was far more emollient than the king in his choice of language."[31] The diplomacy succeeded, as the Commons approved a grant for five subsidies. **Charles** happily declared: "Now I see with this I shall have the affection of my people. I love parliaments. I shall rejoice to meet with my people often."[32]

But his newfound love did not last long because the Commons made the grant conditional on Charles accepting as law a statute forbidding taxation without parliamentary approval, imprisonment without trial, or billeting soldiers without consent. Charles balked, refusing to accept any statutory limitations on his prerogative. The Commons could not decide on how to proceed until **Sir Edward Coke** offered an alternative: in place of a bill, the House would offer a **Petition of Right**. This document, widely considered a landmark in England's constitutional history, reiterated the main points found in Magna Carta and Sir John Fortescue's *In Praise of English Law* while also reminding the king of the many statutes he had trampled. The fourth item, for example, states: "And in the eight and

twentieth year of the reign of King Edward III it was declared and
enacted by authority of Parliament that no man, of what estate or
condition that he be, should be put out of his land or tenement, nor
taken, nor imprisoned, nor [disinherited], nor put to death without
being brought to answer by due process of law."[33] "Nevertheless,"
the **Petition of Right** continues, "against the tenor of the said statutes and other good laws and statutes of your realm to that end
provided, divers of your subjects have of late been imprisoned without any cause shown," and so

> [we] do therefore humbly pray your most excellent Majesty that no
> man hereafter be compelled to make or yield any gift, loan, benevo-
> lence, tax or such like charge without common consent by act of par-
> liament, and that none be called to make answer or take such oath
> or to give attendance or be confined or otherwise molested or dis-
> quieted concerning the same or for refusal thereof. And that no
> freeman in any such manner as is before mentioned be imprisoned or
> detained .... All which [we] most humbly pray of your most excellent
> Majesty as their rights and liberties according to the laws and statutes
> of this realm.[34]

Significantly, while Charles had his supporters, the **Petition of
Right** won the approval of both Houses of Parliament. Even though
one observer said that "the greater part of the Lords stand for the
King's prerogatives over the subjects' liberties," yet at least 50 "lords
and earls" sided with the subjects.[35] Ultimately, the House of Lords
combined with the Commons to present Charles with the **Petition**.
The Lords, **Sir Edward Coke** reported, "have conferred about the
manner [of presenting the Petition of Right] and are agreed that no
addition or preface be used to the King, but that our petition of right
be preferred to His Majesty by command of the Lords and this House
[the Commons] ...."[36] **Charles** first answered the petition by granting
"that right be done according to the laws and customs of the realm,
and that the statutes be put in due execution."[37] This evasive response
was manifestly unsatisfactory, and the Commons started preparing a
much more aggressive document about the illegality of Charles's
acts. This problem was seemingly resolved only when Charles backed

down and used the phrase that was employed to turn statutes into law: "Le roy le veult" (The king wills it). However, relations between Parliament and Charles went very quickly downhill. First, the House of Lords considered the **Petition of Right** so important that they ordered the immediate publication of the petition and the king's reply. However, in an echo of Attorney General Heath's attempt to falsify the legal record, Charles ordered that the parliamentary text be destroyed, and another one printed that included his first, equivocal response replace "le roy le veult" alongside his declaration that while he was glad to confirm the "ancient liberties," nothing in the Petition of Right reduced the scope of the royal prerogative, and he maintained his right to collect duties regardless of regardless of parliamentary approval. **Charles's** "warrant to destroy the first printing, his warrant for the second, were calculated moves in his effort to minimize the significance of the petition to which he had given such a welcome answer on June 7 [1628]."[38] More amorphously, this second attempt at doctoring the record made the relationship between the governor and the governed even more tenuous and fraught with suspicion. It did not help that after the Petition of Right finally passed, the Commons tried once more to impeach **Buckingham**, and **Charles** responded by dissolving Parliament, asserting "I owe an account of my actions to none but to God alone."[39]

While **Charles** could stop the Commons from moving against his favorite, the king could not protect **Buckingham** from all the vicissitudes of fortune, and on August 23, 1628, John Felton, a disaffected veteran of the La Rochelle campaign who had not been paid, stabbed the Duke to death. While **Charles** was distraught, others rejoiced at his violent demise. Indeed, the Duke was so hated that a rumor circulated claiming that he was actually a Spanish agent, sent to destroy the English fleet, giving rise to this manuscript libel celebrating Buckingham's demise:

> Great Buckingham's buried under a stone
> 'Twixt heaven and Earth not such a one,
> Pope and Papist's friend, the Spaniard's factor,
> The Palatine's bane, The Dunkirk's Protector,

> The Dane's disaster, The French king's intruder,
> Netherland's oppressor, the English deluder,
> The friend of Pride, the peer of Lust
> The avaricious actor of things unjust.[40]

Other libels were meaner still. A court observer noted in a letter that when Felton passed through Kingston-upon-Thames on his way to the Tower, "an old woman bestowed this salutation upon him, "Now, God bless thee, little David!," quoth she, meaning he had killed Goliath."[41]

The nation, however, still had to be governed, and the Duke's assassination did not obviate the need for funding the nation's military ventures. **Charles** tried once more, in January 1629, to work with parliament, but this session too ended in chaos with both sides blaming each other. The Commons accused the King of breaking with the Ancient Constitution, while **Charles** in turn accused the Commons, led by the "malevolent dispositions of some ill-affected persons," of so insulting the dignity of monarchy that it made no sense to continue:

> It hath so happened by the disobedient and seditious carriage of those said ill-affected persons of the house of Commons that we and our regal authority and commandment have been so highly condemned as our Kingly office cannot bear, nor any former age can parallel.[42]

Parliament would not meet again for 11 years: the period of **Personal Rule** had begun.

Personal Rule (1629–40)

Historians have diametrically opposed views of this period, with some viewing it as 11 years of tyranny and others regarding the period, as Sir Edward Hyde wrote in the 1640s, as "the greatest calm and fullest measure of felicity that any people in any age hath been blessed with."[43] Certainly, this period had its benefits. Buckingham's death seems to have freed **Charles I** to come into his own, both personally and politically. By all accounts, Charles turned to his wife, **Henrietta Maria**, for support after the Duke's assassination, and the remarkable happened: they fell in love. Eight children followed in due order: **Charles** (the future **Charles II**, 1630); Mary (1631); **James** (the future **James II**, 1633); Elizabeth (1635); Anne (1637); a stillborn girl (1638); Henry (1639); and Henrietta (1644). Moreover, he was a devoted father (he kept a silver staff which recorded their growth).[44] Indeed, Charles "was the first English monarch for well over a hundred years to enjoy anything approaching a happy and fulfilled family life and it did much to define his kingship."[45] While **Charles** always set the tone and direction of his court's policies, he seems to have reacted to Buckingham's death by placing himself even more firmly at the center of government: "the king," an observer reported, "in fourteen days after the duke's death dispatched more business than the duke had done three months before."[46]

Several major developments contributed to the serenity of the Personal Rule's first few years. The first was foreign peace. For different reasons, **Charles** concluded peace treaties with France (1629) and Spain (1630), the former because once the Protestants at La Rochelle had admitted defeat, there was nothing to fight about, the latter because of Charles's admiration for the Spanish court and because he hoped to enlist Spain as an ally in retrieving the Palatine for his sister, Elizabeth. Peace meant that the government no longer had the huge expenses associated with arming and maintaining a fleet, so that pressure was finally relieved. Even more profitably, English merchants took full advantage of their country's neutrality in the Thirty Years War by picking up the slack in trade, leading to a major increase in customs fees. Next, **Sir Richard Weston** (c. 1577–1635), the Lord Treasurer, renewed **Lionel Cranfield's** attempt under King James to tame royal spending by reducing outlays and increasing revenue by such expedients as raising the fines for recusancy. For the first time in a long time, royal revenues actually started showing a surplus.

Charles also reformed the culture of the English court. We have already noted how **Charles** imposed order on the chaos surrounding his father, and he was no hypocrite. **Charles I** was one of the few (possibly the only) male monarchs who did not have a mistress or a lover, did not dress ostentatiously, and did not drink excessively. Instead, **Charles** I "set an example of decorum, upright behavior and self-control, which he expected to see emulated by others."[47] Furthermore, the King imported a "new cosmopolitanism into English court culture."[48] He especially loved painting, not only purchasing major collections but also attracting leading painters to England, the most important being the Flemish artist, **Sir Anthony Van Dyck** (1599–1641), who created many truly exquisite portraitss of **Charles** and his family. Spain's king, **Philip IV**, perceptively chose the great Baroque painter, **Peter Paul Rubens**, for several diplomatic missions, and he described **Charles** as "the greatest amateur of painting of all the princes of the world."[49] The period of **Personal Rule** thus began with peace abroad, prosperity at home, and a sophisticated, cultured court that was the opposite of an embarrassment. What could go wrong?

A great deal, it seems. First, while the constitutional arguments of the first four years of Charles's reign were muted during most of the Personal Rule, thanks in good part to the absence of parliaments, the concerns lurked in the background, and in 1638, **Charles** imposed yet another extra-parliamentary tax that eventually revived the controversy over the royal prerogative and the threat to English liberties. Charles needed to refurbish the English fleet for two reasons: pirates had become active in the Channel, leading to demands from merchants for protection, and Charles wanted to continue his quest to restore the Palatine to his sister, and that also required naval power. Therefore, in 1634, **Charles** revived the levy known as **Ship Money**, traditionally restricted to port towns. Charles and his Privy Council were mindful of the past, and consequently, the decision "was carefully formulated and demonstrated royal concern to avoid the appearance of illegality" because the government based the decision on "the king's emergency power to provide for the safety of the realm."[50] **Ship Money** did not, therefore, contravene the **Petition of Right's** objections to extra-parliamentary taxation. At first, the tax was entirely successful and non-controversial. Nobody doubted that the king should act to protect the nation, and he taxed the people who traditionally supported the levy.

But in 1635, Charles (as always) overstepped his bounds: he extended **Ship Money** to inland communities, and that is where the trouble started. **John Hampden (1595–1643)** of Buckinghamshire, an inland county in the southeast of England, refused to pay a nominal amount of the tax because he believed it was illegal, since the tax was not approved by parliament, and he wanted a court to say so, leading to **Hampden's Case**, sometimes called **The Case of Ship Money**, in 1636. Technically, the Crown won this case, but only by a razor-thin margin, and once more, Charles lost the public relations battle. The case had attracted wide national attention, and so the fact that five of the twelve judges decided for Hampden meant that the victory was hardly resounding. Furthermore, news of the Crown's legal victory only exacerbated the constitutional worries. When the decision was publicly announced in Kent, a contemporary diarist recorded that the auditors in the town square not only sensed that the decision did not square with **the Ancient Constitution**, but that their objections were grounded in a sophisticated and detailed understanding of the law and of contemporary history:

> They confessed ... that the whole discourse of Fortescue in the commendation of the laws of England was to show the king had not an absolute power, they considered in especial the 9, 14, 18, 34, 35, 37, 53 chapters; that it was the opinion and resolution of Sir Thomas Fleming, Sir Edward Coke, the two chief justices, Sir Laurence Tanfield, Chief [Law] Baron, and Baron Altham on conference with the lords of the privy council term ... that the king hath no prerogative but that which the law of the doth give and allow, and therefore his subjects could not with justice bee denied a trial .... That the first king there [in France] imposed taxes at his pleasure was Charles VII without the consent of the estates of his kingdom, that the misery of that realm was enough showed by Fortescue of the Laws of England cap. 35, composed about those times .... [They said that] this king [Charles] took it [Ship Money] by privy seal, it being never granted by parliament to him, which all kings had formerly. They said if the king's council could make this good by law, the subject could not say he had property in ought.[51]

The legal victory had the precise opposite effect than the one **Charles** desired: instead of affirming the legitimacy of Ship Money, the victory only made the tax harder and harder to collect. While the Crown collected 96% of the amount demanded in 1636, that shrank to 20% in 1639.[52] The revival of the constitutional debate (which as the reaction from Kent over the Ship Money decision demonstrates, was not restricted to London or to lawyers) could not have come for a worse time for **Charles**, as he had also decided to declare war on Scotland.

Religion: Arminius, Laud, and Absolutism

To understand how **Charles** came to this point, we need to go back over some of the history of religious controversy in the Tudor–Stuart era. Protestantism, we need to remember, from the start was a house divided that would continue to subdivide. From **Henry VIII** onward, English Protestants disagreed, sometimes violently, over the fundamentals of their creed, such as the legitimacy of bishops, and how closely Protestant worship could or should resemble Catholic ceremonies. **Elizabeth I**, **James VI/I**, and now **Charles I** were all subject to the constant pressure, largely resisted, from the "hotter" Protestants who advocated even more radical reforms and an aggressive foreign policy against Catholicism. Continental Protestantism also had serious controversies over the nature and content of their religion, and the key issue for our purposes was the problem of predestination. **Jean Calvin** proposed that God had already determined ("predestined") who would be saved and who would be damned. Even more starkly, human beings could do nothing to alter their fate.

During the reign of King James, a Dutch theologian named **Jacobus Arminius** (1560–1609) proposed that God's judgments could be influenced by human free will, and while the **Synod of Dort** (1618–19), a meeting of English, Dutch, German, and Swiss Protestants, condemned the **Arminian heresy**, the views of the **Remonstrants**, as Arminius's followers called themselves, penetrated into England anyway.

The Arminian heresy deeply influenced **John Milton**. In *Areopagitica* (1644), he argued against pre-publication censorship because it took away the option of choosing right from wrong, good over evil. "I cannot praise," Milton famously writes, "a fugitive and cloistered virtue, unexercised and unbreathed, that never sallies out and sees her adversary, but slinks out of the race where that immortal garland is to be run for, not without dust and heat."[53] But in *Paradise Lost*, Milton is more equivocal. While God declares that "Man shall not quite be lost, but saved who will," meaning that those who desire salvation will be saved, he qualifies the Arminianism of this statement by adding the Calvinist assertion that humanity will owe their deliverance "to me / …/ and to none but me" (3.174, 181–2).

Charles started favoring a group of bishops who adhered more to **Arminian** views of salvation than **Calvin's**, chief among them being **William Laud** (1573–1645), made bishop of London in 1628 and Archbishop of Canterbury in 1633. **Laud's** preference for **Arminius's** views on salvation led to a number of important doctrinal and practical changes in the English Church. The Laudian church de-emphasized scripture, preaching and sermons, placing emphasis instead on the sacraments, which are available to everyone. The clergyman became central to worship, and Laud insisted on the wearing of vestments. **Laud** placed much more importance on ceremony than on interiority because ceremonies strengthened faith: they are the "hedges that fence the substance of religion from all the indignities which profaneness and sacrilege too commonly put upon it."[54] In short, under **Laud**, the English church became much more hierarchical, much more attentive to aesthetics (in Laud's phrase, the "beauty of holiness), and much less tolerant of dissent. Uniformity, **Laud** argued, was essential for maintaining piety: "No one thing," Laud wrote," hath made conscientious men more wavering in their own minds, or more apt and easy to be drawn aside from the sincerity of religion professed in the church of England than the want of uniform and decent order in too many churches of the kingdom."[55] To ensure uniformity, **Laud** banned preaching by anyone without a license, increased policing visits by bishops and archbishops to the various parishes, imposed strict censorship on the press, and persecuted dissenters in the courts of **Star Chamber** (which concerned itself mainly with crimes against public order, such as sedition) and **High Commission** (which dealt with ecclesiastical matters).

> The most infamous example of Laudian persecution occurred in 1637, when the radical polemicist **William Prynne** (in 1632, he published a gargantuan attack on drama, *Histriomastix*) once more crossed the line. In 1633, Prynne had his ears cropped for his anti-episcopal writings, but that seemed to only encourage him. His next punishment was even more horrible: "his nose was slit, and the initials 'S. L.' burnt into his cheeks. They stood for 'Seditious Libeller'; to **Prynne** they stood for 'Stigma of Laud.' ... The executioner had heated the iron very hot, and burnt one of his cheeks twice. After this he cut one of Prynne's ears so close that he cut off a piece of cheek, and cut him deep in the neck near the jugular vein. Then, hacking the other ear until it was almost off, he left it hanging and went down from the scaffold. He was called back by the surgeon, who made him perform a complete amputation."[56]

Laud's changes were both abstract and very concrete. For example, his first major initiative was to order the communion table moved to the eastern end of the church, where the entire congregation could see it, and to have it surrounded by rails. Why did this seemingly innocuous rearrangement of furniture set off a firestorm? First, unlike shifts in doctrine, this was an innovation that everybody had to notice, and furthermore, "the removal of family pews which was sometimes necessary to accommodate the communion table in its new 'altar-wise position and to enable the congregation to see the communion being celebrated, was a clear instance of how Laudian innovations could upset the social status quo."[57]

The religious poetry of the 1630s reflects some of the conflicts over the Laudian church. **George Herbert's** (1593–1633) *The Temple*, with its stress on ritual and the importance of clergy, especially resonates with Laudianism. On the other hand, according to the note **John Milton** added to the poem in 1645, *Lycidas* prophesizes the overthrow of "our corrupted clergy, then in their height."[58]

Laud's actions and his theology did more than demonstrate the top-down authoritarianism of Charles's administration; moderate and "hot" Protestants alike believed that the king and his archbishop were dragging the English Church closer and closer to Catholicism. In 1629, one "J.P." wrote a polemic whose purpose, as the subtitle puts it, aims at *Convincing Jews of obstinacy, Romish Catholics of Conspiracy, Seducers of Sedition, [and] Arminians of Apostasy*; "Arminianism," J.P. writes in the body of his work, "is a mere stirrup to help men into the saddle of popery, that to suffer these [Arminianism's supporters] is to provide the Romish adversaries friends in court and country...."[59] The same year, the committee for religion in the House of Commons wrote a petition to the king denouncing "the subtle and pernicious spreading of the Arminian faction," and like "J.P.," the committee members warned that Arminians "have kindled such a fire of division in the very bowels of the State, as if not speedily extinguished, it is of itself sufficient to ruin our religion."[60] The fact that **Henrietta Maria** was Catholic didn't help matters, and the fact that neither **Laud** and nor **Charles** had any sympathy at all for Catholicism, and actually increased pressure and fines on recusants, did not seem to register. Public perception trumped the realities of policy. Equally importantly, **Laud's** vision of the Church overlapped with and supported **Charles's** vision of absolute monarchy, and indeed, given that **Laud** largely followed **Charles's** lead, the Laudian Church may well be the religious analogue for **Charles's** privileging of royal prerogative over the liberties of the subject. They are the secular and religious sides of the same coin, as evidenced by how the same people in the Commons who created the Petition of Right also protested the rise of Arminianism.

The Bishops' Wars: The Beginning of the Civil Wars

The desire for conformity, intolerance of differing views, absolutism, and **Charles's** tone-deafness when it came to politics all combined disastrously in 1637. **Charles** decided, without consulting either parliament or the Scots Privy Council, to impose the Book of Common Prayer, revised in a Laudian direction, in Scotland, which, as we have noted in previous chapters, fervently resisted both Catholicism and Protestant bishops. When the new rite premiered in St. Giles's Cathedral in Edinburgh on July 23, pandemonium resulted, with cries of "the mass is entered among us."[61] In February 1638, a petition circulated throughout the country, the **National Covenant**, pledging to oppose the king's religious policies and maintain true religion. Despite the rhetoric of obedience ("we have no intention nor desire to attempt anything that may turn to the dishonor of God, or to the diminution of the King's greatness and authority"), the signers pledged to oppose "all innovations already introduced in the matters of the worship of God."[62] Consequently, the Scots bishops had their powers abolished and episcopacy declared incompatible with the Kirk. Rather than attempting diplomacy, negotiation, and compromise, **Charles** considered the **National Covenant** and the subsequent acts as outright rebellion deserving violent suppression, and so he formed an army to fight what would come to be known as the **First Bishops' War**.

The Scots formed an army of their own, and unlike the English force, which suffered from poor morale because of reluctance to fight for policies many considered oppressive, illegitimate, and irreligious, the Scots were motivated and united. The royal army essentially melted away, and **Charles** agreed to a truce in June 1639. By this point, the royal coffers were empty, and **Charles** had no choice but to call a parliament for the first time in eleven years. As one might expect, the members did not gather in a co-operative mood. They wanted to discuss grievances, **Charles** wanted money to fight the Scots, but the Commons refused to vote supply before the grievances were addressed. As the parliamentarian, **John Pym** (c. 1584–1643) ... said in a speech on April 17, 1640, "our many grievances I take to be first in order ... and which have disabled us to administer any supply until they be redressed ..."[63] When he realized he was not going to get his way, **Charles** dissolved the **Short Parliament** (April 13 to May 15, 1640). Order started to break down in the land. There was a widespread tax strike; London refused to lend the king any money, and there were riots demanding a parliament. The Scots decided to press their advantage, and they marched across the Tweed River in August 1640 – the **Second Bishops' War**, soundly defeating a hastily assembled English force led by **Thomas Wentworth, Earl of Strafford** (1593–1641). The invading army occupied Newcastle (where London got its coal), and after a week more, two northern counties (Durham and Northumberland). Charles was forced to conclude a humiliating truce which obligated him to pay the Scots army £850 a day until a permanent solution was found. With no royal army in between the Scots and London, **Charles** had no choice at all. He had to call another parliament, and this one would sit for at least eight years, from 1640 to 1648, when it would be purged (see the next chapter): the **Long Parliament**.

The Long Parliament and the Descent into Civil War

Nobody in November 1640, on either side of the divide, thought that England was on the brink of civil strife, but a dizzying series of events led to war and in time, the execution of **Charles I**. While the outbreak of the **Civil Wars** (see the box at the chapter's end on what to call the events of 1641–49) might seem, from our perspective, a foregone conclusion, there was nothing inevitable about it. As we will see, a combination of events and personalities led to war.

At the beginning of the **Long Parliament** along with the abolition of the Court of Star Chamber and censorship, there was an extraordinary and unprecedented explosion of book publication. Over the course of the 1600s, roughly five hundred books were printed each year. But in 1640, approximately *four thousand* titles survive, ranging from the high level of political thought represented by John Milton and Thomas Hobbes to pamphlets by the radically egalitarian Diggers and Ranters (see the next chapter). Almost "anyone could publish almost anything," and they did, from Royalist defenses to demotic ballads, from defenses of Laud to prophecies by women attacking the same, booksellers offered them all.[64] Book publication had become, for the first time, a major forum for political debate, despite the efforts by parliament and **the Protectorate** to re-impose press controls. Extremely fortunately for posterity, in 1640, the bookseller, **George Thomason** (c. 1602–66) started collecting every book, pamphlet, and newspaper published in London, and as many as he could get from the provinces. "The Thomason Collection," as it came to be known, eventually comprised more than 22,000 items, and has become an invaluable resource for studying this period. "His practice of adding the dates of publication or acquisition on the works' title-pages has proved invaluable in establishing the chronology of events during this turbulent period, and his marginal notes identify anonymous authors and the clandestine manner in which some works were distributed."[65] The complete collection is now available through Early English Books Online.

The members of the 1640 Parliament gathered, determined to remedy 11 years' worth of grievances, including Arminianism (or Laudianism) in the church, extra-parliamentary taxation, such as Ship Money, and the prerogative courts of Star Chamber and High Commission. The newly elected members of the House of Commons brought with them formal lists of grievances complaining about financial exactions, Arminian innovations, and the dangers of papistry. Perhaps the most famous of these lists of complaints arrived on December 11, 1640, **The Root and Branch Petition**, which asked that all bishops be abolished "with all its dependencies, roots and branches" because "said government is found by woeful experience to be a main cause and occasion of many foul evils, pressures and grievances of a very high nature unto his Majesties subjects ...."[66] The leaders of this parliament were people "whose reputations had been forged in previous disagreements with King Charles," in particular, in the House, **John Hampden** (of Hampden's Case fame), **Denzil Holles** (1598–1680), and especially the parliamentary leader, **John Pym**; in the House of Lords, **Robert Devereaux, Earl of Essex** (1591–1646), son of Elizabeth's ill-fated favorite and later leader of the Parliamentary army, Francis Russell, Earl of Bedford (c. 1587–1631), Robert Rich, Earl of Warwick (1587–1658), **William Fiennes, Viscount Saye and Sele** (1582–1662). In short order, the **Long Parliament** passed legislation prohibiting the financial policies of the 1630s (Ship Money and all other taxation without parliamentary consent) and dissolving the prerogative courts, Star Chamber and the High Commission. To prevent Charles from stopping reform by dissolving parliament, they also passed the Triennial Act (February 15, 1641), which mandated that parliament must meet at least once every three years, and on May 10, 1641, they passed an act declaring that the present parliament could be dissolved only by its own consent.

The leaders of the **Long Parliament** were not content to legislate their way into reforming the king's policies: they also went after the king's advisers, and their first victim was the king's chief councilor, **Strafford**, who had made himself hated when, as Lord Deputy of Ireland, he forced the Scots immigrants to Ulster to reject the National Covenant (see earlier in this chapter), and parliament essentially used him as a scapegoat for all the errors of the king's policies during the Personal Rule. The House charged Strafford with treason, but these charges were bogus, as **Strafford** quickly demonstrated, and so, having failed with a trial, the House moved to a Bill of Attainder. The desire for someone to pay for the last eleven years was so strong that no amount of reason could sway Strafford's enemies. One member of the House of Lords coldly said: "Stone dead hath no fellow."[67] **Charles** agreed to all this legislation because he had no choice: it was either give in, or not get money for an army against the Scots. But by signing the bills, including **Strafford's** death warrant, he was not necessarily agreeing with them, but biding his time until better circumstances allowed him to deal with a parliament that he firmly believed had overstepped its bounds. At the same time, parliament was not about to create an army that they feared (again, not incorrectly) would be used against them. The **"Army Plot"** – a failed attempt to rescue Strafford from the Tower – drove the wedge between parliament and the King even deeper.

Two events moved the pendulum back towards **Charles**. First, in August, he left London to negotiate with the Scots, bringing the legislative juggernaut against him to a halt. Then, in October 1641, **Ireland** exploded in violence. The descendants of the people displaced in the Jacobean **Plantation of Ulster** rose up against the English and Scots settlers, and there were lurid reports of horrible massacres of Protestants by Catholics. One report claimed that the rebels "stripped naked [their prisoners]; some bloodily wounded, even to death, but left alive languishing, their bellies being ripped and guts issuing, cast upon dung-hills; some butchered and cut into gobbets; some men, some women hanged, yea, many hanged, or otherwise put to death by them ...."[68] Rumors that hundreds of thousands of Protestants were massacred, and equally horrible, that Irish Catholics, with the help of Spain, were about to invade England to re-establish their religion, circulated throughout England. Obviously, an army was needed to quell this uproar, but who would command it? Parliament did not trust Charles to use the army against the Irish, not against them. Furthermore, when Charles returned from Edinburgh, he was greeted by cheering crowds.

To counter this swell of support for the King, **Pym** brought before the House of Commons **The Grand Remonstrance**, which declared that the "root of all this mischief we find to be a malignant and pernicious design of subverting the fundamental laws and principles of government, upon which the religion and justice of this kingdom are firmly established."[69] The document summarized everything Charles had done wrong, including matters that parliament had already taken care of, such as the prerogative courts, and everything that parliament had done to rectify those wrongs. The passage in November, 1641 of the **Grand Remonstrance** by a vote of 159 to 148 marked a key development: Parliament's unity had broken into two groups: **the Parliamentarians**, who believed that reform was necessary to safeguard the subject's liberties and Protestant Church; and **the Royalists**, who thought that Pym had gone too far in his demands and who wanted a negotiated settlement with Charles. In December, Parliament passed the **Militia Act**, which mandated that Parliament must approve whoever would lead the army. It took away, in other words, the king's ability to appoint whoever he desired to the post. As one might expect, Charles did not react well to both the Act and the Grand Remonstrance, and he decided to go on the offensive by issuing a proclamation requiring conformity to the Laudian rituals (exactly why the Scots were parked in the north of England), and also in December, he rejected the **Grand Remonstrance** completely. "By God," the King is reported to have exclaimed, "you have asked that of me never asked of a king."[70] Indeed, **Charles** was right: Parliament's demand to approve counselors, eradicate Arminianism and bishops, and run the military expedition to Ireland certainly encroached on royal prerogative, but they did so to the same extent that extra-parliamentary taxation, denial of habeas corpus, and rule without parliament threatened the liberty of the subject.

Charles tried to retaliate against **Pym** and four other leading members of the House by marching into the House of Commons to arrest them, but they had gotten wind of Charles's plan and fled before the king and his guards arrived. Charles's attempt proved that there could be no peace between him and parliament, and matters very quickly reached the point of no return. Realizing that London was no longer safe, Charles left for York in January 1642; the next month, parliament passed an act excluding Bishops from the House of Lords, and **Henrietta Maria** went abroad to seek help for her husband. In March, Parliament reached another milestone by passing the Militia Ordinance without the king's consent, which authorized them to raise troops and seize garrisons.

Not coincidentally, **John Milton** published his attack on bishops in February 1642: *The Reason of Church Government.* While Milton would demand the "removal of your criminous [criminal] hierarchy in the Church," he does not yet extend his argument to the removal of monarchy, granting that "the civil magistrate [the monarch] wears an authority of God's giving, and ought to be obeyed as his vicegerent." Milton also rejects James's dictum, "no bishop, no king"–"your typical chain of king and priest must unlink."[71]

In June, Charles reciprocated, forcing local leaders to choose their side. Finally, on August 22, 1642, **Charles** raised the royal standard at Nottingham, officially starting the **Civil Wars** by summoning his subjects to repress the rebellion headed by the **Earl of Essex**. Despite the king's issuing a proclamation ten days before announcing the event, the ceremony was so poorly attended there was talk of postponing the event. A few nights later, a strong wind blew it down. The first victims of the Civil Wars, however, might be the companies of players and their audiences: on September 2, 1642, because of the "distracted estate of England, threatened with a cloud of blood by a civil war," Parliament closed the public theaters.[72]

There is no universally agreed-upon term for the events of 1642–49, and some of the many include (in no particular order): the English Revolution, the British Revolution, the Great Rebellion, the Puritan Revolution, the Wars of the Three Kingdoms, the Wars of Religion, the Civil War, the British Civil War, and the term I prefer, **the Civil Wars**. Each connotes a particular view, and each carries significant ideological weight. Royalists preferred "the Great Rebellion" because they did not want to grant any legitimacy to their opponents, although some twentieth-century historians use it as well; contemporary left-leaning historians, such as Christopher Hill, prefer "the English Revolution" because of the connotations of an oppressed class overthrowing an evil regime. Revisionist historians tend toward "the English Civil War." Each term has its drawbacks. The problem with "the Puritan Revolution," in addition to using that doubtful term, "Puritan," is that the phrase assumes one cause, and the problem with any term using "English" is that it assumes one country, eliding both Scotland and Ireland. "The Wars of the Three Kingdoms" acknowledges the three very different polities are involved, but the Irish might object, since England was really a colonial occupier. Adding to the confusion, some historians use different terms, sometimes within the space of a single paragraph. For example, the great nineteenth-century historian, Samuel Rawson Gardiner, uses "Puritan Revolution" in the title of one book, "Civil War" in another; Christopher Hill refers to "The English Revolution" in one sentence, which in the next becomes "The Civil War." I have chosen to use **"the Civil Wars"** because that seems the most accurate (there was more than one war, and the wars were internal) and the least judgmental.

Notes

1 *Calendar of State Papers and Manuscripts, relating to English Affairs, Existing in the Archives and Collections of Venice*, ed. Horatio F. Brown (London: HMSO, 1900), vol. 19, 21 (hereafter referred to as *CSPV*).

2 Quoted in Thomas Corns, *A History of Seventeenth-Century English Literature* (Oxford: Blackwell, 2007), 168.

3 *King James VI and I: Political Writings*, ed. Johann P. Sommerville (Cambridge: Cambridge University Press, 1994), 181.

4 *King James VI and I: Political Writings*, 184.

5 Quoted in David L. Smith, *The Stuart Parliaments 1603–1689* (London: Arnold, 1999), 113.

6 Dr. Meddus to the Rev. Joseph Meade, Thomas Birch, *The Court and Times of Charles I* (London: Henry Colburn, 1849), vol. 1, 30.

7 Mark Kishlansky, *A Monarchy Transformed: Britain 1603–1714* (London: Penguin, 1996), 106.

8 Roger Lockyer, *Buckingham: The Life and Political Career of George Villiers, First Duke of Buckingham 1592–1628* (London: Longman, 1981), 250.

9 Kishlansky, *A Monarchy Transformed*, 107–8.

10 Quoted in Lockyer, *Buckingham*, 266.

11 Smith, *The Stuart Parliaments*, 115.

12 "Rev. Joseph Mead to Sir Martin Stuteville," Birch, *Court and Times*, vol. 1, 93–4.

13 *Proceedings in Parliament, 1626*, ed. William B. Bidwell and Maija Jansson (New Haven: Yale University Press, 1991), vol. 2, 395.

14 Quoted in Kevin Sharpe, *The Personal Rule of Charles I* (New Haven: Yale University Press, 1992), 3.

15 John Rushworth, *Historical Collections of Private Passages of State* (London, 1659), sig. Aaa2r; also quoted in Samuel. R. Gardiner, *History of England from the Accession of James I to the Outbreak of the Civil War* (London: Longmans, Green, 1896), vol. 6, 110.

16 *CSPV*, vol. 19, 508; quoted in Richard Cust, "Charles I, the Privy Council, and the Forced Loan," *Journal of British Studies* 24.2 (1985), 212.

17 *CSPV*, vol. 19, 508.

18 Birch, *Court and Times*, 112; emphasis in the original.

19 *CSPV*, vol. 19, 213.

20 *CSPV*, vol. 19, 217.

21 "Rev. Joseph Mead to Sir Martin Stuterville," Birch, *Court and Times*, vol. 1, 30.

22 "Rev. Joseph Mead to Sir Martin Stuterville," Birch, *Court and Times*, vol. 1, 131.

23 "Rev. Joseph Mead to Sir Martin Stuterville," Birch, *Court and Times*, vol. 1, 230.

24 Quoted in Nick Bunker, *Making Haste from Babylon: The "Mayflower" Pilgrims and Their World* (New York: Alfred A. Knopf, 2010), 358.

25 Quoted in Barry Coward, *The Stuart Age: England 1603–1714*, 3rd ed. (London: Longman, 2003), 162.

26 John Guy, "The Origins of the Petition of Right Reconsidered," *The Historical Journal* 25.2 (1982), 292. Mark Kishlansky, however, fervently disagrees with Guy's conclusions. See "Tyranny Denied: Charles I, Attorney General Heath, and the Five Knights' Case," *The Historical Journal* 42.1 (1999): 53–83.

27 John Rushworth, *Historical Collections of Private Passages of State* (London, 1659), sig. Ttt2v.

28 Rushworth, *Historical Collections*, 296.

29 Kishlansky, *A Monarchy Transformed*, 110.

30 *Commons Debates 1628*, ed. Robert C. Johnson and Maija Jansson Cole (New Haven: Yale University Press, 1977), vol. 2, 8–9.

31 Richard Cust, *Charles I: A Political Life* (Harlow: Pearson/Longman, 2007), 71.

32 Kishlansky, *A Monarchy Transformed*, 111.

33 "The Petition of Right (1628)," *Divine Right and Democracy: An Anthology of Political Writing in Stuart England*, ed. David Wootton (Harmondsworth: Penguin, 1986), 169.

34 *Divine Right and Democracy*, 169, 170.

35 "Rev. Joseph Mead to Sir Martin Stuterville," Birch, *Court and Times*, vol. 1, 346–7.

36 *Commons Debates 1628*, vol. 4, 7.

37 Quoted in Austin Woolrych, *Britain in Revolution 1625–1660* (Oxford: Oxford University Press, 2002), 57.

38 Elizabeth Read Foster, "Printing the Petition of Right," *Huntington Library Quarterly* 38.1 (1974), 85.

39 Quoted in Woolrych, *Britain in Revolution*, 58.

40 "Great Buckingham's buried under a stone," *Early Stuart Libels*, ed. Alistair Bellamy and Andrew MacRae. http://www.earlystuartlibels. net/htdocs/buckingham_assassination_section/Pi15.html.

41 "Rev. Joseph Meade to Sir Martin Stuterville," Birch, *Court and Times*, vol. 1, 395–6.
42 "A Proclamation about the Dissolving of Parliament" (London, 1629).
43 Quoted in Coward, *The Stuart Age*, 165. The most extensive and sympathetic treatment of this period is Kevin Sharpe, *The Personal Rule of Charles I* (New Haven: Yale University Press, 1992).
44 Sharpe, *Personal Rule*, 185.
45 Cust, *Charles I*, 148.
46 "Rev. Joseph Meade to Sir Martin Stuterville," *Court and Times*, vol. 1, 396. Sharpe reproduces two letters representative of the marginal notes Charles regularly scribbled on governmental correspondence (200–7).
47 Sharpe, *Personal Rule*, 190.
48 Cust, *Charles I*, 161.
49 Cust, *Charles I*, 161.
50 Kishlansky, *A Monarchy Transformed*, 121–2.
51 Kenneth Fincham, "The Judges' Decision on Ship Money in February 1637: the Reaction of Kent," in *Bulletin of the Institute of Historical Research* 57 (1984), 233–4.
52 Robert Bucholz and Newton Key, *Early Modern England 1485–1714: A Narrative History* (Oxford: Blackwell, 2004), 230.
53 *Areopagitica, Complete Poetry and Essential Prose of John Milton*, ed. William Kerrigan, John Rumrich, and Stephen M. Fallon (New York: Modern Library, 2007), 939.
54 Quoted in Sharpe, *Personal Rule*, 289.
55 Sharpe, *Personal Rule*, 288.
56 William Lamont, "Prynne, William (1600–1669)," *Oxford Dictionary of National Biography*, Oxford University Press, September 2004; online edn., January 2008. http://www.oxforddnb.com/view/article/22854, accessed July 1, 2010.
57 Coward, *The Stuart Age*, 175.
58 *Complete Poetry and Essential Prose*, ed. Kerrigan, Rumrich, and Fallon, 100.
59 J. P., *Christ's Confession and Complaint* (London, 1629), sig. G1v; Sharpe, *Personal Rule*, 295.
60 J. P. Kenyon, ed., *The Stuart Constitution 1603–1688* (Cambridge: Cambridge University Press, 1966), 157.
61 Quoted in Bucholz and Key, *Early Modern England*.

62 "National Covenant." http://www.covenanter.org/Westminster/ nationalcovenant.htm. Accessed July 1, 2010.

63 *Proceedings of the Short Parliament of 1640*, ed. Esther S. Cope and Willson H. Coates (London: Royal Historical Society, 1977), 148–9.

64 David Cressy, *England on Edge: Crisis and Revolution 1640–1642* (Oxford: Oxford University Press, 2006), 295. See also Sharon Achinstein, "Texts in Conflict: the Press and the Civil War," *The Cambridge Companion to the Writing of the English Revolution*, ed. N. H. Keeble (Cambridge: Cambridge University Press, 2001), 50–70.

65 David Stoker, "Thomason, George (c. 1602–1666)," *Oxford Dictionary of National Biography*, Oxford University Press, September 2004; online edn., October 2008. http://www.oxforddnb.com/view/article/27250, accessed July 11, 2010.

66 Kenyon, *Stuart Constitution*, 171–2.

67 Quoted in Kishlansky, *A Monarchy Transformed*, 144. On Strafford, see Ronald G. Asch, "Wentworth, Thomas, first earl of Strafford (1593–1641)," *Oxford Dictionary of National Biography*, Oxford University Press, September 2004; online edn., October 2009. http://www.oxforddnb.com/view/article/29056, accessed July 3, 2010.

68 Henry Jones, *A perfect relation of the beginning and continuation of the Irish-rebellion, from May last, to this present 12th, of January, 1641* (London, 1641), sig. B1v.

69 Kenyon, *Stuart Constitution*, 231.

70 Quoted in Kishlansky, *A Monarchy Transformed*, 149.

71 *Reason of Church Government*, in *The Riverside Milton*, ed. Roy Flannagan (Boston: Houghton Mifflin, 1998), 911.

72 *Acts and Ordinances of the Interregnum*, ed. C. H. Firth and R. S. Rait (London: HMSO, 1911), vol. 1, 26.

8

The Civil Wars, the Commonwealth, and the Early Restoration (1642–71)

Historiography

How did England move from the adulation heaped upon Queen Elizabeth to a revolt against the monarchy that ended with Charles I being executed for crimes against the "fundamental laws" of the nation? This is a question, one distinguished scholar admits, about which "historians of seventeenth-century England are in complete disarray."[1]

For the "Whig" historians (see note 14 in Chapter 6), the answer was simple: Charles I tried to rule without parliament, and thus got swept away by the ongoing march to liberty. The "Whig" preference for long-term causes, however, did not die out with the advent of the twentieth century. Rather, the economic historian, **R. H. Tawney**, and the Marxist historian, **Christopher Hill**, gave the Whig narrative a different content.

A Short History of Early Modern England: British Literature in Context, First Edition.
Peter C. Herman.
© 2011 Peter C. Herman. Published 2011 by Blackwell Publishing Ltd.

For **Tawney** and his extremely influential disciple, **Lawrence Stone**, the rise of the "gentry" and the decline of the aristocracy ultimately led to the revolt.

Tawney's and Stone's work unleashed an academic quarrel fought during the 1950s in the pages of the *Economic History Review* known as the "Storm of the Gentry," in which their use of statistics was subject to withering criticism. Wealth, for example, does not seem to have determined political allegiances. While an academic quarrel from over 60 years ago might seem irrelevant today, literature students should be mindful that despite their popularity among literary critics, Stone's works, including *The Crisis of the Aristocracy* and *The Family, Sex, and Marriage*, remain highly suspect by historians, and so should be used with caution.[2]

Marxist historians, including the young **Christopher Hill**, attributed the Civil Wars to a crude form of class warfare, but while **Hill** has long since abandoned this kind of reductive analysis, his interest in the "fourth sort," to use William Harrison's term (see Chapter 1, text accompanied by note 34) in the underclass rather than the relatively wealthy and the elite, led directly to one of his most influential books, especially for literature majors, *Milton and the English Revolution*, which investigated the connections between John Milton and the radicals of the 1640s and 1650s.

Historians today largely now shy away from the kind of "long-term" model represented by Hill, Stone, and Tawney. Just about everything else, however, remains in dispute. Three examples: Against the argument that "Puritanism" constituted the driving force of the Civil Wars, **Nicholas Tyacke** has proposed that Arminianism shattered the religious consensus, thus forcing Calvinist Protestants into opposing Laud not just with books, but arms as well; **Kevin Sharpe** seeks to exonerate Charles I and Laud, arguing the Personal Rule was not a period of festering resentment against tyranny, but an oasis of calm and order; and, finally, **Brian Manning** and **David Underdown** (following Hill's lead) have replaced the conventional focus on parliament and the ruling classes with investigations of the role of "popular grievances, popular movements and popular aspirations in the revolutionary struggles of the decade 1640 to 1649." In short, literature students should know that nearly every aspect of the Civil Wars (including what to call this period) remains the subject of intense debate.[3]

1642–45: First Civil War

As the tepid response to Charles's raising his standard in Nottingham suggests, the Civil Wars did not begin with the nation enthusiastically choosing sides and plunging into war. Both parliament and the king, to be sure, had their partisans, but a very significant proportion of England opted for neutrality. Some counties did so overtly, others engaged in passive neutrality, choosing a side only when forced to do so. One reason for this resistance was the widespread coverage of the Thirty Years War, whose devastation was very much on people's minds. A 1643 Norfolk petition for neutrality begged that the authorities to keep Germany in mind before doing anything rash: "Oh let the miserable spectacle of a German devastation persuade you to decline those perilous casualties which may result from a civil war."[4] But despite the unwillingness, both sides were determined to fight. **Prince Rupert** (1619–82; son of **Frederick of Bohemia** and James's daughter, **Elizabeth**) led the Royalist forces; **Robert Devereaux, Earl of Essex** led the Parliamentary army. In 1642, each side had advantages and disadvantages.

The Royalists came to be known as **Cavaliers**, from the Spanish, *caballero*. Like "Puritan," this was originally a term of abuse, signifying a courtier who was all flash but no substance. The Parliamentarians adopted the term, **Roundheads**, transforming a term of abuse aimed at the short hair of low-class apprentices into an assertion of political identity.

Curiously, the two sides in this conflict anticipate in some ways the American Civil War 200 years later. While the divisions were not as sharp as they would be between the Union and the Confederacy, generally speaking, the English Civil Wars pitted the North against the South: the Royalists had the loyalty of the North and West of England, while the Parliamentarians held the South and East. But there were pockets of sympathy for the Parliamentarians in the North, just as one found Royalists in the South. The Royalists, at the conflict's start, enjoyed the advantage of better, more experienced soldiers. Despite his young age, **Prince Rupert** had extensive military experience, although in 1637 he was captured by the Holy Roman Empire. He spent his three years' captivity studying war and armaments. On the other side, the Parliamentarians (like the Union) enjoyed the advantage of greater wealth and a much larger population from which to draw soldiers. Plus, the Parliamentarians had London, England's nerve center. While more of the nobility and the clergy sided with the king, as the **Earl of Essex** demonstrates, there were peers who chose to side with Parliament, as did many clergymen. Religious affiliation rather than class seems to have been a better predictor of which side one would choose, with Arminians tending toward the Royalists and the more committed Protestants tending toward Parliament. While some Catholics fought for Charles, most tried to stay out of the conflict altogether.

The two forces met for their first serious encounter on October 23, 1643 in the **Battle of Edgehill**. Both sides proved their mettle that day. Prince Rupert's cavalry chased the Parliamentary horsemen from the field and sacked the baggage train. But they could not regroup, and the Parliamentary foot soldiers broke the Royalist infantry. Only nightfall prevented a massacre. While the battle ended in a draw, the king's forces had an unimpeded road straight to London, but they moved too slowly, and allowed Londoners to create a force of 24,000 to defend the city. **Charles** headed south to Oxford, his winter headquarters.[5]

The uncertain result of these first encounters proved that there would be no quick end to the Civil Wars, which led to a split within the Parliamentary ranks. The "peace group," led by **Denzil Holles**,

217

was so appalled by the prospect of civil war as well as the percolating radicalism of the Commons that they were willing to negotiate a settlement, and until then, carry on a strictly defensive war.

Holles began his memoirs, written in 1648, by denouncing the threat to the class structure posed by the radicals who, in his view, had hijacked the Commons:

The wisest of men saw it to be a great evil that servants should ride on horses; an evil, now both seen and felt in this unhappy kingdom. The meanest of men, the basest and vilest of the nation, the lowest of the people, have got the power into their hands ... making their will their law; their power their rule; their hair-brained, giddy, fanatical humor and the setting up of a Babel of confusion, the end of their actions.[6]

The "war group" wanted to impose terms on the king, and demanded an offensive war aiming at total military victory. They were led by, among others, the younger **Sir Henry Vane** (1613–62; in 1635, **Vane** emigrated to New England and served for a brief time as governor. Caught up in a controversy over religious toleration, Vane lost the election to John Winthrop, and returned to England in 1637). **John Pym** (who by this time was dying of cancer) mediated between the two sides, advocating a forward military strategy while at the same time promoting a more traditional division of powers afterward.[7] This split in the Parliamentary ranks would only deepen. In any event, **Charles** had no interest in a negotiated settlement, although the terms offered by parliament in early 1643 (abolishing bishops; controlling who advises the king; confirming parliament's ancient rights and privileges, among other provisions) hardly gave him any incentive.[8] No wonder **Charles** said, "no less power than his who made the world of nothing can draw peace out of these articles."[9] By April, talks had collapsed.

In the absence of a national, centralized military, both sides organized their armies through local militias and regional forces, commanded by local leaders or aristocrats. One of the cavalry colonels of the Eastern Association (comprising the wealthy, agricultural countries in England's mid-eastern region) was **Oliver Cromwell.**

In addition to a few Royalist victories, the most important being the capture of the port city of **Bristol** (on England's southwest coast), both sides spent most of 1643 reinforcing their armies for the next round of hostilities. **Charles** looked to **Ireland** for help, seeking to free up the Royalist army there by promising Irish Catholics religious toleration and permission for their bishops to sit in the Irish House of Lords, if they would cease their rebellion. Parliament looked to **Scotland**. According to **the Solemn League and Covenant**, as the agreement was called, the Scots, in return for a commitment to "the reformation of religion … according to the Word of God and the example of the best reformed churches" and a very great deal of money every month, would deliver an army to help the Parliamentarians.[10] To meet the needs for men and money to pay both the English and Scots armies, Parliament resorted to forced impressments of soldiers (conscripting men to fight whether they wanted to or not), compulsory assessments, and a new tax on necessary commodities, such as beer and cider. The irony was lost on nobody that Parliament now turned to the same sort of financial measures that **Charles** resorted to earlier. Indeed, the huge cost of the war may have made more than a few nostalgic for the previous decade. In Kent, for example, where we should recall that the Ship Money decision was received with considerable grumbling about how it contradicted the Ancient Constitution (see the previous chapter), the *"yearly* payment for Ship Money in the 1630s equaled that county's *monthly* payment to Parliament in 1645–6."[11]

In 1643, Parliament established the **Westminster Assembly** to debate reforms to the English Church, and as part of the **Solemn League**, the Scots sent representatives. Two years later, the Assembly abolished the Book of Common Prayer and replaced it with the **Directory of Public Worship**, which suggests but does not prescribe how services ought to be conducted. For example,

> The Communion, or Supper of the Lord, is frequently to be celebrated, but how often may be considered and determined by the ministers and other church-governors of each congregation, as they shall find most convenient for the comfort and edification of the people committed to their charge.[12]

The **Directory** was far from popular, and many parishes continued with the old liturgy through the 1650s. The Book of Common Prayer would be officially reinstated after the Restoration.

Furthermore, the alliance with the Scots proved a mixed blessing for the Parliamentary side. On the one hand, they threatened the Royalist control of England's north, and to counter that threat, Prince Rupert marched north. The Parliamentary force, comprised of the Scots and the Eastern Association, met his forces at **Marston Moor** on July 2, 1644, the bloodiest battle of the Civil Wars. In a letter to his brother, **Cromwell** ascribed the victory to "the Lord's blessing upon the Godly Partly." God, Cromwell and others sincerely believed, was on their side, as shown by how easily the Parliamentarians defeated the Royalists: "We never charged but we routed the enemy … God made them as stubble to our swords."[13] For many, the Civil Wars were as much a holy war as the Israelite's conflict with the Philistines. York fell to the Parliamentarians the following week. On the other hand, the Parliamentary victories in the North were undercut by Royalist victories in the South, and the alliance with the Scots, while obviously beneficial militarily, was ruinously expensive. Equally importantly, the Scots insistence on imposing their vision of church government on England started causing significant resistance from the more radical elements in the Parliamentary forces. **Cromwell** had a public quarrel with the Scots major-general, Lawrence Crawford, who accused Cromwell of purging his forces of Presbyterians and replacing them with "such as were of the Independent judgment."[14]

This spat indicated a larger splintering within the Parliamentary forces. To simplify greatly, the "peace party," led by **Essex** and **Holles**, fought to bring Charles back to the negotiating table. They understood the fragility of the Parliamentary position, as expressed by the commander of the Eastern Association, Edward Montague, Earl of Manchester (1602–71): "if we beat the King ninety and nine times, yet he is King still, and so will his posterity be after him, but if the King beat us once, we shall be all hanged, and our posterity made slaves."[15] This group was generally known as the **Presbyterians**. Against them we have the more radical Protestants, the spiritual heirs of the Elizabethan and Jacobean **Brownists** or **Separatists** (see chapter 5) and the author of the **Marprelate tracts** (see Chapter 4); these people, the **Independents**, wanted each congregation to have the freedom to make their own individual decisions about governance and ritual; religious tolerance, in short. They were led in Parliament by **William Fiennes, Viscount Saye and Sele** in the Lords and **Oliver St. John** in the Commons. They comprised the "war party"; the Independents fought to defeat the king, and then negotiate with him. These differences may seem clear-cut, and at their extremes, the distinctions are easy to see. But once one moves toward the middle, the boundaries separating **Independents** and **Presbyterians** can be maddeningly vague, as demonstrated by "people labeled as both Presbyterians and Independents seeking out the ministry of an Anglican Archbishop, albeit a conspicuously modern one …."[16] But within their broad definitions, the intensifying conflict between the **Presbyterians** and the **Independents**, and between the various factions within each group, would be of crucial importance.

> In 1643, Parliament tried to re-impose order in the book world by prohibiting all unlicensed publications. As a response, **John Milton** composed *Areopagitica*, printed in June 1644 without a license and without identifying either the printer or the publisher (however, the title page boldly proclaims Milton's authorship). While *Areopagitica* made no impact at the time, it would become one of the most famous briefs against censorship.

The internal divisions among the Parliamentarians, and the divisions between the Parliamentarians and the Scots, led to their not immediately following up their victory at **Marston Moor**. While the "peace group" put forward another set of proposals to the king, the "war group" decided to completely revamp the structure of their military forces. In place of the various county and regional units (such as the Eastern Association), there would be one army under a single, unified command: **the New Model Army**. Concomitantly, in the spring of 1645, Parliament passed the **Self-Denying Ordinance**, ordering everyone, peer and commoner alike, to resign their commands: promotion from the ranks would now be based exclusively on merit, not one's family (**Cromwell**, due to his evident military skill, was granted an exception). **Sir Thomas Fairfax** (1612–71) became captain-general; **Cromwell** was put in charge of the cavalry. The **New Model Army** proved itself at the **Battle of Naseby** on June 14, 1645, which effectively broke the Royalist side and made a Parliamentary victory all but inevitable. Further Parliamentary victories ensued, including the recapture of Bristol in September. The first part of the Civil Wars (known as the **First Civil War**) ended in October 1646, when Oxford surrendered. The military juggernaut accompanied Parliament's legislative remaking of England. **Archbishop Laud**, accused of treason and imprisoned in the Tower in 1640, was finally put on trial for treason in 1644, but charges against him were bogus, and a guilty verdict could not be assured.

Parliament, therefore, used the same expedient employed against Strafford: passing a bill of attainder, which resulted in **Laud's** beheading on January 10, 1645. In August that year, Parliament established a national Presbyterian church (bishops would be outlawed in 1646). Given these two events, it might seem that the religious battle had ended and peace would reign, but victory over Arminianism and Laudianism only created more suspicion and outright hostility between the moderate **Presbyterians** and the radical **Independents**, who accused their opponents of attempting to impose a religious conformity equivalent to Laud's. "New *Presbyter*," concludes **Milton** in his sonnet, "On the New Forcers of Conscience," "is but old *Priest* writ large."

1646–49: Radicalism, the New Model Army and the Execution of King Charles I

Victory, as the Parliamentarians quickly discovered, brought its own problems. While the Parliamentarians were focused on defeating the king's forces, their own differences, while simmering, could be papered over. In a letter describing the taking of Bristol in 1645, **Cromwell** wrote, "Presbyterians, Independents, all have here the same spirit of faith and prayer, the same presence and answer. They agree here, have no names of difference."[17] Perhaps assuming that Cromwell correctly described the situation, **Holles** devised a very simple plan. He would, along with the Presbyterian majority in parliament, reform England's religious and political structure to prevent royal abuses from ever occurring again. He would then invite Charles back to rule within the newly established rules and constitutional boundaries. **Holles** did not take into account how the armed conflict between parliament and the monarchy gave free rein to all sorts of radical ideas or how **Charles** would try to take advantage of the divisions within the Parliamentary ranks by negotiating first with Parliament, then with the Scots, then with the Independents, sometimes all three simultaneously, but with none sincerely.

In May 1646, **Charles** decided that he might get better terms, and so, after first disguising himself as a servant, he presented himself to the Scots, who (after discovering that Charles had no intention of relinquishing the Episcopal structure of the Church), promptly handed the king over to parliament in return for a very substantial sum of money. It must have seemed to **Holles** that he held all the cards: the Presbyterians enjoyed a majority in parliament, and now he held the king. **The New Model Army**, restive because they had not been paid for months, despite the crippling taxes imposed by Parliament to support them, appeared more of a liability than an advantage. Therefore, **Holles** proposed disbanding the majority of the **New Model Army** (without paying them first) and sending the rest to fight the Irish.

The soldiers of the **New Model Army** had other ideas, and it is a moot point whether **Holles's** callous attitude toward Parliament's soldiers radicalized the army, or if the army had already been gripped by radical ideas about religious toleration and secular government. **Holles's** refusal to grant a hearing to the petitions of grievances sent by the army to Parliament provoked them to mutiny, to invade London, and on June 3, 1647, to take possession of the king. **Charles I**, seeing an excellent opportunity to further divide his enemies, was all too happy to accompany his new captors.

Fascinatingly, the **New Model Army** became a vehicle for the kind of democratic principles that would be enshrined a century later in the American Constitution. For the first time in English history, political proposals were put forward in the name of "the people," regardless of their rank. As a declaration sent to parliament on June 14, 1647 demonstrates, the **New Model Army** had a very different sense of itself than any force before it: we are "no mere mercenary army hired to serve any arbitrary power of a state, but called forth and conjured by the several declarations of Parliament to the defense of our *and the people's* just rights and liberties" (my emphasis).[18] In the past, one's worth was directly pegged to one's place in the social order, and those on the bottom (the fourth sort) were hardly worth mentioning. Now, the army, led by the radical egalitarianism of **the Levellers**, conceived of their mission as fighting for *everyone's* rights, regardless of their birth. In October or

November 1647, the army issued *An Agreement of the People*, which implicitly did away with monarchy; in its place this document proposed that "the people do of course choose themselves a parliament once in two years [and] that the power of this and all future representatives of this nation is inferior only to theirs who choose them"; the *Agreement* further proposed "that in all laws made or to be made, every person may be bound alike" and "That as the laws ought to be equal, so they must be good and not evidently destructive to the safety and well-being of the people."

The radicals and their officers, pejoratively called **"the grandees,"** met to debate these proposals at a church in Putney (**the Putney Debates**), and the verbatim record of these proceedings provides a truly gripping account of the unprecedented arguments over who could participate in the nation's governance. One on side, **Colonel Thomas Rainsborough** (c. 1587–1648) argued **the Leveller** position that *all* inhabitants of England should have the vote regardless of economic circumstances:

> I think that the poorest he that is in England has a life to live as the greatest he; and therefore truly, sir, I think it's clear, that every man that is to live under a government ought first by his own consent to put himself under that government; and I do think that the poorest man in England is not at all bound in a strict sense to that government that he has not had a voice to put himself under.[19]

Colonel Henry Ireton (1611–51), Cromwell's son-in-law, answered that the vote should be restricted to men with a certain amount of property (nobody argued for enfranchising women):

> I think that no person has a right to an interest or share in the disposing of the affairs of the kingdom, and in determining or choosing those that shall determine what laws we shall be ruled by here, no person has a right to this that has not a permanent fixed interest in this kingdom … But that by a man's being born here he shall have a share in that power that shall dispose of the lands here, and of all things here, I do not think it is a sufficient ground. … All the main that I speak for, is because I would have an eye to property.[20]

Rainsborough responded by coming very close to anticipating the anarchist quotation, "Property is theft":

> To the thing itself – property – I would fain know how it comes to be the property … and I would fain know what we have fought for; and this is the old law of England and that which enslaves the people of England, that they should be bound by laws in which they have no voice at all.[21]

As for **Cromwell**, who moderated the debate, he clearly sided with **Ireton**, and tried to lower the debate's temperature:

> I know nothing but this, that they that are the most yielding have the greatest wisdom; but really, Sir [Col. Rainsborough], this is not right as it should be. No man says that you have a mind to anarchy, but the consequence of this rule tends to anarchy, must end in anarchy, for where is there any bound or limit set, if you take away this, that men that have no interest but the interest of breathing [should have no voice]. Therefore I am confident on't, we should not be so hot with one another.[22]

The Levellers were not alone in their visions of a new society. Throughout the 1640s and 1650s, all sorts of radical groups sprung up seeking to remake society in one way or another. Some of the most famous are **the Diggers**, who held that all property should be held in common and started a utopian agrarian community on common land; they are best known through the writings of **Gerrard Winstanley** (c. 1609–76), who in 1649 asserted that since the monarchy had been abolished and all the "prerogative customs … cast out, [England] now ought to be a free land, and a common treasury to all her children";[23] **the Ranters**, who believed that they were among the elect, and so laws no longer applied to them; and **the Quakers**, the pejorative name for **the Society of Friends**, who also held that God was the only source of authority and did away with any formal religious service. **Quakers**, morever, believed in gender equality, and women wrote many of their early tracts.

While the army debated, **Charles** escaped to the Isle of Wight, and after more fruitless negotiations (the king having answered their proposals with "an absolute negative"), Parliament gave up and in January 1648 voted to "declare that they will make no further addresses or applications to the King."[24] This resolve, however, ran ahead of popular sentiment for a settlement with the king, but the **New Model Army** was now driving policy, and they were determined to rid the nation of **Charles** and indeed, monarchy itself. As always, Charles managed to make a bad situation worse by concluding an agreement with the Scots that traded an army and support for a promise to impose Scots Presbyterianism for three years (who knows if Charles actually meant to hold up his end of the bargain). The military result of this agreement was the **Second Civil War**, a series of Royalist revolts in the South, Wales, and Scotland that were easily defeated by Cromwell and Fairfax. The larger effect, however, was to erase all sense of mercy among the Parliamentarians towards their enemies. Many, including **Cromwell**, thought that by taking up arms on behalf of the king, the Royalists defied clear evidence that God sided with the Parliamentarians: "their fault who have appeared in this summer's business is certainly double to theirs who were in the first, because it is the repetition of the same offence against all the witnesses that God has borne."[25] Army leaders also started to believe that God wanted them "to call Charles Stuart, that man of blood, to an account for that blood he had shed, and mischief he had done to his utmost against the Lord's cause and people in these poor nations."[26]

The Presbyterians of the House of Commons (led by **Holles**), however, took a different lesson from these events. Believing that the majority in England wanted an accommodation with the monarchy, they voted 129–83 to overturn the **Vote of No Addresses** and to restart negotiations with **Charles**. That was too much for the army, and the next day (December 6, 1648), **Colonel Thomas Pride** stopped those who had voted for continuing to talk to the king from entering the House, arresting some 45 members and secluding 18 – **Pride's Purge**. **Pride** may have politely asked **William Prynne** to accompany him, but when he refused, **Prynne**, whom we should remember in

1637 was barbarically mutilated for his anti-Laudian views (see the previous chapter in this book), was dragged away, calling on bystanders to witness how the soldiers, "being more and stronger than he, and all armed, and he unarmed, they might forcibly carry him whither they pleased, but stir he would no thence of his own accord."[27]

Holles fled England to Normandy, where he lived until 1654, when **Cromwell** offered amnesty to Presbyterian exiles such as himself. Holles returned to live quietly on his estate until the Restoration, when he returned to politics and served as **Charles II's** ambassador to Paris from 1662 to 1665. He died in 1680.[28]

The remainder, known as the **Rump** or the **Rump Parliament**, in January 1649 created a High Court of Justice to do something all but unthinkable: put the king on trial for high treason against the Ancient Constitution of England. The Act creating this court begins:

> Whereas it is notorious that Charles Stuart, the now King of England, not content with the many encroachments which his predecessors had made upon the people in their rights and freedom, hath had a wicked design totally to subvert the ancient and fundamental laws and liberties of this nation, and in their place to introduce an arbitrary and tyrannical government, and that besides all other evil ways and means to bring his design to pass, he hath prosecuted it with fire and sword, lived and maintained a civil war in the land, against the Parliament and Kingdom.[29]

On January 20, 1649, **Charles** was brought into the courtroom to answer these charges, but when asked how he pled, **Charles** refused to enter a plea because he did not recognize the authority of this court to try him:

> I would know by what authority – I mean lawful – there are many unlawful authorities in the world – thieves and robbers by the highways – but I would know by what authority I was brought from

Figure 8.1 Historiaels verhael, Van de Geboorte, Leven en Sterven, van …
Carolvs Stvarts, Coningh van Engelandt, Schotlandt, en Yerlandt, 1649.
© The Trustees of the British Museum.

thence and carried from place to place, and I know not what. And
when I know by what lawful authority, I shall answer. Remember, I
am your King – your lawful King.[30]

A contemporary account gives the flavor of the sharp back-and-
forth between **Charles** and his judges:

Answer was made [to the king's questioning the authority of this court]
by authority of the Parliament of England, and that if he had marked
what was read he might have understood that before. Then the King
said, they had not a lawful authority, and that he saw none of his Lords
here. The Lord President told him that they sat by the authority of the
Commons of England in parliament assembled who had chosen him to
be their king, and to whom he must give an account. The King denied
that he was chosen by the people, but that he had it by inheritance, and
said that it hath been hereditary above a thousand years.[31]

It didn't matter because the verdict was already known. On January
27, he was condemned, and on January 30, 1649, after stating that he
moved "from a corruptible to an incorruptible crown," **Charles I**

lost his head.[32] Two months later, Parliament abolished the monarchy along with the House of Lords, and on May 19, 1649, declared:

> that the people of England ... are and shall be, and are hereby constituted ... to be a Commonwealth and Free State, and shall from henceforth to be governed as a Commonwealth and Free by the supreme authority of this nation, the representatives of the people in Parliament.[33]

England's experiment in republican rule had begun.

The Interregnum (1649–60)

The Commonwealth: The Rump and Barebone's Parliament (1649–53)

From the start, **the Rump Parliament** found itself under attack from all sides. As one might expect, the Royalists would attempt to overthrow the Commonwealth by force. But the military campaign was accompanied by an equally important, international pamphlet war. Books were as important as bullets in determining and maintaining legitimacy. To defend the new regime overseas, Cromwell's government asked **John Milton**, on the basis of *The Tenure of Kings and Magistrates* (published February 13, 1649) to join the counsel as Secretary for the Foreign Tongues. While **Milton** would handle Latin diplomatic correspondence, his real job was to defend Charles's execution against Continental accusations of regicide. The Council of State also charged **Milton** with answering *Eikon Basilike* (The Image of the King), a book that appeared ten days after **Charles's** execution containing the late king's final meditations (while ascribed to Charles, at least some of the book was written by John Gauden, the king's chaplain, although the exact proportion remains in dispute). The *Eikon*'s phenomenal popularity (35 editions the first year alone) so worried the new government that they asked **Milton** to pen a reply, and the much less popular *Eikonoklastes* (The Image-Breaker) went on sale on October 6, 1649. Ominously, Milton's rejoinder to *Eikon Basilike* did not sell anywhere near as many copies (only two editions appeared, although a French translation came out in 1652).

> **Milton** wrote three books defending the new regime: *Defensio pro populo Anglicano* (Defense of the English people; 1651), vindicating Charles's execution to Europe; *Defensio Secunda* (Second Defense; 1654); and *Defensio Pro Se* (Defense of Himself; 1655). **Milton** went totally blind in 1652, and so the latter two works were dictated, as would be *Paradise Lost* (1667), *Paradise Regained*, and *Samson Agonistes* (published together in 1671).

While **Milton** attended to the propaganda war, **Cromwell** dealt with the military threats emanating from **Ireland** and **Scotland**. Following the execution of Charles, **James Butler, Duke of Ormond** (1610–88), whom Charles had appointed lord lieutenant of Ireland, created an alliance between the Royalist Old English Catholics and the native Irish, eventually occupying the eastern shoreline and threatening to take Dublin. In August 1649, the Rump sent **Cromwell** at the head of a well-paid, well-supplied army to put a stop to this threat, and within a week, he had defeated Ormond's largest army. Cromwell achieved his victory in Ireland, however, through a brutality that shocks even today. After taking the town of **Drogheda**, Cromwell, according to his own report, had all the officers "knocked on the head; and every tenth man of the soldiers killed; and the rest shipped for the Barbadoes," as slaves.[34] As for **Wexford**, "an even more brutal massacre took place when [Cromwell's] soldiers broke the leash of military discipline" and killed every man, woman and child they could find.[35] While **Cromwell** allowed that such actions might be cause for "remorse and regret," he considered this slaughter divinely justified as both vengeance for earlier rebellions and as a way of discouraging future rebellions against English rule: "I am persuaded that this is a righteous judgment of God upon these barbarous wretches, who have imbrued their hands in so much innocent blood; and that it will tend to prevent the effusion of blood for the future."[36]

Andrew Marvell's (1621–78) notoriously ambiguous poem, "An Horatian Ode upon Cromwell's Return from Ireland" (likely written soon after Cromwell came back in May 1650, but not printed until 1681), praises Cromwell's victory ("And now the Irish are ashamed / To see themselves in one year tamed" [ll. 73–4]) while warning that he might become a tyrant ("Nor yet grown stiffer with command" [l. 81]) and casting doubt on the deeper legitimacy of Parliament's ascendance: "The same arts that did gain / A power must it maintain" (ll. 119–20).[37]

Having successfully squashed the Irish threat, the Rump then sent **Cromwell** to deal with Scotland, which had declared **Charles II** their rightful king two days after his father's execution. After some resistance on his part, **Charles II** agreed to accept the Covenant and repudiate his father's treaty with the Irish guaranteeing toleration of Catholicism in return for their invading England on his behalf. For their part, the English were not as keen to fight the Scots as they were the Irish. The commander of the New Model Army, **Thomas Fairfax**, refused to lead an army against the Scots because they had not yet invaded England – "Human probabilities are not sufficient grounds to make war upon a neighbor nation, especially our brethren of Scotland, to whom we are engaged in a solemn league and covenant"[38] – but the real reason was that he did not want to fight against fellow Presbyterians. Cromwell, therefore, took charge, and he crushed the Scots army on September 3, 1650, and then, exactly one year later, at Worcester defeated a Scots Royalist force led by **Charles II**, who ignominiously hid in an oak tree to avoid capture. After a few weeks of evading Cromwell's army, **Charles II** managed to escape to the Continent where he would keep a "small, shabby, peripatetic court" for the next decade.[39] While on the field of battle, **Cromwell** fought against both the Irish and the Scots with equal ferocity and brilliance, yet he put the latter in a fundamentally different category: "I had rather be overrun with a Cavalierish interest, than a Scotch interest," Cromwell said, "I had rather be overrun with a Scotch interest, than an Irish interest; and I think of all this [the Irish] is the most dangerous ... all the world knows their barbarism."[40]

While **Cromwell** successfully dealt with these two external threats, the Rump also had to confront its internal critics. The Civil Wars seemed to release, as has been noted previously in this chapter, all sorts of radical ideas about reshaping religion. As a contemporary put it, "as wars increased, so variety of judgments increased."[41] The **Ranters**, for example, were an **antinomian** group (meaning, they did not recognize the authority of any laws other than inspiration) who believed, as one of their members said in his recantation of his wild spiritual past, that "there is no act as drunkenness, adultery and theft in God ... Sin hath its conception only in the imagination ... No matter what Scripture, saints or churches say, if that within thee do not condemn thee, thou shalt not be condemned."[42] Such opinions could not be allowed to stand, and so, **the Rump** reinstated licensing in 1649 and passed the Blasphemy Act in 1650 against "monstrous opinions and wicked and abominable practices."[43] While this Act mandated prison, the government also imposed barbaric punishments on those deemed to have transgressed. After the Quaker **James Nayler** (1618–60) imitated Christ's entry into Jerusalem by riding into Bristol (in pelting rain) surrounded by a few followers singing "Holy, holy, holy, Lord God of Sabbath," Parliament had him whipped until the skin on his back was completely torn off, his tongue bored through with a red-hot iron, and the letter "B" (for "blasphemer") branded on his forehead.[44]

Cromwell and his council were hardly more tolerant of those who criticized their political legitimacy. The Leveller **John Lilburne** (c. 1615–57) regularly accused the Rump of having no legitimate authority and effectively erasing the distinction between themselves and the prerogative government of Charles I. An "aghast" and "astonished" **Lilburne**, in his aptly titled pamphlet, *England's New Chains Discovered* (1649), gave a long list of how Cromwell's government had betrayed its ideals:

> And lastly, for completing this new kind of liberty, a Council of State is hastily erected for guardians thereof, who to that end are possessed with power to order and dispose all the forces appertaining to England by sea or land, to dispose of the public treasure, to command any person whatsoever before them, to give oath for the discovering of truth, to imprison any that shall disobey their commands, and such as they shall judge contumacious [disobedient or insubordinate]. What now is become of that liberty "that no man's person shall be attached or imprisoned, or otherwise disseised of his freehold, or free customs, but by lawful judgment of his equals?"[45]

Lilburne claimed that before he was brought in for his examination, he overheard through a closed door **Cromwell** say very loudly while "thumping his fist against the counsel table 'til it rang [that] you have no other way to deal with these men but to break them pieces [or else] they will break you,"[46] and Cromwell meant it. While the means were not anywhere near as savage as those applied to **Nayler**, Levellers, including **Lilburne**, often found themselves imprisoned and Leveller mutinies in the New Model Army were quickly repressed, and their leaders executed.

The achievements of the Rump Parliament were few, but they did try to implement some reforms. In 1651 they passed the **Navigation Act** forbidding foreign powers from trading with their colonies. The resulting trade frictions led to the **First Anglo-Dutch War**, which the English, thanks to superior naval tactics, handily won. **The Rump** also tried to reform the law courts, the Poor Law, the clergy, and the morals of the nation. Ultimately, they overstayed their welcome, and more dangerously, when they finally decided to dissolve, they proposed no limits on who could vote, thus opening the door for the return of Royalist Presbyterians. That could not be allowed, and so **Cromwell** entered the House with a group of soldiers and summarily dissolved **the Rump** himself:

> [He] told the House that they had sat long enough … that some of them were whoremasters … that others of them were drunkards, and some corrupt and unjust men and scandalous to the profession of the gospel, and that it was not fit that they should sit as a parliament any longer.[47]

Parliaments now served, it seems, at the pleasure of the army and its Lord General, **Cromwell**. The next parliament, known as either the **Nominated Assembly** or **Barebone's Parliament**, after one of its lesser members, the leather-seller and lay preacher, **Praisegod Barebone** (c. 1598–1679), would also run afoul of their approval.

After Cromwell dissolved **the Rump**, he and a council of army officers debated over what should come next: **Major-General John Lambert** (1619–84) wanted a single ruler with a council that would be balanced by mandatory parliaments, while **Major-General Thomas Harrison** (1616–60) proposed a nominated assembly modeled after the Sanhedrin (the High Court of ancient Israel, which ruled until the fourth century CE). **Harrison** belonged to a sect known as the **Fifth Monarchists**, who believed in the imminent second coming of Christ and the thousand year rule of the saints. While the council did not necessarily subscribe to this form of religious enthusiasm, they liked the idea of an assembly of men drawn from "the various forms of godliness in this nation,"[48] and so they asked churches to send in names. Only a small minority belonged to the **Fifth Monarchy** sect, yet they set the tone. While **Barebone's Parliament** passed some legitimate reforms, such as regulating the conditions for the incarceration of the insane and mandating that the courts use English rather than law French, many of their initiatives, such as replacing the common law with Mosaic Law and trying to abolish the court of Chancery, would have been disastrous. **Cromwell** had initially welcomed this group in fervently religious terms – "Truly," he said in his opening speech, "God hath called you to this work by, I think, as wonderful providences as ever passed upon the sons of men in so short a time" – but he quickly grew disillusioned, grumbling that he was "more troubled now with the fool than before with the knave."[49] As the more pious attended a prayer meeting, the few moderates in the Assembly voted to "deliver up unto the Lord General Cromwell the powers which they received from him ...."[50] While **Lambert** was behind this development, Cromwell was not, and he was as surprised as anybody at this turn of events. **Barebone's Parliament** lasted from July to December 1653, hardly six months.

Recent historians have been more sympathetic to **Barebone's Parliament**, downplaying the centrality of religious fanatics,[51] yet **Cromwell** and his army council evidently perceived in them a very serious threat to the commonwealth, and a pamphlet they commissioned from the amazingly adaptable **Marchamont Nedham** (see the box below) explains some of the thinking behind returning to military rule. **Nedham** fully admits the army's role in England's governance is "unaccustomed," claiming that they acted "not without much regret and hazard to themselves." But, **Nedham** goes on, they had to act for the good of the nation, because the consequences of their proposed reforms "would have been a subverting [of] the fundamental laws of the land, the destruction of propriety, and an utter extinguishing of the ministers of the gospel. In truth, their principles led them to a pulling down all and establishing nothing, so that instead of the expected settlement, they were running out into mere anarchy and confusion."[52] In addition to threatening "the extirpation of Law and government itself," **Nedham** noted the specific dangers posed by the Fifth Monarchists.[53] In the name of establishing Christ's rule on earth, they would declare "war with all other powers, and break them in pieces"; moreover, these people were deeply intolerant of any views other than their own, "fastening a mark of anti-Christianism upon everything they liked not ... [they would] have introduced a new fury of persecution more high than ever, and by decrying all other ways to establish their own, have imposed a more than antichristian yoke upon the necks of believers."[54]

236

Marchamont Nedham (c. 1620–78), one of the most important journalists of the era, changed sides no fewer than four times. His career started in 1643 as editor and author of the Parliamentary weekly, *Mercurius Britannicus*, but following a stint in prison he shifted to the Royalist side with another newsbook, *Mercurius Pragmaticus*, which lasted from 1647 to 1649. Following a second short stint in prison, this time at Parliament's order, Nedham started writing pamphlets defending the Commonwealth and editing his third weekly newsbook, *Mercurius Politicus* (1650–60). After the Restoration, Nedham was pardoned, and returned to writing Royalist propaganda. While a contemporary called him a political "shuttlecock," **Nedham** was also a "great crony" of **John Milton**, who licensed the *Mercurius Politicus*.[55]

The Cromwellian Protectorate (1654–58)

Civil authority had yet again passed into the hands of the army, but not for long, as **Major-General Lambert** had prepared an extraordinary document, England's only written constitution, the **Instrument of Government**, which established that "the supreme legislative authority ... shall be the Lord Protector," who will rule with a council and Parliament.[56] The first version of this document offered Cromwell the crown, but he refused, as he would throughout the Protectorate, and he pointedly refused to wear anything ostentatious or grand at his installation.[57] Yet that did not stop others from treating Cromwell like a monarch. The Venetian ambassador noted that he sat on a luxurious chair that rested on opulent carpets, and that men accorded Cromwell "the obsequious and respectful form observed to the late kings."[58] Indeed, **Cromwell** could not escape the shadow of monarchy. His enemies referred to him as "King Cromwell,"[59] and his iconography often echoed the imagery used for earlier kings (compare Figure 8.2, Robert Walker's 1649 portrait of Cromwell, with Figure 7.1, van Dyck's portrait of Charles I).

Figure 8.2 Oliver Cromwell by Robert Walker. © National Portrait Gallery, London.

Cromwell looked at the beginning of the Protectorate as a fresh start; he told the first Protectorate Parliament that its "great end" was "healing and settling," and he warned against "remembering [that] might set the wound fresh a-bleeding."[60] Yet that task was not so easily accomplished. In the same speech, Cromwell reminded his audience that the class structure, the "natural magistracy of the nation [was] almost trampled under foot, under despite and contempt, by men of Levelling principles."[61] Others returned the favor by describing the Protectorate's government as nothing but "a monarchy bottomed by the sword and 30000 men"; the monarchy may have been "somewhat too tenacious of power," but "the present government is yet more autocratic and arbitrary."[62]

The four years of the **Protectorate** present something of a paradox. On the one hand, with the major exception of **the rule of the Major-Generals** (see later in this chapter), the Cromwellian government ruled England well during this period. The Poor Laws were administered with efficiency and compassion, and the government "launched a much needed reform of the law and sought to make education more accessible" as well as pursuing "a broadly tolerant religious policy, which allowed for much individuality of practice among the congregations; left adherents of the old Prayer Book and Catholics to live in peace if they would live peacefully; and allowed Jews to return to England for the first time since their official expulsion in 1290."[63] Cromwell also pursued an aggressive, largely successful foreign policy. The trade wars against the Dutch provoked by the **Navigation Act** ended well for the English, and upon concluding hostilities with one enemy, Cromwell declared war against Spain, England's traditional enemy. Rather than a land war on the Continent, Cromwell settled on the policy known as the **Western Design**, an attempt to undermine Spain by conquering Spain's possessions in the Caribbean. The attempt in 1655 at capturing Hispaniola (the island containing the modern nations of Haiti and the Dominican Republic) was a dismal failure, as was the attempt to capture a Spanish treasure fleet. Cromwell's navy did seize Jamaica from the Spanish and while it seemed at the time a consolation prize, this island's plantations would become a major source of wealth in the eighteenth century.

But the **Cromwellian Protectorate** did not enjoy deep support, and their Royalist and radical enemies continually harried them. In March 1655, a royalist rising in Wiltshire led by one John Penruddock (hence the name, **Penruddock's Rising**), was handily put down, but it led to the division of England into twelve administrative districts, each overseen by one Major-General, In addition to being charged with keeping order and collecting taxes, the Major-Generals were enjoined to "encourage godliness and virtue," opening the door for some to attempt to suppress alehouses, Sunday sports, and other forms of supposed immorality. Possibly the most rigorous was **Major-General Thomas Pride**, of **Pride's Purge** fame, whose territory included Southwark, the sketchy area where the brothels and the theaters were located. Supposedly, Pride tried to ban bear-baiting "not because it gave pain to the bears, but because it gave pleasure to the spectators."[64] The rule of the Major-Generals lasted only a year, failed dismally, and largely caused Cromwell's later reputation as a "Puritan" kill-joy.

Oliver Cromwell died on September 3, 1658, and his son, **Richard** (1626–1712) inherited the position of Lord Protector. Oliver, however, was the glue holding together England's experiment in non-monarchic rule. Without him, matters swiftly descended into chaos, and Richard did not have skills to maintain control. First Parliament tried to control the army, then the army dissolved Parliament, banished Richard, and recalled **the Rump**, who then tried to exert authority over the army, who then (perhaps unsurprisingly) re-dissolved the Rump on October 13, 1659. The political philosopher, **Thomas Hobbes** (1588–1679), details no fewer than eight "shiftings of the supreme authority."[65] Sensing that his time had come, on April 4, 1660, **Charles II** issued the **Declaration of Breda,** offering a general amnesty ("excepting only such persons as shall hereafter be excepted by parliament, those only to be excepted") and religious toleration (so long as the opinions "do not disturb the peace of the kingdom") in return for restoration.[66] It worked. The Royalists and Presbyterians dominated the parliament elected that month, and they issued a fleet to bring **Charles II** home. Accompanied by **General George Monck** (1608–70), once Cromwell's protégé but now disillusioned with "the fanatical party" who had overtaken Parliament and threatened to dismantle the Church of England, the restored king re-entered London as England's monarch on 29 May 1660, his birthday.[67]

John Milton tried to stem the tide by publishing two editions of *The Ready and Easy Way to Establish a Free Commonwealth* in late February and early April 1660 (the latter an expansion of the former). Famously, Milton demanded "Is it such an unspeakable joy to serve, such felicity to wear a yoke [?]" and he ended his pamphlet by comparing himself to the prophet, Jeremiah:

"Thus much I should perhaps have said though I were sure I should have spoken only to trees and stones, and had none to cry to, but the prophet, 'O earth, earth, earth!' to tell the very soil itself what her perverse inhabitants are deaf to."[68]

The Early Restoration (1660–71)

Reactions to the Restoration were mixed. As one might imagine, supporters of the monarchy, the vast majority in England, were utterly rapturous at the return of **Charles II**. An anonymous poet exclaimed in a poem that both celebrates the king's restoration and participates in the cult of Charles I as martyr:

> Charles! Glorious name! but glorious more by far
> Of it the subject, our dread sovereign!
> Son of Great Charles, who now a sparkling star
> In Heaven shines, his son (long may he reign!)
>   Our sun on earth, let him excel in glory,
>   His famous father, matchless in any story.[69]

Another anonymous poet, this time from Scotland, equally proclaimed the return of golden days: "With what transcending glory doth he rise, / To clear the shades of our long darkened skies, / The throne's repaired, Majesty restored, / The regal race returned, admired, adored!"[70] "London was in festival for three days after the royal entry, while the corporation of Norwich had to halt the merry-making after the proclamation when it had continued undiminished for nearly a week."[71] The few remaining supporters of "the Good Old Cause," including **John Milton**, obviously had less cause to celebrate and a great deal to fear. An early biographer reported that Milton remained "so dejected that he would lie awake whole nights," and immediately after **Charles II's** return, "by the advice of those that wished him well, and had a concern for his preservation, [Milton moved] into a place of retirement and abscondence, till such time as the current of affairs for the future should instruct him what farther course to take."[72]

Milton had good reason to worry since he was one of the chief defenders of **Charles I's** execution. But for reasons that remain obscure (although an early biographer credited **Andrew Marvell** with the necessary behind the scenes maneuvering), **Milton** was not exempted from the Act of Oblivion. Instead, *Eikonoklastes* and *Defensio Prima* were officially condemned and a few copies of each publicly burned on August 27, 1660.[73]

The new king understood that a blood bath would be in nobody's interest, and the desire for reconciliation expressed in the **Declaration of Breda** was genuine. Consequently, while the core of his Privy Council consisted of those who shared exile with him, he doled out other important posts to former members of the Protectorate, such as **Monck**, who became Captain-General of the army. Charles urged parliament to pass the **Act of Indemnity and Oblivion**, which exempted fewer than 100 people from a full pardon. Only those who signed Charles I's death warrant were subject to full retribution. Given what might have been, 11 public executions (including the Fifth Monarchist, **General Thomas Harrison**), seems light, although **Cromwell** and **Ireton** were disinterred and their corpses dismembered.

If **Charles II** followed through on his promise in the **Declaration of Breda** to abolish "all notes of discord, separation and difference of parties" by not pursuing (with exceptions) "no crime whatsoever, committed against us or our royal father," the **Cavalier Parliament** (1661–78) completely reversed his intentions on religious toleration. **Thomas Venner's** (1608–61) Fifth Monarchist uprising occurred in 1661, when 50 armed men (and one armed woman) proclaimed the reign of King Jesus in the middle of London. This uproar, which was not altogether harmless, as numerous rebels and a few Royalists died, may have posed no real threat to the government, but it cemented the increasingly popular association between religious radicalism and political sedition. The successful candidates to the House of Commons were largely deeply conservative people who wanted vengeance on those who had destroyed (in their view), the Church of England, and between 1661 and 1665 the Cavalier Parliament passed a series of laws – collectively but misleadingly known as the **Clarendon Code**, named after Lord Chancellor **Edward Hyde, Earl of Clarendon** (1607–74), who in fact was no fan of religious intolerance and worked to soften the restrictions – meant to crush **Nonconformists** or **Dissenters**, the terms generally used for anyone disagreeing with official doctrine.

The **Cavalier Parliament** restored bishops to the House of Lords and to their place within the Church, the Book of Common Prayer, and the wearing of vestments. These positive steps were balanced by highly punitive ones. **The Corporation Act** (1661) required municipal officers to renounce the Presbyterian Covenant and to receive the sacrament according to Anglican rites; **the Quaker Act** (1662) rendered illegal the Quaker practice of refusing to plead in court (Quakers avoid swearing all oaths); and **the Act of Uniformity** (1662) required that all ministers swear to consent to everything in the Book of Common Prayer as well as repudiating the Covenant and rebelling against the monarch; and the **Licensing Act** (1662) restored pre-publication and forbade publishing anything contrary to "the doctrine or discipline of the Church of England," all under the watchful eye of the government's chief censor, **Roger L'Estrange** (1616–1704), who "established himself as a spokesman for the most vindictive party of the old royalists."[74] There was more to come. Another pathetic anti-Stuart plot in 1663 led to the **Conventicle Act** of 1664, which ordered crippling fines against anyone attending nonconformist meetings, known as "conventicles," and in 1665, the **Five Mile Act** prohibited any nonconformist preacher from coming within five miles of his former parish.

While these laws (deemed by Andrew Marvell as "the quintessence of arbitrary malice") were aimed at all nonconformists,[75] they fell with greater rigor on the Quakers. According to **Milton's friend**, the Quaker **Thomas Ellwood**, although

> this unlawful, unjust, unequal, unreasonable and unrighteous law took place in (almost) all places, and was vigorously prosecuted against the meetings of dissenters in general … the brunt of the storm fell most sharply on the people called Quakers, not that it seemed to be more particularly leveled at them, but that they stood more fair,

243

steady and open, as a butt to receive all the shot that came, while some others found means and freedom to retire to coverts for shelter.[76]

Since violent resistance was out of the question, most of the sects, including the Quakers, turned inward: "radical religious discourse, particularly Quaker writing, often envisioned the inward-looking saint enduring great opposition and trials and yet remaining, almost in a superhuman fashion, firm and unmoved."[77] As Abdiel says to Satan in *Paradise Lost*: "How few sometimes may know, when thousands err" (6.148).

To his credit, **Charles II** tried in 1672 to issue a **Declaration of Indulgence** granting religious toleration, but the rabidly anti-Catholic parliament forced the king to withdraw it. The king's inability to ameliorate the harshness of parliament's religious policy was a marker of the monarchy's reduced power. While he could dismiss judges at will, the prerogative courts of Star Chamber and High Commission remained abolished. The **Triennial Act** of 1641 was confirmed in 1664, albeit without penalties, and so the monarchy had to call for regular parliaments, and **Charles II** eschewed any rhetoric about not having to account for his actions to anybody other than God. Ironically, if the Parliamentarians lost the battles of the Civil Wars in one sense, in another they actually won the war. **Absolutism,** as conceived by **Charles II's** grandfather and father, had ended in England.

Furthermore, it did not take very long before a strong sense of buyer's remorse set in. While the hysterical excitement accompanying **Charles II's** return could not last, few have plummeted in public estimation so far and so fast. The problem, as one courtier put it in 1663, is that "the King has abandoned himself to his lust and his ministers to their passions against one another."[78] Monarchs, as we have seen in previous chapters, could be lascivious, and their appetites affect national policy, but nothing before matched the erotic circus that featured the king at its center. **Charles II's** and his court's tendency toward sexual excess were public knowledge well before the Restoration. While **Charles** attended services regularly and set aside each Friday for prayers in memory of his father, yet "a Cromwellian spy could describe Charles's entourage as full of drunkenness, fornication, and adultery."[79]

A newsbook from 1660 by the ever-slippery **Marchamont Nedham** gleefully recounts the adventures of "H," ostensibly one of the King's companions, who "swears he hath horn'd 15 Cuckolds within this 14 dayes."[80] And **Charles II** happily led these goings-on. He filled his correspondence from before the Restoration with the details of his "romantic manoeuvers," in particular "the wooing of a young woman at Brussels known as 'the infanta.'"[81] Nor was this woman the sole object of Charles's attention. The man had no fewer than 17 mistresses before the Restoration, fathering 14 illegitimate children, and that was before his marriage in 1662 to the stolid **Catherine of Braganza** (1638–1705). This match brought a dowry that included trading privileges in the Portuguese empire in both Bombay and Tangiers, and a lot of money.

But, fatefully, the match did not provide children, and **Charles** had already started his affair with his long-time mistress, **Barbara Palmer**, née Villiers (1641–1709, a distant cousin of **George Villiers, Duke of Buckingham**). After the wedding, the King returned to her in both mind and body. The entire court took their king's behavior as a model, and by 1661, the incidence of syphilis was a crying scandal; lurid tales of excess circulated widely. Examples included the time in June 1663 that a young gentleman went out on a balcony stark naked to preach a mock sermon accompanied by obscene gestures, or the time a dinner party in Oxford devolved into an orgy.[82]

The sexual escapades of the King and his court were compounded by a series of domestic and foreign policy disasters. **Lord Chancellor Clarendon** may have personally opposed the **Second Anglo-Dutch War** (caused by the renewal of the 1651 Navigation Act and the passing of the Staple Act), which may have begun well with the taking of New Amsterdam – renamed New York – but ended with the Dutch fleet sailing unmolested up the Thames and Medway rivers, burning the docks at Chatham and capturing the flagship of the royal navy, the *Royal Charles*.[83] Adding to the turmoil, in 1665, London endured a terrible outbreak of plague, and then, in 1666, **the Great Fire of London** took place. In addition, that autumn England endured terrible weather leading to crop failures.

Not all, of course, was frivolity and catastrophe. In 1660, **the Royal Society**, England's first organization devoted to the advancement of science and Baconian experimentation, was created, and its first publication was Robert Hooke's *Micrographia* (1665), containing engravings of the "minute bodies" (to quote the title) as seen by the newly invented microscope. The Restoration also led to a tremendous increase in patronage for the arts and the re-opening of the public theaters, this time, however, with women playing women's roles. The plays produced, however, by such authors as George Etheredge (c. 1635–91) and William Wycherly (1640–1716), reflect a fundamentally different sensibility than the one exhibited by Jacobean playwrights, just as the poetry written by John Dryden (1631–1700) and John Wilmot, Earl of Rochester (1647–80) reflects a new sense of aesthetics, one that privileged rhyme, wit, and order.

The positive reception accorded **John Milton's** final poetic works, *Paradise Lost* (1667; revised 1674), and *Paradise Regained. A Poem in IV Books. To which is added Samson Agonistes* (1671), shows that he was not entirely out of step with his times, yet Milton understood that his poetic sensibility fundamentally differed from Restoration fashions. In the note on the verse appended to the 1668 edition of *Paradise Lost*, Milton criticized the "famous modern poets "who, "carried away by custom," preferred "the troublesome and modern bondage of rhyming" to blank verse."[84] Milton's final poems, looking backward to the failure of non-monarchic rule and the restoration of the monarchy, are generally taken as the endpoint of the early modern period; what happens next – the couplets of Alexander Pope, the rakes and fops of Restoration comedy, the complex novels by Fielding and Richardson – is another story altogether.

The End of the Stuart Dynasty

When **Charles II** died in 1685, the throne passed to his brother, **James II**, who had converted to Catholicism years earlier. James II (b. 1633) tried to enforce toleration of Catholic worship, but the rabidly anti-Catholic parliament forced him back down. Parliament in 1688 invited the king's son-in-law,

William of Orange (1650–1702), who belonged to the same family that led the Dutch rebellion against Spain, to invade England, and he seized the Crown without any resistance, becoming **King William III/II: the Glorious Revolution**. James decided to flee rather than fight. He died in France in 1701, and the throne passed to **Elizabeth Stuart's** grandson, **George**, from the House of Hanover. Queen Victoria would be the last of the Hanover monarchs.

Notes

1   Barry Coward, *The Stuart Age: England 1603–1714*, 3rd ed. (London: Pearson, 2003), 186.
2   See David Cressy, "Foucault, Stone, Shakespeare and Social History," *English Literary Renaissance* 21.3 (1991): 121–3.
3   The works mentioned are as follows: R. H. Tawney, "The Rise of the Gentry," reprinted in *Essays in Economic History*, ed. E. M. Carus-Wilson (London: Edward Arnold, 1963, vol. 1, 173–214; Lawrence Stone, *The Crisis of the Aristocracy 1558–1641* (Oxford: Clarendon Press, 1965) and *The Family, Sex and Marriage, 1500–1800* (London: Weidenfield and Nicolson, 1977); Christopher Hill, *The English Revolution 1640* (London : Lawrence and Wishart, 1985) and *Milton and the English Revolution* (London: Faber, 1977); Nicholas Tyacke, "Puritanism, Arminianism and Counter-Revolution," *The Origins of the English Civil War*, ed. Conrad Russell (London: Macmillan, 1973), 119–43); Kevin Sharpe, *The Personal Rule of Charles I*; Brian Manning, *The English People and the English Revolution, 1640–49* (London: Heinemann, 1976), and David Underdown, *Pride's Purge: Politics in the Puritan Revolution* (Oxford: Clarendon Press, 1971). For a full explication and bibliography of the "Storm over the Gentry," see R. C. Richardson, *The Debate on the English Revolution*, 2nd ed. (London: Routledge, 1988), 118–24.
4   Quoted in Coward, *The Stuart Age*, 206.
5   Mark Kishlansky, *A Monarchy Transformed: Britain 1603–1714* (London: Penguin, 1996), 153.
6   *Select Tracts relating to the Civil Wars in England*, ed. Frances Maceres (London: R. Wiles, 1815), vol. 1, 191.
7   Coward, *The Stuart Age*, 210.

8   "The Propositions Presented to the King at the Treaty of Oxford," *The Constitutional Documents of the Puritan Revolution 1625–1660*, ed. Samuel Rawson Gardiner (Oxford: Clarendon Press, 1906), 262–7.
9   Quoted in Richard Cust, *Charles I: A Political Life* (Harlow: Pearson/Longman, 2007), 372.
10 "The Solemn League and Covenant," *Constitutional Documents*, 268.
11 Robert Bucholz and Newton Key, *Early Modern England 1485–1714: A Narrative History* (Oxford: Blackwell, 2004), 241.
12 *A Directory for the Public Worship of God* (Edinburgh, 1645), sig. G4v.
13 Letter VIII, *Oliver Cromwell's Letters and Speeches: with Elucidations*, ed. Thomas Carlyle (New York: Wiley & Putnam, 1845), vol. 1, part 1, 150.
14 Quoted in Coward, *The Stuart Age*, 216.
15 Quoted in Bucholz and Key, *Early Modern England*, 243.
16 Daid Underdown, *Pride's Purge: Politics in the Puritan Revolution* (Oxford: Clarendon Press, 1971), 21.
17 Letter XV, *Cromwell's Letters*, vol. 1 part 1, 181.
18 "A Declaration," *The Stuart Constitution, 1603–88: Documents and Commentary*, ed. Kenyon (Cambridge: Cambridge University Press, 1966), 296.
19 Quoted in *Divine Right and Democracy*, ed. David Wootton (Harmondsworth: Penguin, 1986), 286.
20 *Divine Right and Democracy*, 287, 290.
21 *Divine Right and Democracy*, 294.
22 *Divine Right and Democracy*, 293. Despite the conciliatory rhetoric, sectarians could be treated with the utmost barbarity, as shown by the case of James Nayler.
23 Winstanley, *A Watchword to the City of Longdon* (London, 1649), sig. A4r.
24 "The Vote of No Addresses," *Constitutional Documents*, ed. Gardiner, 356.
25 Quoted in Coward, *The Stuart Age*, 235.
26 "The Windsor Prayer-meeting, 1 May 1648," *The Stuart Constitution*, ed. Kenyon, 319.
27 Quoted in Underdown, *Pride's Purge*, 144.
28 John Morrill, "Holles, Denzil, first Baron Holles (1598–1680)," *Oxford Dictionary of National Biography*, Oxford University Press, September 2004; online edn., January 2008 http://www.oxforddnb.com/view/article/13550, accessed July 21, 2010.
29 "The Act Erecting a High Court," *Constitutional Documents*, ed. Gardiner, 357.

30 Quoted in *The Trial of Charles I: A Documentary History*, ed. David Lagomarsino and Charles T. Wood (Hanover: University Press of New England, 1989), 64.

31 *Collections of Notes taken at the King's Trial at Westminster Hall, on Saturday last, January 20, 1648* (London, 1648), sig. A4v-r.

32 *The Trial of Charles I*, 143–4.

33 *Constitutional Documents*, ed. Gardiner, 388. The acts abolishing monarchy and the House of Lords can be found on pp. 384–8.

34 Letter LXXI, *Cromwell's Letters*, vol. 1, pt. 2, 383.

35 Kishlansky, *A Monarchy Transformed*, 199.

36 Letter LXXI, *Cromwell's Letters*, vol. 1, pt. 2, 383–4.

37 Marvell, "An Horatian Ode," in *The Longman Anthology of British Literature*, gen. eds. David Damrosch, Kevin J. H. Dettmar; vol. eds. Constance Jordan and Clare Carroll (New York: Pearson Longman, 2006), vol. 1B, 155–8.

38 Quoted in Ian J. Gentles, "Fairfax, Thomas, third Lord Fairfax of Cameron (1612–1671)," *Oxford Dictionary of National Biography*, Oxford University Press, September 2004; online edn., January 2008. http://www.oxforddnb.com/view/article/9092, accessed July 22, 2010.

39 Bucholz and Key, *Early Modern England*, 256.

40 Quoted in Coward, *The Stuart Age*, 248–9.

41 Laurence Claxton, *The Lost Sheep Found* (London, 1660), sig. B1v. "Laurence Claxton" is a pseudonym for Laurence Clarkson (1615–67).

42 Quoted in Christopher Hill, *The World Turned Upside Down: Radical Ideas During the English Revolution* (London: Penguin, 1972), 215.

43 Quoted in Kishlansky, *A Monarchy Transformed*, 203.

44 Leo Damrosch, "Nayler, James (1618–1660)," *Oxford Dictionary of National Biography*, Oxford University Press, September 2004. http://www.oxforddnb.com/view/article/19814, accessed July 23, 2010.

45 Lilburne, *England's New Chains Discovered*, in *The English Levellers*, ed. Andrew Sharp (Cambridge: Cambridge University Press, 1998), 145, 148. Lilburne quotes from Magna Carta, clause 29.

46 John Lilburne, Thomas Prince, and Richard Overton, *The Picture of the Council of State, held forth to the Free People of England* (London, 1649), sig B4v-r.

47 Quoted in Blair Worden, *The Rump Parliament, 1648–53* (Cambridge: Cambridge University Press, 1974), 1.

48 Quoted in John Morrill, "Cromwell, Oliver (1599–1658)," *Oxford Dictionary of National Biography*, Oxford University Press, September 2004; online edn., May 2008. http://www.oxforddnb.com/view/article/6765, accessed July 27, 2010.

49 Austin Woolrych, *Britain in Revolution: 1625–1660* (Oxford: Oxford University Press, 2002), 550.

50 Quoted in Marchamont Nedham, *A True State of the Case of the Commonwealth* (London, 1654), sig. B5v; Cromwell, *Letters and Speeches*, vol. 2, pt. 1, 45. While *A True State* was published anonymously and is catalogued as such in Early English Books Online, it has been attributed to Nedham.

51 See for example Barry Coward, *The Cromwellian Protectorate* (Manchester: Manchester University Press, 2002), 813.

52 Nedham, *A True State*, sig. B1v.

53 Nedham, *A True State*, sig. B3r.

54 Nedham, *A True State*, sig. B1v-r.

55 Joad Raymond, "Nedham, Marchamont (*b.* 1620, *d.* 1678)," *Oxford Dictionary of National Biography*, Oxford University Press, September 2004; online edn., January 2008. http://www.oxforddnb.com/view/article/19847, accessed July 26, 2010; on Milton and Marchamont's friendship, see Blair Worden, *Literature and Politics in Cromwellian England: John Milton, Andrew Marvell, Marchamont Nedham* (Oxford: Oxford University Press, 2007), 203.

56 "The Instrument of Government," *Constitutional Documents*, ed. Gardiner, 405.

57 Kishlansky, *A Monarchy Transformed*, 207.

58 Quoted in Ivan Root, *The Great Rebellion 1642–1660* (London: Batsford, 1966), 172.

59 Lilburne, Prince and Overton, *The Picture of the Council of State*, sig. C2v.

60 "Speech II," *Cromwell's Letters and Speeches*, vol. 2, pt. 1, 89.

61 "Speech II," 90.

62 "A Copy of a Letter from an Officer of the Army in Ireland to his Highness the Lord Protector concerning his changing of the Government" [June 24, 1654], *The Manuscripts of Sir William Fitzherbert and Others* (London: HMSO, 1893), 3. The calendar further states that the writer "is in favor of a free and equal commonwealth" (3), a Leveller, in other words.

63 Coward, *The Stuart Age*, 264; Bucholz and Key, *Early Modern England*, 259.

64 Quoted in Kishlansky, *A Monarchy Transformed*, 210.

65 Thomas Hobbes, *Behemoth, or The Long Parliament*, ed. Ferdinand Tönnies (Chicago: University of Chicago Press, 1990), 195–6.

66 "The Declaration of Breda," *Constitutional Documents*, ed. Gardiner, 466.

67 Quoted in Ronald Hutton, "Monck, George, first duke of Albemarle (1608–1670)," *Oxford Dictionary of National Biography*, Oxford University Press, September 2004; online edn, January 2008. http://www.oxforddnb.com/view/article/18939, accessed July 29, 2010.

68 *The Ready and Easy Way to Establish a Free Commonwealth*, in *The Complete Poetry and Essential Prose of John Milton*, ed. William Kerrigan, John Rumrich, and Stephen M. Fallon (New York: Modern Library, 2007), 1136.

69 Anon, *Britain's Triumph, for her Imparalleld [unparalleled] Deliverance, and her Joyful Celebrating the Proclamation of her most Gracious, Incomparable King, Charles II* (London, 660), sig. A4v.

70 *Caledon's Gratulatory Rapture* (Edinburgh, 1660), s.p.

71 Ronald Hutton, *The Restoration: A Political and Religious History of England and Wales 1658–1667* (Oxford: Clarendon Press, 1985), 125–6.

72 Quoted in William Riley Parker, *Milton: A Biography*, 2nd edn. Oxford: Clarendon Press, 1996), vol. 1, 577; Edward Philips, in *The Riverside Milton*, ed. Roy Flannagan, 27.

73 Barbara K. Lewalski, *The Life of John Milton* (Oxford: Blackwell, 2000), 400–1.

74 Quoted in Harold Love, "L'Estrange, Sir Roger (1616–1704)," *Oxford Dictionary of National Biography*, Oxford University Press, September 2004; online edn., October 2007. http://www.oxforddnb.com/view/article/16514, accessed July 30, 2010.

75 Quoted in David Loewenstein, *Representing Revolution in Milton and his Contemporaries: Religion, Politics and Polemics in Radical Puritanism* (Cambridge: Cambridge University Press, 2001), 246.

76 Thomas Ellwood, *The History of the Life of Thomas Ellwood* (London, 1714), 284–5.

77 Loewenstein, 260.

78 Quoted in Hutton, *The Restoration*, 185.

79 Hutton, *The Restoration*, 122.

80 *News from Brussels*, sig. A4r.

81 Hutton, *Charles the Second, King of England, Scotland, and Ireland* (Oxford: Clarendon Press, 1989), 124–5.

82 Hutton, *Charles the Second*, 186.

83 Bucholz and Key, *Early Modern England*, 276–7.

84 "The Verse," *Complete Poetry and Essential Prose of John Milton*, ed. Kerrigan, Rumrich, and Fallon, 291. This note was appended to the 1668 edition of *Paradise Lost*.

Index

A Short History of Early Modern England: British Literature in Context, First Edition. Peter C. Herman.

© 2011 Peter C. Herman. Published 2011 by Blackwell Publishing Ltd.

St. Bartholomew's Day Massacre, 127
St. John, Oliver, 221
Star Chamber, court of, 200, 204, 205
Steere, Bartholomew, 144
Stewart, Henry, Lord Darnley, 125
Stone, Lawrence, 215
Strafford, Earl of; see Wentworth, Thomas, Earl of Strafford
Stubbe, John, 135
Stubbes, Phillip, 19
Surrey, Earl of; see Howard, Henry
Synod of Dort, 198

T.E., *The Law's Resolutions on Women's Rights*, 21–3
Tawney, Richard H., 214–15
Tewkesbury, Battle of, 49
Theaters, closing of, 208–09
Thirty Years War, 168, 216
Thirty-Nine Articles of Faith (1563), 119
Thomas Cromwell, 81–82
Thomas of Woodstock, 33–5
Thomason Tracts, 204
Thomason, George, 204
Throckmorton, Nicholas, 135
Tottell, Richard, 108
Towton, Battle of, 47–8
Treason Act (1534), 80, 94
Treason Act (1563), 119
Treaty of Câteau-Cambrésis, 123
Treaty of Edinburgh, 124
Treaty of London 154, 168
Triennial Act (1641), 205, 244
Tudor Myth, 52–3
Tudor, Owen, 43, 47
Tunstall, Bishop Cuthbert, 108

Tyacke, Nicholas, 215
Tyler, Wat, 32
Tyndale, William, 73, 121; New Testament and Pentateuch, 73, 83; *Obedience of the Christian Man*, 74–5

Underdown, David, 215–16
Union of England and Scotland, 160–1

Van Dyke, Sir Anthony, 196, 237
Vane, Sir Henry, the Younger, 218
Venner, Thomas, 242
Vesalius, Andreaus, 172
Villiers, George, Duke of Buckingham, 165–6, 170, 171, 184, 186–7, 193–5
Vote of No Addresses, 227

Waad, Armigail, 115–16
Walker, Robert, 238
Walsingham, Sir Francis, 117, 130, 140
Warbeck, Perkin, 61
Wars of Religion (France), 127, 137–8
Wars of the Roses, 46–52, 59–61
Warwick, Earl of; see Neville, Richard
Webster, John, 162
Wentworth, Thomas, 162
Wentworth, Thomas, Earl of Strafford, 203; and Ireland, 205–6
Western Rebellion, 99, 101
Westminster Assembly, 220
Weston, Sir Richard, 195
Wexford, 231
Whig view of history, 152–3, 214
Whitgift, Archbishop John, 122